THE
MOSAIC
HANDBOOK

for the X Window System

THE
MOSAIC
HANDBOOK

for the X Window System

DALE DOUGHERTY, RICHARD KOMAN, & PAULA FERGUSON

O'REILLY & ASSOCIATES, INC.
103 MORRIS STREET, SUITE A
SEBASTOPOL, CA 95472
(800) 998-9938 • (707) 829-0515
EMAIL: *nuts@ora.com*

The Mosaic Handbook for the X Window System

by Dale Dougherty, Richard Koman, and Paula Ferguson

Copyright © 1994 O'Reilly & Associates, Inc. All rights reserved.
Printed in Canada

Editor: Dale Dougherty

Production Editor: Stephen Spainhour

Printing History:

      October 1994:   First Edition.

This book is printed on acid-free paper with 80% recycled content, 15-20% post-consumer waste. O'Reilly & Associates is committed to using paper with the highest recycled content available consistent with high quality.

ISBN: 1-56592-095-3

TABLE OF CONTENTS

CHAPTER TWO

CHAPTER THREE

CHAPTER FOUR

ACCESSING OTHER INTERNET SERVICES _____ 75

CHAPTER FIVE

CUSTOMIZING MOSAIC _____ 105

FIGURES

TABLES

FOREWORD

I always enjoy giving demos of Mosaic and showing people interesting places to go on the Internet. At tradeshows or in boardrooms, whether there's one person or many looking over my shoulder or watching it on a big screen, I watch to see when they "get" it. When do they really get the power of Mosaic? When do they really understand what the Internet makes possible? When do they realize that this is something they always wanted to do with a computer?

One thing I usually do when Mosaic appears on the screen is to distinguish between the Mosaic interface and the document that is displayed. I say, "When I use the scrollbar, which Mosaic provides, everything that moves is in the document window, where formatted documents containing text and graphics are displayed. The document itself contains any number of hypertext links, or connections to other documents anywhere on the Net. I move the mouse pointer over a link and click on it. Right away, Mosaic begins retrieving the document from a remote information server."

Then I stop and explain that the document I just retrieved came from Geneva, Switzerland. Usually, someone smiles. Next I get a document from a server in Australia and yet another from a university in Texas. At that point, someone usually asks a question, just to be sure. This gives me the chance to stop and emphasize to the audience that we are traveling great distances across the Internet. Sometimes there is a delay in making a long-distance connection, and then I have the opportunity to make the same point. But often enough the document pops up on the screen, just as if it were on my local system. "Did you see that?" I ask. "I just got that document from a World Wide Web server in Vancouver, B.C."

Mosaic makes it easy to navigate the Internet, and the connections that it makes are transparent to the user. I begin to worry that the audience might not grasp the power behind such a simple interface. So, I explain what the World Wide Web is.

While Mosaic manages the user interface and the display of documents—in other words, what is visible to the user—the World Wide Web (WWW) is invisible. The WWW is an information architecture, developed at CERN, a particle physics lab in Geneva, Switzerland. The WWW defines the components of a global information system and how they work together. I try to explain how clients like Mosaic are used to access information servers out on the network. How the clients and servers talk to each other is established by a WWW protocol specification known as HTTP (HyperText Transfer Protocol).

The World Wide Web specifications are public, and anyone can follow them to build a client; there is even code available that takes care of common functions. Indeed, that is how Mosaic was developed at the National Center for Supercomputing Applications (NCSA) at the University of Illinois. The virtue of public specifications is that from the outset, the World Wide Web recognized the need to have clients for all platforms. This was fully realized when NCSA came out with versions of Mosaic for the X Window System, Microsoft Windows, and the Macintosh.

As a graphical browser, Mosaic has managed to redefine what it means to be on the Internet. Instead of typing long command lines and having to remember a lot of arcane details, users can find the best the Net has to offer with a couple of mouse clicks. As if that isn't enough, when I show people that Mosaic can be used for multimedia, their reaction is one of disbelief, of seeing the future today. "Can you really find sound and video on the Net?" Yes, I answer, and although it may be impractical today for you to download digital sound bites or MPEG movie clips, the capability is there. The result can be stunning, and worth the wait. As the speed of network connections improve, so much more is possible.

The emergence of Mosaic and the WWW is the most exciting computing development in a decade, supplying the infrastructure needed to usher in the Age of Networked Information. Already, it is changing how people think and work, from elementary school children to CEOs. More and more people are discovering that they can move through the rich landscape of the Internet, find its wealth of resources, and contribute to its growth by becoming information publishers themselves.

It is also redefining what it means to be a publisher. With the *Global Network Navigator*, O'Reilly & Associates is exploring this new territory, and learning how to serve a new audience of online customers. Mosaic is also changing the way businesses and other organizations distribute information. Companies like Digital and Boeing, for instance, are setting up Web servers to distribute employee handbooks, sales sheets, and policies. Users are creating their own home pages and listing their hobbies or favorite places to visit on the Net.

All in all, the World Wide Web is becoming an incredible, enormous interconnected network of information, public and private, commercial and educational, free and for-pay. If you have an Internet connection, all you need is Mosaic to begin exploring these resources on your own.

Well, maybe, that's not all you need. Things are not as easy as they seem in a demo. Knowing where to go and what to do on your own can be a lot more challenging, especially given the size of the Internet. Learning how to navigate the Net and keeping up with all the new resources that are added every day is not easy. That's one reason we created *GNN*, so that you can find this information online and not have to spend your time gathering it. It is also why we developed *The Mosaic Handbook*. This book is more than a description of the Mosaic interface; it's a guide to navigating the Internet.

Dale Dougherty
Publisher, *GNN*

PREFACE

Welcome to Mosaic, the program that turns most folks' conception of the Internet on its ear. Forget about the Net being hard to use. Forget about command-line interfaces. Forget about UNIX commands.

You are about to enter the World Wide Web—a strange and fascinating land of hypertext, color graphics, digital video, interactive maps, and other cool stuff. Follow its strands and you'll wind a path through underground music archives, online newspapers and magazines, a warehouse of scientific knowledge, up-to-the-minute weather maps and traffic reports, interactive services, and so much more.

But Mosaic is more than just a Web browser. In fact, it's an integrated interface for the entire Internet. Most services on the Net—including Gopher, WAIS, FTP, newsgroups and more—can be accessed through Mosaic.

How big is the Web? No one's really sure, since there's no central server registration point, but Matthew Gray, an MIT student who is the author of a program that travels the Internet seeking out new forms of Web life, sums it up pretty well: "Wow, it's big," he says.

But what exactly *is* the World Wide Web? It's a seemingly infinite system of servers on the Internet all tied together by hypertext links. Hypertext is a technology for linking collections of documents. On the Internet, these collections are distributed among a web of information servers. Using a mouse, you can click on a hypertext link in one document and retrieve the linked document from an information server out on the Internet. That server could be anywhere in the world.

The documents that you get can have a lot more than just text. Mosaic supports multimedia documents, and on the Web you can find graphics, video, audio, and other digital media.

The Best of the Net

What kind of information servers will you find on the Web? We'll cover that in some depth in this book, but to give you an idea of what's out there, here are some of the servers that in 1994 were named the "Best of the Net" by the *Global Network Navigator* (*GNN*), O'Reilly & Associates' online publications center and guide to Internet resources. In the images that accompany the descriptions of these servers, you'll see different documents displayed within the Mosaic interface. Mosaic displays documents within the area surrounded by the scroll bars.

International Teletimes

This general-interest magazine is published online from Vancouver, B.C., on a shareware model. According to its writer's guidelines, "Teletimes seeks to present informed opinion and observation drawn from the experience of living in a particular place." International Teletimes is a collaboration of many volunteers from around the world, but perhaps most notable is the fact that its editor-in-chief, Ian Wojtowicz, was 16 years old when he received the Best of the Net award.

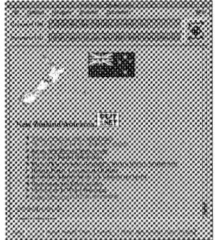

New Zealand Information

Perhaps you are traveling to New Zealand, or teaching a class about it. A server at Carnegie-Mellon University will tell you more than you might want to know. Want to know about the climate, or locate Auckland on a map? Listen to a speech in the native Maori language? Want to know what a tuatara is? The most ancient of all living reptiles, and the sole survivor of the beak-heads family, the tuatara lives to be over 100 years old. What's more, while young the tuatara has a third eye. You'll also find out that the main difference between Marmite and Vegemite, two types of yeast extract, is that the latter is Australian and tastes awful.

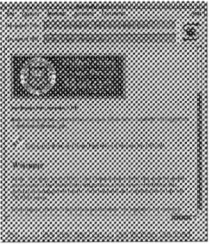

U.S. Bureau of the Census

The self-proclaimed "Factfinder for the Nation," the Census Bureau has created a model server for government agencies to follow. In short, it organizes information so that citizens can make their own use of it. You can get financial data on state and local governments as well as schools. The Bureau's statistical briefs are PostScript documents describing poverty in the U.S., analyzing housing changes from 1981–1991, or profiling people of Asian and Pacific Island heritage in the American population. In the Census Bureau Art Gallery, there is a display of posters used to promote participation in the census.

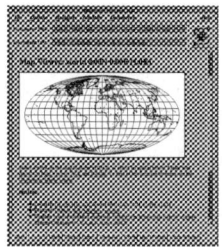

Xerox PARC Map Viewer

From the famous research lab that gave birth to the technologies that would become the Apple Macintosh and Adobe PostScript (among others), here's one of the most interactive applications on the Net. MapViewer is an application that dynamically renders a map based on user input. Click on a region and MapViewer will zoom in on it. You can also use a geographic name server to locate a particular location by name. Typing in "San Jose, California," we find that it is the county seat, and had a population of 62,000 in 1980. Its latitude and longitude are also given, and we can click on this information to display a map of the U.S. and a map of Northern California showing where San Jose is.

The Geographic Name Server happens to be located at the University of Buffalo, but that's how the Net works—one computer connects to another, just as one person's work connects to what other people are doing. A map of the world that is created dynamically seems the best way to think of our own new world, where the boundaries of nations and the limits of individuals can be overcome by making so many different connections possible.

Those are just four of the thousands of servers on the Web, with new ones coming online every day. Of course, not all of them are absolutely riveting. Helping you find the ones that interest you is what this book is really all about.

"Wherever you go, there you are," a line from the movie *Buckaroo Bonzai*, sort of sums up what Mosaic and the Web are all about. The Web is made for browsing, for following trains of thought, for taking interesting detours whenever they crop up. Mosaic users have a sense of the explorer about them, an excitement about discovering new information, a lust for links.

What This Book Is About

The Mosaic Handbook for the X Window System is aimed at everyone who uses Mosaic—or who wants to use Mosaic—to access the Internet. Whether you're a rank beginner or an experienced Net-surfer who wants a guide to Web sites or help with customizing Mosaic, we think you'll get something out of this book.

Chapter 1, *The Wide World of Internet Services*, provides an overview and history of the Internet, including the development of the World Wide Web and Mosaic.

Chapter 2, *Getting Started with Mosaic*, describes how to begin using NCSA Mosaic and covers the most important aspects of the Mosaic interface.

Chapter 3, *Exploring the World Wide Web*, covers how to navigate through the World Wide Web. It includes a tour of *GNN* and provides pointers to some of the more fascinating places on the Web.

Chapter 4, *Accessing Other Internet Services*, describes how to use Mosaic as a browser for Gopher, FTP, WAIS, TELNET, and NetNews.

Chapter 5, *Customizing Mosaic*, explains how to make changes in Mosaic's default behavior.

Chapter 6, *Using Mosaic for Multimedia*, gives the lowdown on using other programs to play audio, video, and other multimedia files.

Chapter 7, *Creating HTML Documents*, gives a tutorial in how to write your own Web documents.

Chapter 8, *Future Directions*, discusses future development of the Web. It introduces the new World Wide Web Organization (W3O), which is a development consortium founded by MIT and CERN.

Appendix A, *Mosaic Reference Guide*, describes all the user functions available from Mosaic's interface and menus.

Appendix B, *HTML Reference Guide*, describes the tags used to create World Wide Web documents.

Appendix C, *List of X Resources*, lists all the X resources you can use to customize Mosaic's appearance and behavior.

Appendix D, *Installing Mosaic*, describes how to install Mosaic from the CD-ROM provided with this book.

NCSA Mosaic

The Mosaic Handbook for the X Window System includes NCSA Mosaic Version 2.4 on CD-ROM. Future editions will include Enhanced NCSA Mosaic, a commercial version that was not available at the time this book went to the printer. If you register your copy of NCSA Mosaic by sending us the registration form in the back of this book, we will upgrade you to Enhanced NCSA Mosaic as soon as it becomes available.

Enhanced NCSA Mosaic is based on the original Mosaic developed at the National Center for Supercomputing Applications (NCSA). However, it is not a public domain program, nor is it the same as the versions that can be downloaded from the Net.

Spyglass, Inc. was chosen by NCSA as the master licensee of NCSA Mosaic. They will license Enhanced NCSA Mosaic to other vendors, who will then distribute copies to end users. Spyglass is committed to maintaining a single code base for all three Mosaic platforms and keeping a consistent interface across all platforms. Thus, all three versions should be consistent in their reliability and functionality, which has not been true in the versions on the Net.

Enhanced NCSA Mosaic features a number of improvements over the original NCSA version, including:

- Dramatically faster performance

- Easier installation

- Simplified interface for easier browsing

- Support for forms, allowing for two-way communication between users and Web servers

- Proxy gateway support for security in networked environments

- Online help system

NCSA is now focusing on research into advanced features for the next generation of Mosaic, such as voice recognition, full-motion video, and intelligent agents for searching on the Internet. NCSA will continue to offer a public-with-copyright version of Mosaic over the Internet, which you can download for free. As part of the NCSA-Spyglass agreement, Spyglass will provide many of its improvements to NCSA, which will incorporate them into their version.

Support and Registration

As we just said, this book includes NCSA Mosaic. When Enhanced NCSA Mosaic for the X Window System becomes available, we will upgrade users of this edition of the Mosaic Handbook and begin to supply it with future editions. To ensure that you get the upgrade, be sure to fill out and send us the registration card in the back of the book, or complete the online registration form accessible from the Mosaic Handbook Home Page. Check the *Mosaic Handbook Support Center* to learn about updates to the program.

If you have problems with the software, check the online Support Center. If you cannot solve your problem using the online resources, you can send email to *support@gnn.com.* We generally cannot deal with the specifics of your Internet connection other than what we describe in Chapter 2. Be sure to ask your system administrator or your Internet service provider if you are having problems using Mosaic to access documents on the Internet.

The Home Page

The CD-ROM that comes with this book also includes the Mosaic Handbook Home Page, which is the first page you see when you start this version of Mosaic.

During the installation process, you will copy the Mosaic Handbook Home Page to your system. The Home Page contains links to the *Global Network Navigator*, the *Mosaic Handbook Hotlist*, which provides online links to all the Internet resources mentioned in this book, and the *Mosaic Handbook Support Center*. It also has a link to a document that allows you to register your copy of NCSA Mosaic. These resources are *not* on the CD-ROM shipped with this book; they are on the Internet. If you don't have an Internet connection up and running, you will not be able to access these resources.

The Home Page provides an easy way for you to start using the World Wide Web and the Internet. Later in the book, we will show you how to modify the Home Page and add links to your favorite resources.

Throughout the book, we'll refer to the Mosaic Handbook Home Page as your Home Page (with initial capital letters) to distinguish it from other home pages in general. Most servers have a home page, which is the first document you come to when connecting to a server. We'll refer to these pages by their full names, such as the NCSA Mosaic Home Page.

The Mosaic Handbook Hotlist

Because filenames and server locations change with great frequency, we have created the *Mosaic Handbook Hotlist*. This document will be maintained on the *GNN* server (rather than put on this book's disk) so that it can be updated in case the network addresses of the resources described in this book change. Online access will also make it more convenient for you because you don't have to type the long addresses yourself.

Conventions

The following font conventions are used in this book:

Italic	is used for file and directory names, USENET newsgroups, and to emphasize new terms.
Bold	is used for commands, command-line options, hypertext links, and Internet names and addresses.
`Constant Width`	is used for HTML tags, X resource names and values, and the contents of files or the output of commands in examples.
`Constant Italic`	is used within examples for variables that the reader will replace with an actual value.
`Constant Bold`	is used within examples for text that is literally typed by the user.

Acknowledgments

This book was produced as the result of a collaborative effort over a fairly short period of time. Ron Petrusha provided an early draft of the book, and a number of other people contributed throughout the process. In particular, we'd like to thank the entire staff of *GNN*, who are responsible for developing the Internet's premier Web site. We'd especially like to recognize Joan Callahan, Ellie Cutler, John Labovitz, Jennifer Niederst, and D.C. Denison. Joan, Ellie, and John contributed to Chapter 3. In Chapter 8, we used articles that D.C. wrote for *GNN* to describe the World Wide Web organization. Jennifer, *GNN*'s Art Director, designed the Mosaic Handbook Home Page and its supporting documents.

Richard Koman did a terrific job of coming in under pressure to help get this book together. He wrote chapters 2, 4, 5, 6, and 7. Dale Dougherty, publisher of *GNN*, wrote chapters 1, 3, and 8. Paula Ferguson did a great job of reviewing the book and adapting it for the X Window System, rewriting chapters 5 and 6 and revising chapters 2 and 4.

Stephen Spainhour handled the production duties in getting this version of the book into print. Clairemarie Fisher O'Leary also steered the various versions of the book through production and caught a few errors of ours based on her own knowledge of HTML. Edie Freedman designed the cover art, capturing our navigation theme. Chris Reilley handled the illustrations throughout the book. Frank Willison, O'Reilly's Managing Editor, coordinated this effort and kept us on track. Chris Tong and Susan Reisler did the indexing. Frank Howard captured the screenshots for the Windows version. Valerie Quercia wrote the glossary. Lenny Muellner and Jessica Hekman provided technical support. Sheryl Avruch and Sue Willing also provided invaluable help with various production and administrative tasks.

Thanks also to Tim O'Reilly, whose company has made it possible to grow in so many interesting and worthwhile directions.

## CHAPTER ONE

THE WIDE WORLD OF INTERNET SERVICES

What Is the Internet?
The Internet and Online Services
The Client and the Server
The Development of WWW and Mosaic
Developing The Global Network Navigator

Without the Internet, Mosaic wouldn't make much sense. Using Mosaic on a computer that's not connected to the Internet is like having a car that sits in the driveway. Before you go to visit the many services that the Internet has to offer, there are a few things you should know about this global network.

This chapter contains basic information about the Internet, which is useful for understanding how Mosaic works. It explains the client/server architecture behind most Internet information services. We also examine the development of the World Wide Web and how Mosaic came to be. If you find yourself itching to get started, please feel free to jump ahead to the next chapter. This chapter isn't "required reading" because it contains information that most people on the Internet already know.

What Is the Internet?

Not so long ago, if you asked "What is the Internet?" you'd get a technical answer. A longtime Internet user would usually make the following points:

- The Internet is a network of networks, with hundreds of thousands of computers connected to one another.

- The TCP/IP protocols at the core of the Internet describe how messages are addressed and sent as packets from one computer on the network to another computer. A packet may be routed through several computers to reach its destination.

- The Internet came into being as a U.S. Defense Department network, ARPAnet, that was designed to withstand a nuclear bomb attack. It is a distributed network without a vulnerable central hub.

- The National Science Foundation (NSF) built a network, NSFNET, on the same model as ARPAnet to connect research and educational institutions. Because of the government funding, commercial traffic was restricted by an Acceptable Use Policy. In the early 1990's private, commercial networks joined the Internet, and restrictions on commercial activity were relaxed.

Today, the Internet has come to mean something much more than a physical network with historical ties to research, education, and national defense. It has become a cultural icon, emblazoned on the cover of *Time* magazine, and the subject of many stories in your hometown newspaper and the *Wall Street Journal.* The Internet has come to represent what the future looks like today, and to suggest what is possible when people can communicate with each other around the world.

The Internet has been variously characterized as the Information Superhighway, the Infobahn, and Cyberspace. It has been called the best reason to have a personal computer at home. John Markoff of *The New York Times* has written that the PC, not the set-top box, will rule the consumer market and that services such as those provided on the Internet will be available sooner and prove more valuable than video-on-demand and 500-channel cable systems.

So, what do people do on the Internet? They exchange email, follow newsgroups, and download files. They also find information and other people. These are things that many people have done for years on traditional online services such as CompuServe and America Online. What's so fascinating about the Internet? How does it differ from these online services?

The Internet Is Distributed

You could say that CompuServe is a big computer and hard disk in Columbus, Ohio. CompuServe users dial in via modems to access that computer and its data. It is a centralized network, completely owned and operated by CompuServe.

The Internet, in contrast, is completely distributed. Your computer connects to another computer that is connected to another computer. That's how the Internet works. You are accessing not one computer, but many. You connect to your Internet service provider and from that point you can access any computer on the network.

The Internet Is International

Perhaps the most exciting thing about the Internet is its sheer size. While the Internet has its origins in America and most of the Internet traffic originates here, it is a global network. The fact that we can retrieve a document from Switzerland, Germany, Japan, or New Zealand demonstrates that we live in an interconnected global community.

The Internet Is Wide Open

Nobody really runs the Internet—at least not yet. Some have compared the Internet to the Wild West, with arguments escalating into flame wars instead of gunfights. There are few rules, at least written ones, but there is a culture that tends to support and enforce its wishes. In contrast, CompuServe is controlled and institutional, like a hospital or an airport.

The Internet is wide open in a technical sense. Nobody owns the Internet, and there is little proprietary technology involved in its operation. This means that people have lots of choices.

The Internet and Online Services

One of the most interesting developments on the Internet is its potential to redefine how we obtain online services via a public network. The Internet effectively unbundles the services that a traditional online service provides; that is, the charge for network access is separated from the charge for content. For instance, a customer of Mead Data, which provides Lexis and Nexis online services, uses a private network, a software interface, and a delivery system, all built and maintained by Mead Data in order to supply the content to their users. Users pay high hourly rates for the amount of time they are on Lexis or Nexis accessing content.

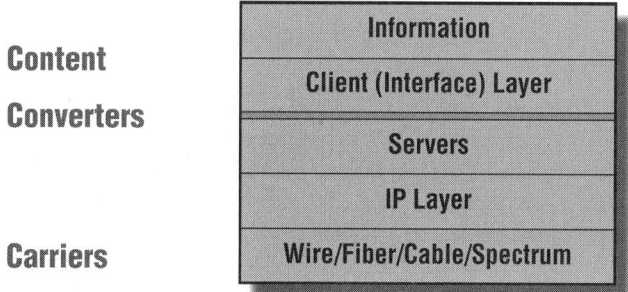

Figure 1-1. Layers of the Internet

Figure 1-1 shows the layers of the Internet. Each layer may be supplied by a different vendor. At the bottom is the carrier, the wire over which the bits are transmitted. These are typically phone lines leased from the local and national phone companies, but the carrier can also be a cable company.

The next layer up from the bottom is the IP (*Internet Protocol*) layer. Each Internet service provider has a network of computers that it serves, and it routes Internet traffic to and from those machines. At the next layer, you have client and server software. In short, the server software distributes information on the Net, while users run client software to access and display that information.

A traditional online service often supplies a single interface program—usable only with that service. On the Internet, you have lots of tools to choose from, including programs to exchange email, participate in newsgroups, and search and gather information. In many cases, there are shareware or public domain versions of these programs as well as fuller-featured, commercially supported programs. The point is that there are many sources that can supply you with an Internet connection and the kinds of tools that you use while connected.

Because the Internet is a general-purpose network that has many uses, a company might install an Internet connection just as it does a phone system. It allows users within the company to communicate with the rest of the world. The general-purpose network serves those who want access to information as well as those who want to provide information to others. In fact, with this information infrastructure in place, it becomes easier and cheaper to become an information provider and more people can do it. That has great potential for revolutionizing the business of online information services.

The Client and the Server

A key to making Internet information services more accessible is making them easier to use. For many users, their first experience with the Internet was a UNIX command-line prompt:

```
unix%
```

At this prompt, the user would type in various commands such as "who am i" or "ftp" or "rlogin."

Until recently, UNIX was the interface of the Internet and you had to learn something about the UNIX command set to navigate successfully. UNIX is a very powerful operating system (and the Internet, as well as O'Reilly & Associates, owes a lot to UNIX), and networking is part of its basic design. From the very beginning UNIX computers were networked to each other, and programmers found useful ways to take advantage of the benefits. On UNIX systems, many programs were designed with a client/server architecture, which means that a program was divided into two parts that could run on different computers.

Take a word processing program as an example. Imagine that all the file handling routines are executed on a computer dedicated to that task. This software is the *server*. On your personal computer, meanwhile, a program controls the user interface and responds to your interactions. This is the *client*. When you ask for a file, the client program sends a message to the server to send that file. The server complies with the request, and the client then interprets and displays the file.

In other words, the server software on one computer manages the information and access to it, and the client program on another computer manages the user's interactions with the information.

One exciting aspect of client/server design is that multiple clients can interact with a single server or with many different servers. In addition, clients can fit into the user's enviroment and assume the likeness of other locally run programs.

In short, this means that Windows users can run a Windows client that interacts with servers on powerful UNIX machines. As a user, you get the benefit of using a client that fits into your computing environment, while accessing a central file server that can handle lots of requests at once.

Mosaic is client software, and there are Mosaic clients for the Windows, Macintosh, and X Window System environments. All three programs receive the same information from the server, but they may display it differently. Mosaic is specifically designed to access World Wide Web servers, but it can also access other types of information servers.

Information Servers

An Internet-based information server is a computer that runs a program to handle incoming requests for information. There are actually many different types of information servers on the Internet. In this section, we will survey FTP, Gopher, and WAIS. Each provides a different way to access information, and user interactions range from the simple to the arcane. When we get to the World Wide Web in the next section, you will better understand how information access can be even easier.

FTP

If you run an FTP (*File Transfer Protocol*) server, you allow users on other computers to log on to your computer and retrieve files that you have put in a public area. Since giving each user an account would be a problem, an FTP server is set up to accept anonymous logins.

When O'Reilly & Associates first published our computer books, we made sample source code available on our FTP server. One server that we use for this is **ftp.ora.com**. We told our readers how to come in using the Internet and retrieve the files. Below you can see a sample FTP session, in which, after logging in, we change directory (**cd**) and then use the **get** command to retrieve the file named *bookcat.txt*.

```
dale % ftp ftp.ora.com
Connected to ruby.ora.com.
220 ruby FTP server (Version wu-2.4(1) Fri Apr 15 14:14:30 EDT 1994) ready.
Name (ftp.ora.com:dale): anonymous
331 Guest login ok, send your complete e-mail address as password.
Password:
230-Welcome to O'Reilly & Associates, Inc. FTP Archive.
230-
230-If your ftp client chokes on this message, log in with a '-' as the
230-first character of your password to disable it.
```

```
230-
230-If you have problems with or questions about this service, send mail to
230-ftp-manager@ora.com; we'll try to fix the problem or answer the
230-question.
230-
230-Current local time is Mon Aug 1 00:02:24 1994
230-
230 Guest login ok, access restrictions apply.
ftp> cd /pub
250-This directory includes...
250-
250-book_covers Image files of the covers of O'Reilly's books
250-book* Book catalog in four different formats
250-errata/ Errata and updates for various O'Reilly titles
250-examples/ Example files and programs from O'Reilly publications
250-
250-"Index" files in this directory and subdirectories have more information.
250-
250-Please read the file Index
250- it was last modified on Thu Jul 21 08:44:06 1994 - 11 days ago
250 CWD command
successful.
ftp> get bookcat.txt
200 PORT command successful.
150 Opening ASCII mode data connection for bookcat.txt (124651 bytes).
226 Transfer complete.
local: bookcat.txt remote: bookcat.txt
127533 bytes received in 31 seconds (4 Kbytes/s)
ftp> quit
```

The advantage of FTP is that any kind of file can be made available, whether
ASCII text, PostScript, or various graphics formats. Almost anyone on the Internet
can access a file via FTP, although the commands make it feel like a lot of hard
work. With FTP, if you know what you want and where it is located, then it works
reasonably well.

Gopher

Gopher originated at the University of Minnesota where the varsity is known as
the Golden Gophers. Gopher made things easy for users looking for information,
as well as for organizations wanting to provide information. From the user's point
of view, information on a Gopher server is organized as a series of hierarchical
menus. Using a Gopher client, you choose a particular item on a menu and
receive either a submenu or a text file.

Putting up a Gopher server requires not much more effort than running an FTP
server. You arrange files in a set of directories, with each directory corresponding
to a menu of choices presented to the user. At O'Reilly & Associates, we set up a

Gopher server to provide information about our books. You can access this server by running the Gopher client on your local machine. The UNIX command for doing this is:

```
unix% gopher gopher.ora.com
```

There are different Gopher clients available, including several commercial clients for Windows and the Macintosh. Here is the opening screen from our server:

```
Internet Gopher Information Client v2.0.12

Root gopher server: gopher.ora.com

--> 1. About O'Reilly & Associates
    2. News Flash! -- New Products & Projects/
    3. Detailed Product Descriptions/
    4. Ordering Info/
    5. Complete Listing of Titles
    6. FTP Archive & Email Information/
    7. Feature Articles/
    8. Errata for "Learning Perl"/
    9. Bibliographies/

Press ? for Help, q to Quit Page: 1/1
```

Gopher was responsible for the first big surge in Internet traffic as people began exploring what was available on servers throughout the world. Anyone can quickly understand how to move through the network of Gopher servers.

Unfortunately, what Gopher gained in ease of use, it lost in flexibility. Users felt as though they were always moving from one menu list to another, and when you finally got somewhere, you ended up with a ASCII document that wasn't very enjoyable to read.

WAIS

WAIS (*Wide Area Information Servers*) was developed by a consortium of four companies interested in developing an easy-to-use searching system. The consortium, consisting of Thinking Machines Corp., Apple Computer, Dow Jones, and KPMG Peat Marwick, was lead by Brewster Kahle, then at Thinking Machines in Cambridge, Massachusetts. Brewster saw that there was so much information available on the Internet that anyone would have trouble locating the most relevant documents.

Each WAIS server contains a full-text index of all the documents on the server. A user of a WAIS client submits a simple query, such as a keyword or phrase, and the WAIS server returns a list of the documents that contain those words. If you select one of the documents from the list, it will be displayed on your computer.

Although WAIS was originally developed for use with a graphical client on the Apple Macintosh, in practice most people do not use a WAIS client. They access a

WAIS server using either a Gopher client or a WWW client. Therefore, searching for a document has become an alternative to browsing. For instance, on the O'Reilly Gopher server, you can access a WAIS server to perform a keyword search of the book descriptions online. This is what a WAIS query looks like:

```
+----------------------Keyword search on Descriptions----------------------+
| |
| Words to search for |
| _____ |
| |
| |
| [Help: ^_] [Cancel: ^G] |
+--------------------------------------------------------------------------+
```

If we enter the keyword "Internet" in the search field, WAIS will return a list of books whose descriptions contain that word. The result looks like this:

```
Keyword search on Descriptions: Internet

--> 1. !%@:: A Directory of Electronic Mail Addressing & Networks
    2. Computer Security Basics
    3. Connecting to the Internet: An O'Reilly Buyer's Guide
    4. DNS and BIND
    5. European Networking
    6. Global Network Operations
    7. Learning the UNIX Operating System
    8. Mobile IP Networking
    9. Networked Information and Online Libraries
    10. Notable Speeches of the Information Age, John Perry Barlow: USENIX
Conferen..
    11. Security and Networks
    12. TCP/IP Network Administration
    13. The Future of the Internet Protocol
    14. The Whole Internet User's Guide & Catalog
    15. Volume 6A: Motif Programming Manual
```

Selecting any book by number will display the book's description. Note that WAIS tries to rank the list in order of importance, but you usually have to scan the list and select the most appropriate choice. For instance, the book that is most clearly about the Internet, *The Whole Internet User's Guide and Catalog*, shows up 14th on the list.

WAIS is a valuable tool for indexing large bodies of information and helping users locate specific documents in a collection. However, most users do not find searching alone to be an intuitive way to work. Therefore, WAIS servers typically run alongside other servers.

For more information about information servers and how to set them up, see *Managing Internet Information Services* by Cricket Liu, Jerry Peek, Bryan Buus, Russ Jones, and Adrian Nye, published by O'Reilly & Associates.

The Development of WWW and Mosaic

The World Wide Web is very similar in design to the Internet-based information servers we examined in the last section. However, WWW offers several advances, including a document-oriented view of computing that offers formatted text and graphics instead of menu lists.

The World Wide Web at CERN

The World Wide Web originated at the European Particle Physics Laboratory (CERN) in Geneva, Swizterland. Tim Berners-Lee, an Oxford University graduate who came to CERN with a background in text processing and real-time communications, wanted to create a new kind of information system in which researchers could collaborate and exchange information during the course of a project. For most scientists, a publication presents a record of what a project accomplished; that is, you read it after the project is long over. Tim saw the need for physicists to collaborate in real-time, and not just on one project, but on the many that were ongoing.

Tim used hypertext technology to link together a web of documents that could be traversed in any manner to seek out information. The web does not imply a hierarchical tree, the structure of most books, or a simple ordered list. In essence, it allows many possible relations between any individual document and others. Tim implemented hypertext as a navigational system, allowing users to move freely from one document to another on the Net, regardless of where the documents are located.

The term "hypertext" was coined in the 1960's by Ted Nelson, who defined it as "non-sequential writing." He wanted to emphasize that hypertext applied to not only locating and reading information, but also to creating it. Nelson popularized the idea in his books and his vision of a global hypertext system called Xanadu. This was a project designed to remain incomplete, rather like building a library to contain all the world's information. Surprisingly, the World Wide Web comes as close to realizing Xanadu as anything Nelson and his associates have achieved. (Nelson has argued that WWW lacks several key aspects of his system.)

While the WWW does present a navigational model that is much easier for users, it also presents some problems for information providers. It requires authoring documents in a particular format defined by the system. Specifying a document format is necessary if hypertext links are to be embedded in the document.

There were many implementations of hypertext systems before the World Wide Web. What Tim did, in cooperation with others at CERN, such as Robert Caillau, was to define an Internet-based architecture using open, public specifications and free, sample implementations on the client and server end. Because the specifications are public, anyone can build a client or a server. Because there are sample implementations and the code can be obtained for free, developers can choose to build or refine parts of the system. Both factors encourage other people to contribute to the project, and as is true of many things on the Internet, the WWW effort has turned into a collaborative project involving people and organizations from around the world.

WWW specifications

Let's look briefly at the WWW specifications. While this is not necessary for you to become a Mosaic user, it will help you understand how Mosaic works.

The World Wide Web is a set of public specifications and a library of code for building clients and servers. There are three key specifications:

- URL (*Uniform Resource Locator*)

- HTTP (*HyperText Transfer Protocol*)

- HTML (*HyperText Markup Language*)

Figure 1-2 illustrates how these specifications work together. A URL is the address of a document on a network server. If a user clicks on a link in a document, the link contains a URL which the client interprets and then initiates a session with the specified server. HTTP is the protocol, a fixed set of messages and replies, that both the client and server understand. Thus, the client sends a message to the server requesting a document and the server returns it. The document itself is coded in HTML, and the browser interprets the HTML to identify the elements of the document and to render it. The use of HTML allows documents to be formatted for presentation using fonts and line justification appropriate for the system on which it is displayed.

The format of a URL is discussed in Chapter 2, *Getting Started with Mosaic*. The HTTP protocol is not discussed further in this book. The basics of HTML are covered in Chapter 7, *Creating HTML Documents*.

Early Browser Development

The team at CERN implemented a line-mode browser, which is the lowest common denominator among browsers, and can be used from almost any kind of terminal.

```
Welcome to the World-Wide Web
THE WORLD-WIDE WEB

This is just one of many access points to the web, the universe of
information available over networks. To follow references, just type the
number then hit the return (enter) key.

The features you have by connecting to this telnet server are very primitive
compared to the features you have when you run a W3 "client" program on your
own computer. If you possibly can, please pick up a client for your platform
to reduce the load on this service and experience the web in its full
splendor.
```

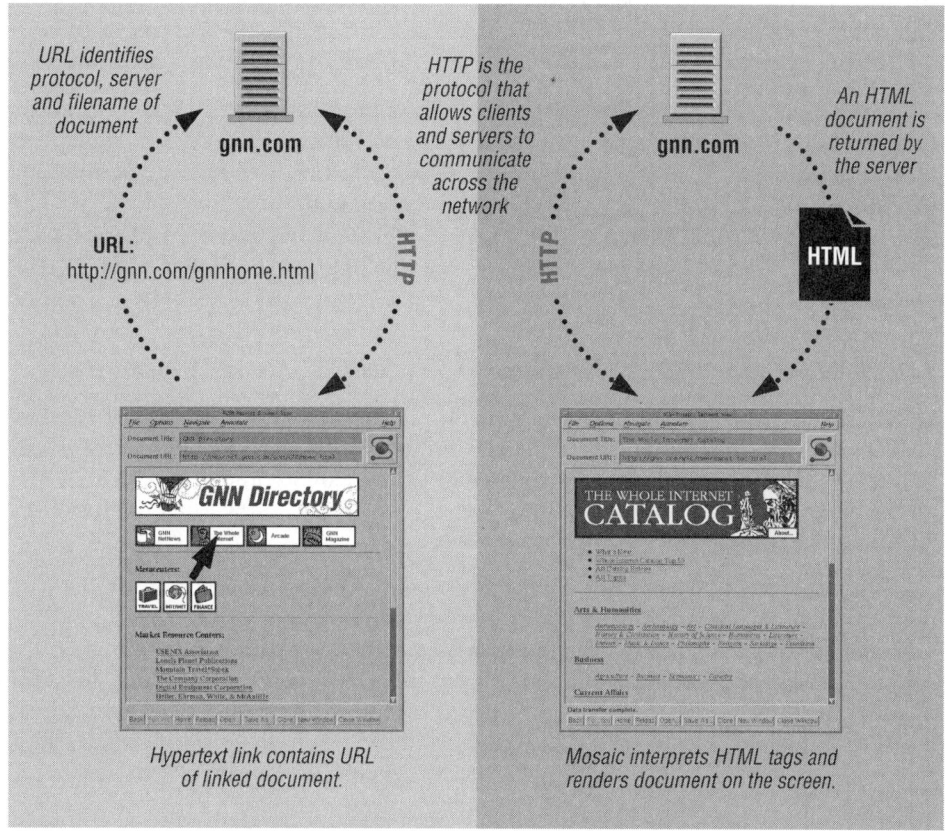

Figure 1–2. Key specifications of WWW

```
For more information, select by number:

A list of available W3 client programs[1]
Everything about the W3 project[2]
Places to start exploring[3]
The First International WWW Conference[4]

This telnet service is provided by the WWW team at the European Particle
Physics Laboratory known as CERN[5]
[End]
1-5, Up, Quit, or Help: q
```

The example above shows the initial login session with the line-mode browser, using TELNET to access the CERN server (**info.cern.ch**). As you can see, the screen is formatted ASCII text. Links are numbered and appear inside brackets. To follow a link, you enter the number of the link at the prompt at the bottom of the screen.

Another browser with a better interface was developed for Steven Jobs' NeXT computer. However, it did not receive wide usage outside CERN. Lynx, a browser with a full-screen interface, was developed at Kansas University by Lou Montulli.

With these early browsers, WWW had reached proof-of-concept stage when the first versions of Mosaic became available in the spring of 1993, but it had not achieved widespread use. While multiple clients existed, none of them suggested the potential of combining text and graphics in a graphical Web client. With an easy-to-use interface that lets you click on a link to navigate the Web, as well as the ability to display graphics, Mosaic made the Internet accessible to a broader group of users.

The Development of Mosaic at NCSA

The National Center for Supercomputing Applications (NCSA), located at the University of Illinois at Urbana-Champaign, is funded by the National Science Foundation to provide supercomputing resources to the research community. NCSA is part of a wider effort by Congress to fund a national infrastructure for high-performance computing and communications.

It would be nice to write that such government funding directly resulted in the development of Mosaic. However, Mosaic came rather unexpectedly. Marc Andreessen was an undergraduate student at UIUC. He had a part-time job at NCSA, building tools for scientific visualization. He began working on Mosaic as one of those tools, but pretty soon, he knew he was on to something bigger. From that point on, Marc was racking up far more hours than his part-time status required. Eventually, Eric Bina joined Marc in developing Mosaic.

To Marc's credit, when he started building Mosaic, he looked around on the Internet and discovered that he didn't have to start from scratch. He found the WWW and saw that it was intended to serve a community similar to the one served by NCSA. Having an existing code base available from CERN meant his work could progress very quickly, even if he had to re-write some of the code to make it usable. It is hard to point out any single new feature that Mosaic introduced, either as a hypertext browser or a WWW client. Rather, Marc made available a solid program with the right number of features for users to feel amazed and empowered by their ability to navigate the riches of the Internet. Figure 1-3 shows Mosaic viewing the *GNN Home* page. Marc was not only the developer of Mosaic, he was also its champion. He spent lots of time on the Web developer mailing list, talking about various development issues. Sometimes he would introduce minor improvements overnight, and sometimes major changes, and send out a new version for immediate distribution on the Net. While many people anxiously awaited the updates, NCSA wasn't sure what Marc had created, and where it fit inside their organization. Nonetheless, the excitement of government supporters, the press, and the Internet user community was overwhelming. NCSA expanded its Mosaic development efforts, hiring students to develop Windows and Mac versions.

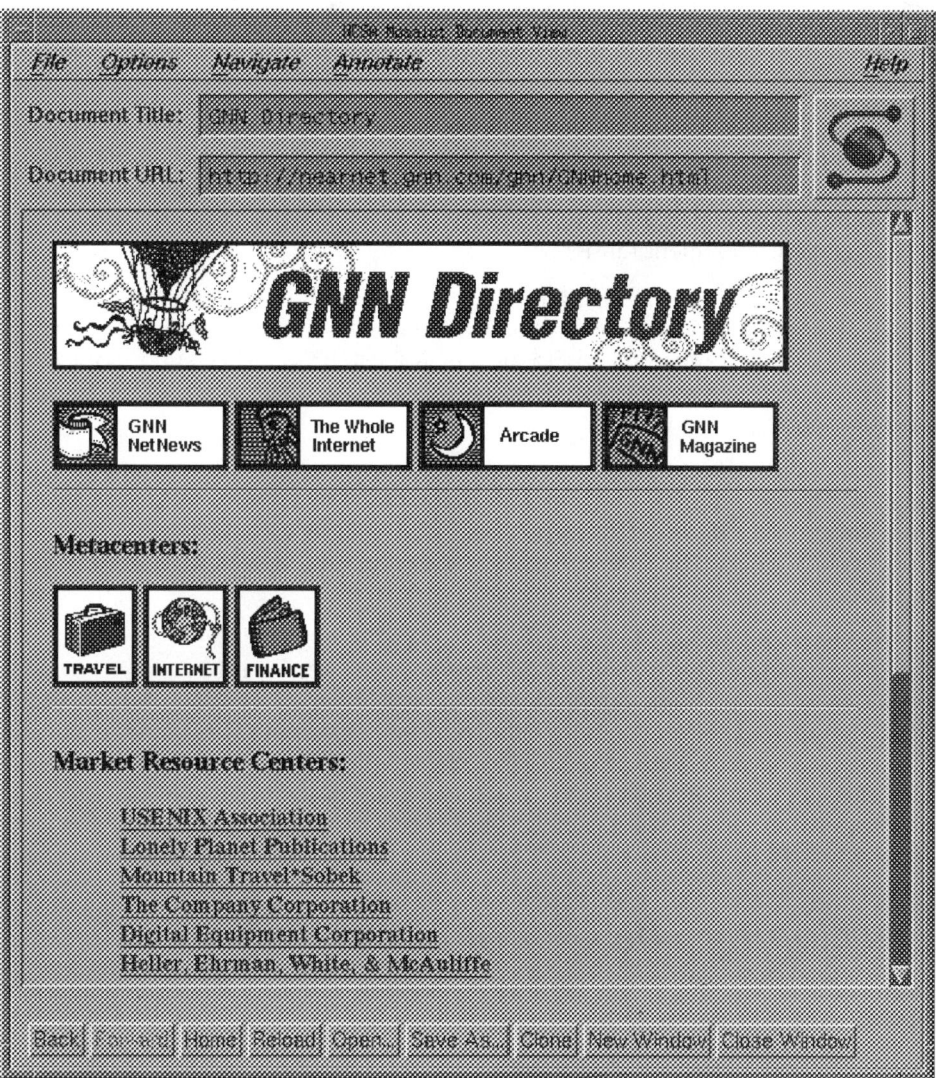

Figure 1-3. Sample Mosaic screen

With the April 1993 release of Mosaic 1.0 for the X Window System, Mosaic began to drive the explosive growth of the World Wide Web. By the fall, Version 2.0 of Mosaic for X came out, and the first beta versions of Windows Mosaic and MacMosaic were released. By September 1993, the WWW was responsible for 1% of the traffic on the NSF backbone, and as of June 1994, the Web accounts for at least 6% of the traffic.

Commercialization and Future Developments

NCSA is not a commercial software development organization; it was chartered to create software for scientific researchers and place it in the public domain. NCSA made Mosaic freely available on the Internet "for academic, research, and internal business purposes only." No doubt these terms have helped make Mosaic popular. Anyone can get a copy, try it out, and realize how useful it is. Naturally, commercial software developers have taken notice of Mosaic. Many of them are interested in taking its development further.

Because Mosaic is copyrighted, anyone wanting to modify the source code or distribute binaries of Mosaic must obtain a license to do so from NCSA. Initially, NCSA handled the licensing of Mosaic. In August 1994, NCSA announced that it had reached an agreement with Spyglass Inc. to have them serve as the licensing agent for Mosaic.

As a result of the various licensing deals by companies that will continue development of Mosaic, we may wind up with many different versions of Mosaic. Future editions of *The Mosaic Handbook for the X Window System* will come with Enhanced NCSA Mosaic from Spyglass, which we have chosen because it is likely to define the core feature set for Mosaic.

In the long run, NCSA Mosaic may be viewed as the application that made the Internet important, just as Lotus 1-2-3 created a market for IBM personal computers. Others are at work on products that will compete with Mosaic, including Marc Andreessen himself. Marc left NCSA in December 1993 and eventually founded a company with James Clark, one of the founders of Silicon Graphics, Inc. Mosaic Communications Corp. has hired many of the original Mosaic developers from NCSA, and it will be interesting to see what they create in light of such high expectations.

Developing The Global Network Navigator

At O'Reilly & Associates, we had been looking at various methods of publishing online. After all, we wrote books about computers, and it seemed to make sense to deliver books about computers on computers. We had developed a number of requirements for online publishing and as we began learning about the World Wide Web, we got very excited. At the time, we were just about to publish the best-selling Internet book, Ed Krol's *The Whole Internet User's Guide and Catalog*.

We began to explore the Web and wonder what uses a publisher could make of it. One of our first efforts was an online demo of the resource catalog in the Krol book. It was so well received that we began to think of making it into a product, and that led to the development of the *Global Network Navigator*. Using a Web server to put the resource catalog online was the obvious part of it; we also saw the opportunity to create online magazines. The magazine format could be used to portray what people were doing on the Internet, what they were interested in.

As Mosaic became available in the summer of 1993, we began doing demos and showing people just what was possible with the new technology. In fact, we had to take great pains to make people understand where Mosaic ended and *GNN* began—that Mosaic was intended to retrieve documents from network servers, and we ran a network server ready to deliver our documents upon request to Mosaic users.

We launched *GNN* in August 1993 at the InterOp tradeshow in San Francisco, and it went online officially October 1. We made *GNN* available for free, but asked that users register and become subscribers. As of August 1, 1994, we have over 40,000 subscribers.

GNN introduced advertising in our online publications. We make it possible for advertisers to deliver a message in an editorial context which we have created for users. We also think, perhaps ambitiously, that we can change the nature of advertising by asking advertisers to take advantage of this new medium and provide users with only as much information as they are interested in receiving. We call it "content-driven" advertising.

That is all said to give you some flavor of *GNN* as a pioneering effort in online publishing, an ongoing experiment in creating online audiences. As it grows, *GNN* will continue to change, making it difficult to describe on paper especially using black-and-white screenshots. The real thing is online and in living color. Online, *GNN* may differ some from what you see in this book, but it is a good way to show off the capabilities of Mosaic and to help you explore the World Wide Web.

## CHAPTER TWO

GETTING STARTED WITH MOSAIC

The Right Kind of Internet Connection
Starting Mosaic
Connecting to GNN
Mosaic's Navigation Tools
Document-based Features
When Things Go Wrong

Now that you understand something about how Mosaic, the World Wide Web, and the Internet all fit together, you can start using Mosaic to explore the Web. This chapter will show you how to navigate the Web using hypertext, Mosaic's controls, and Internet path names (called Uniform Resource Locators, or URLs). Once you understand the basic navigation techniques, you can travel the Web to visit an incredibly wide variety of information sources all over the world.

This chapter covers starting Mosaic, navigating with hypertext and URLs, and using Mosaic's feature set. We assume you are familiar with the X environment, so we don't cover the basics of using Motif-based X applications. For guidance in this area, see Volume Three, *X Window System User's Guide, Motif Edition*, from O'Reilly & Associates.

We also expect that Mosaic is installed on your system. If you are using a machine, such as X terminal, that is part of a larger network at your company or school, Mosaic is probably already installed. If it isn't, you'll need to talk to your system administrator. If you manage your own UNIX workstation and you don't yet have Mosaic installed, follow the instructions in Appendix D, *Installing Mosaic*.

Before getting started, however, we must make sure you are on the Internet and have the right kind of connection to use Mosaic. You can't get started without it.

The Right Kind of Internet Connection

You probably already have access to the Internet if you are using a UNIX system at work or at school. If you aren't on the Internet, however, perhaps the most difficult part of using Mosaic is understanding how to obtain the right kind of Internet connection. Fortunately, it is getting a lot easier to get an Internet connection these days, especially if you know which applications you want to use, such as email and Mosaic.

In this section, we give an overview of your options for getting on the Internet. If you want more detail, consult Susan Estrada's *Connecting to the Internet: A Buyer's Guide*, also from O'Reilly & Associates.

First of all, you need to find a local Internet Service Provider. The ISP essentially maintains a computer network of customers who are connected to the Internet through their computers. There are two major lists of Internet service providers—the Public Dialup Internet Access List, or PDIAL, maintained by Peter Kaminski, and Susan Estrada's Internet Access Provider List, or DLIST. To get a copy of PDIAL, send an email message to **info-deli-server@netcom.com** with the text "Send PDIAL" in the body of the message. For information about getting the DLIST, send email to **dlist@ora.com**.

Before you contact an ISP, you should decide which type of connection is best for you. You need to make an assessment of your needs and what you can afford. (It is similar to buying a computer in that regard.)

There are basically three kinds of Internet connections: dialup shell, PPP/SLIP, and dedicated lines.

Dialup Shell Account

> A dialup shell account is usually the cheapest and easiest type of connection you can get. Unfortunately, you can't use Mosaic over that connection. (You have to run a browser such as Lynx on your Internet host computer.)

PPP/SLIP Account

> A PPP/SLIP account usually runs over a high-speed modem (14,400 or 28,000 bits per second, or bps) that connects to your ISP. The main difference between a shell account and a PPP/SLIP account is that the latter puts your computer on the network. Both operate over standard phone lines, and both require you to dial up and connect to an ISP. However, to use a shell account, you typically use a telecommunications program to dial the Internet host and log in. If you have PPP or SLIP, these programs establish the connection and then you can route Internet traffic to and from your machine.

> PPP/SLIP also provides an important piece of the connection puzzle—TCP/IP, the protocols that allows data to traverse multiple networks on the way to its final destination. With a PPP/SLIP account or a dedicated line connection you will be able to use Mosaic just fine.

> While PPP/SLIP connections over fast modems offer reasonable speed, they are still quite a bit slower than dedicated lines, so it's best to get as fast a modem as possible. While you can use a 9600 bps modem with Mosaic, it will seem rather slow. Anything less than 9600 baud is unacceptable.

Dedicated Line

Many organizations connect to the Internet via a dedicated line, which is a separate telecommunications line that connects you to your ISP. Both of you have a piece of equipment known as a router that routes the traffic between your local area network and the computer network maintained by your ISP. Dedicated lines come in various speeds; the slowest is a 56K line, which is four times faster than a 14.4K bps modem.

Peak Performance

When you use Mosaic to retrieve a document from the Internet, there are a number of factors that affect performance. You may click on a link and not get an immediate result. If you understand that your computer is responsible for only a portion of the final result, then you may be more patient. Here are some of the factors affecting performance:

- The speed of your Internet connection

- The amount of traffic on the Internet, which includes all points between you and your destination

- The load on the server from which you are retrieving the document, perhaps along with thousands of other users at the same time

- The size of the document, which often depends on whether or not you are retrieving documents with graphics, or even larger data objects, such as sound or video files

Of these factors, only the first one is really within your control. You may be able to get a higher speed connection by obtaining a faster modem, using ISDN if available, or making arrangements for a dedicated phone line into your business.

Starting Mosaic

Now you're ready to use Mosaic to start navigating the Web. Launch Mosaic using the following command:

```
% Mosaic &
```

Mosaic starts by opening a home page, or start-up document. The version of Mosaic on your CD comes with a special home page created just for this book. If you've installed Mosaic from the CD, you copied this document, the Mosaic Handbook Home Page, to your system during the installation process. Figure 2-1 shows what you will see when Mosaic starts up and displays the Home Page.* If

---

* If your system uses the public domain version of NCSA Mosaic available on the Net, you will not have this special home page. Instead, the public domain version of Mosaic retrieves the NCSA Mosaic home page on the NCSA WWW server. You aren't stuck with this home page, however. It's easy to select another home page, as we'll explain in Chapter 5, *Customizing Mosaic*.

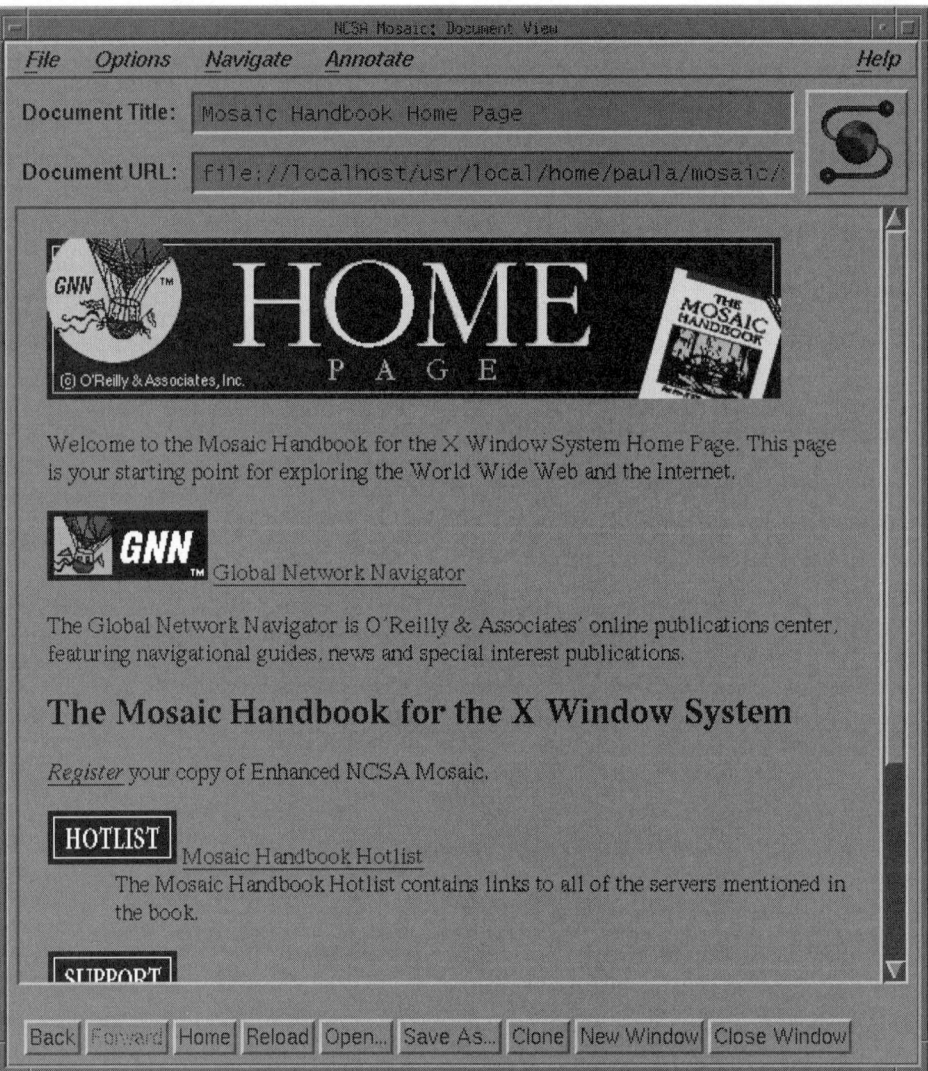

Figure 2-1. Mosaic displaying the Home Page

you are not connected to the Internet, Mosaic will still display the Home Page because it is on your system. However, if you aren't connected, you won't be able to view the linked documents, as they are only available via the Internet. If you are using a modem, make sure that PPP or SLIP is able to connect to your Internet Service Provider. PPP and SLIP can be difficult to configure correctly, so talk to your ISP if you're having a problem.

When you start Mosaic, you will see the home page banner, some introductory text, and several graphics that provide links to Registration, *GNN*, the *Mosaic*

Handbook Hotlist, and Mosaic Support. We'll start our introduction to Mosaic by clicking on these links and exploring some of the resources on *GNN.*

The Mosaic Interface

Before we get started, let's take a minute to get familiar with the Mosaic interface. Figure 2-2 identifies the elements of the interface. Some of these will be discussed in more detail later in the chapter, so at this point we'll move quickly through the interface.

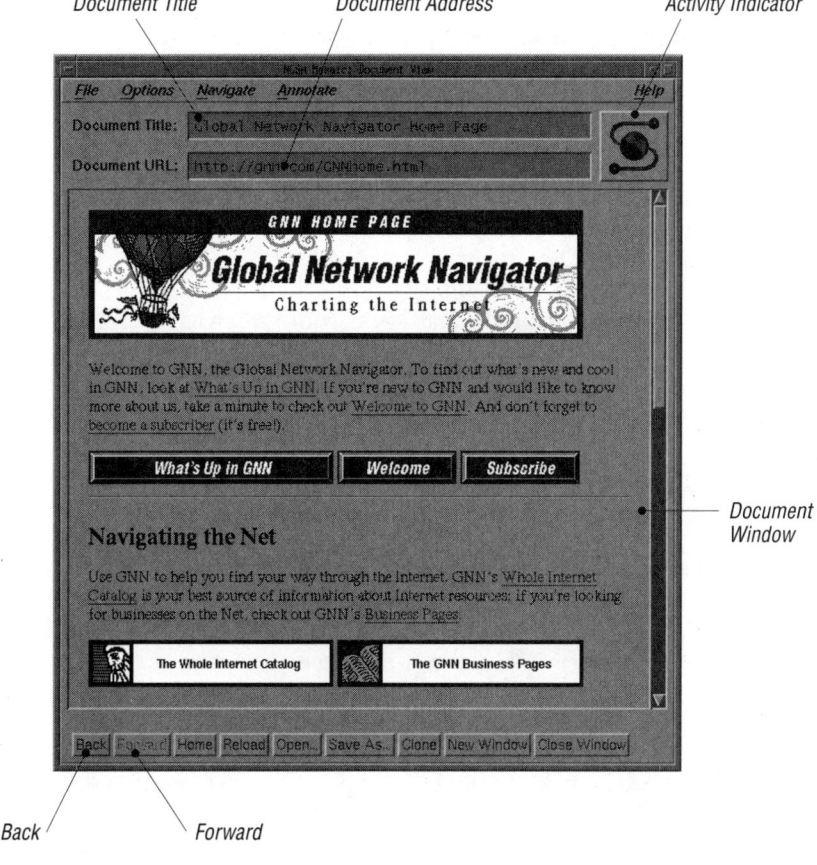

Figure 2-2. Elements of Mosaic's interface

It is important to make a distinction between Mosaic itself and the document it is displaying. In Figure 2-2, Mosaic is displaying the *GNN Home* page in the browsing area of the document window, but the *GNN Home* page is not part of Mosaic. In the title bar displayed by the window manager, you see the words "NCSA

Mosaic: Document View". Mosaic's menu bar is immediately below the title bar; we'll be exploring many of the menu items later in this chapter.

Beneath the menu bar are two fields that display the title and URL of the active document. In this example, the title is "Global Network Navigator Home Page." The globe in the S-shaped icon at the right spins when Mosaic is busy retrieving a document.

The browsing area takes up most of the space in the Mosaic window. Underneath the browsing area is the status area, which displays messages about what Mosaic is doing. The control panel is below the status area. The control panel contains buttons that you use to navigate through the Web with Mosaic.

The uses of these different elements will become clear as we start using the program.

Connecting to GNN

To get started with Mosaic, let's visit *GNN*. You'll notice that the **GNN** icon on the Home Page is surrounded by a heavy border, as are the other icons. That tells you that it's a hypertext link. Click on it to go to *GNN*. Mosaic then goes out on the Internet and downloads the *GNN Home* page. When it's finished, it displays the formatted page—complete with graphics—on your screen, as in Figure 2-2. Each of the graphics on the *GNN Home* page is surrounded by a border, so you know that they're hypertext links. Try clicking on the **What's Up in GNN** bar near the top of the page. After a little while, the *What's Up in GNN* page will be displayed.

A Look at GNN

Congratulations, you've just mastered the most important navigation skill for using Mosaic and the World Wide Web. Clicking on hypertext links is also the easiest and most enjoyable way to navigate the Web. By just clicking on links, you can explore the Web by following subjects and ideas that interest you, discovering new areas of interest in the process. Hypertext links one document to another, which is linked to another, and so on, through literally thousands of documents. This system of links gives the World Wide Web its name; the links are like threads in a spider's web, connecting all the different servers together into a single system. Some servers, like the NCSA and CERN servers, have huge numbers of links pointing to them; others have relatively few.

Now that you have hypertext down, let's throw in one of Mosaic's navigation tools. From the *What's Up* page, click on the **Back** button in the control panel to go back to the *GNN Home* page. Clicking on the **Back** button tells Mosaic to display the last document you were looking at.

Let's take a more in-depth look at the *GNN Home* page. Under the **What's Up in GNN** bar are icons for the four main sections of *GNN*—*NetNews*, *The Whole Internet Catalog*, *Arcade*, and *GNN Magazine*—plus three metacenters—*Travel*,

Internet, and *Finance.* You can visit any of these sections by clicking on the graphic. Next 'is a section called *Market Resource Centers* and a list of company names. This is *GNN*'s advertising section. The company names are hypertext links. To learn about one of the advertisers in this section, click on a name.

At the bottom of the page is a graphic labeled **Subscribe to GNN.** You can click here to fill out a subscription form, which helps us learn who is using *GNN* and what parts of the service are most useful. Let's get started by going to *NetNews,* shown in Figure 2-3. Click on the **NetNews** graphic, and Mosaic gets and displays the *NetNews* home page.

Multimedia in Mosaic

The *GNN* pages integrate text and graphics in one document. These graphics are called *inline graphics* because they are displayed in the document. You can also view full-size images and photographs, animations and video, and listen to sound files. Mosaic cannot display these files directly but relies on "viewer" programs to display them.

Often you'll see a postage stamp-size graphic that is also a link. This image may be linked to a full-size version of the image, which can be displayed in a graphics viewer program. Other links may take you to video, audio, PostScript files, and many other kinds of files. We'll discuss multimedia in more depth in Chapter 6, *Using Mosaic for Multimedia.*

Getting Your Page

How does hypertext work? Basically, when you click on hypertext—whether it's text or graphics—you are telling Mosaic that you want to get the document that is linked to the hypertext. When you clicked on the **NetNews** graphic, you told Mosaic that you wanted to see the *NetNews* home page.

But how does Mosaic know, of all the millions of documents on the Internet, which page is the *NetNews* home page, where it is, or how to get it? It knows because every hypertext link has embedded in it a URL that gives the name of the computer where the document is stored, the path and name of the document, and the protocol for transferring the document. Every computer on the Internet has a unique name and every document has a unique URL.

When you click on the **NetNews** graphic, for instance, a number of things happen:

- Mosaic looks up the URL for that link. In this case it is:

    `http://gnn.com /news/index.html`

- Mosaic opens an HTTP (the Web protocol) connection to the GNN server.

- Mosaic sends the URL to the server to request the *NetNews* home page.

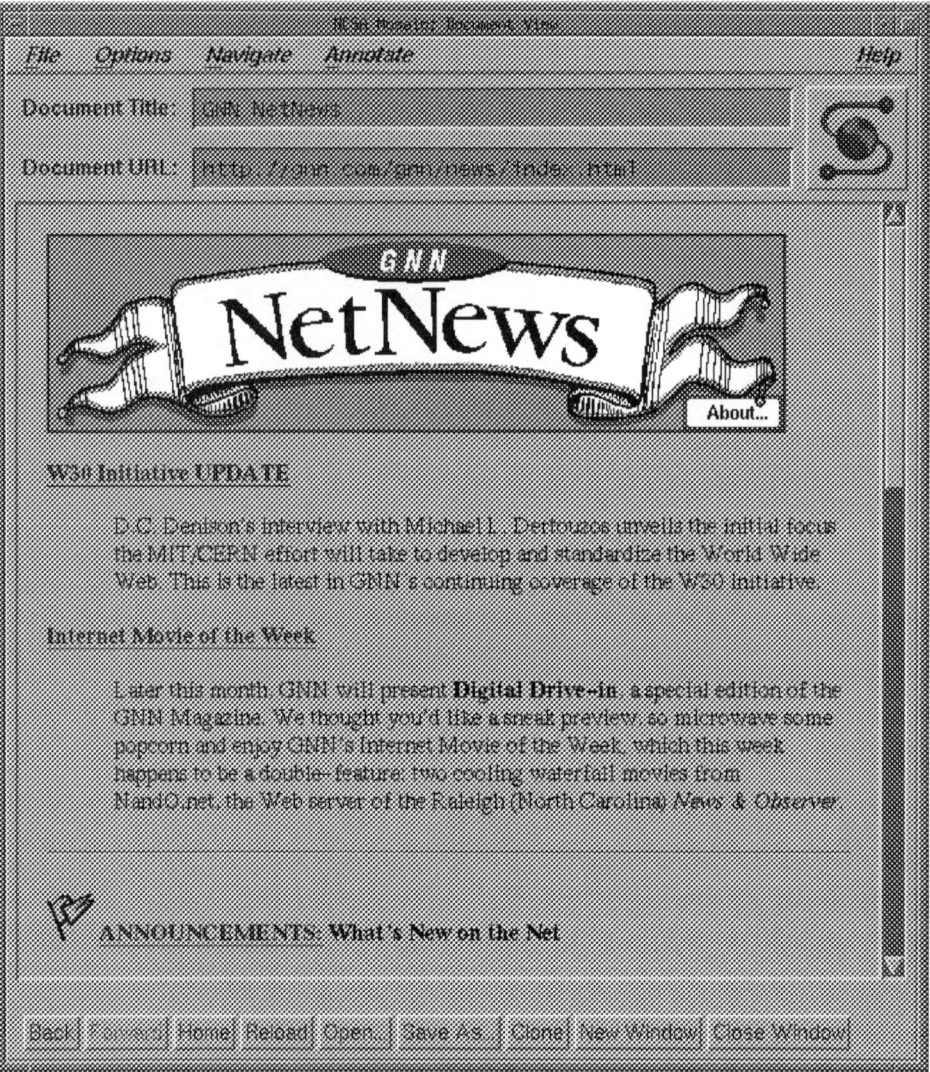

Figure 2-3. NetNews

- The GNN server sends the *NetNews* home page, which is an HTML (Hypertext Markup Language) document. HTML is a simple tagging language that tells Mosaic how to format the document on your computer.

- Often, as with this page, the HTML document includes instructions for graphics files to be displayed at certain positions on the page. Mosaic contacts the server again to download the graphics files.

- When all the related files have been received, Mosaic interprets the HTML tags and displays the document on your computer.

If this all seems complicated, you can be grateful that Mosaic shields you from so much of it. As a Mosaic user, you don't need to know which document you're asking for, what computer it lives on, where that computer is, what the protocol is, or many other things Internet users used to have to know. All you need to be able to do is point at a hypertext link and wait for the document to be delivered.

Mosaic's Navigation Tools

As you link your way around the Web, you'll make the online equivalent of a wrong turn, and you'll want to go back where you came from. Other times, you'll find some pages you really like and want to return to often. And you'll probably forget many the places you've been, but you may want to revisit some of them.

Mosaic provides tools to deal with each of those situations, to give you more control over your Mosaic session than you could possibly have just by following links. The major tools are:

- **Back** and **Forward** buttons (found on the control panel)
- **Window History** (found in the **Navigate** menu)
- **Hotlist** (found in the **Navigate** menu)
- **Home** button (found on the control panel)

Using **Back** and **Forward** is like walking around your neighborhood—it's the quickest way to get to your neighbor's house. **Window History** is like driving your car on the interstate—you have to start it up and pay attention to the exit signs, but it's the best way to cover distance. Using **Hotlist** is like taking a plane to your destination—you have to make arrangements first but once you do, you'll get where you're going in a flash. Finally, no matter how far you travel, you can always use **Home** to return home.

Back and Forward

To check out these tools, let's return to *NetNews*. At the top of the page are two news story headlines. (*NetNews* is a constantly changing section, so the version you see when you connect will be different than the version printed here.) Click on the top story, "W3O Initiative Update," to read that story. The article, which is reprinted in Chapter 8, *Future Directions*, is shown in Figure 2-4.

After you read this article, you may want to go back to the *NetNews* page. To do so, click on the **Back** button at the far left of the control panel. Now click on the second headline, and Mosaic will display the "Internet Movie of the Week" article. Again, clicking on the **Back** button takes you to back to *NetNews*. But if you click on the **Back** button again, you'll return to the W3O article. That's because you're

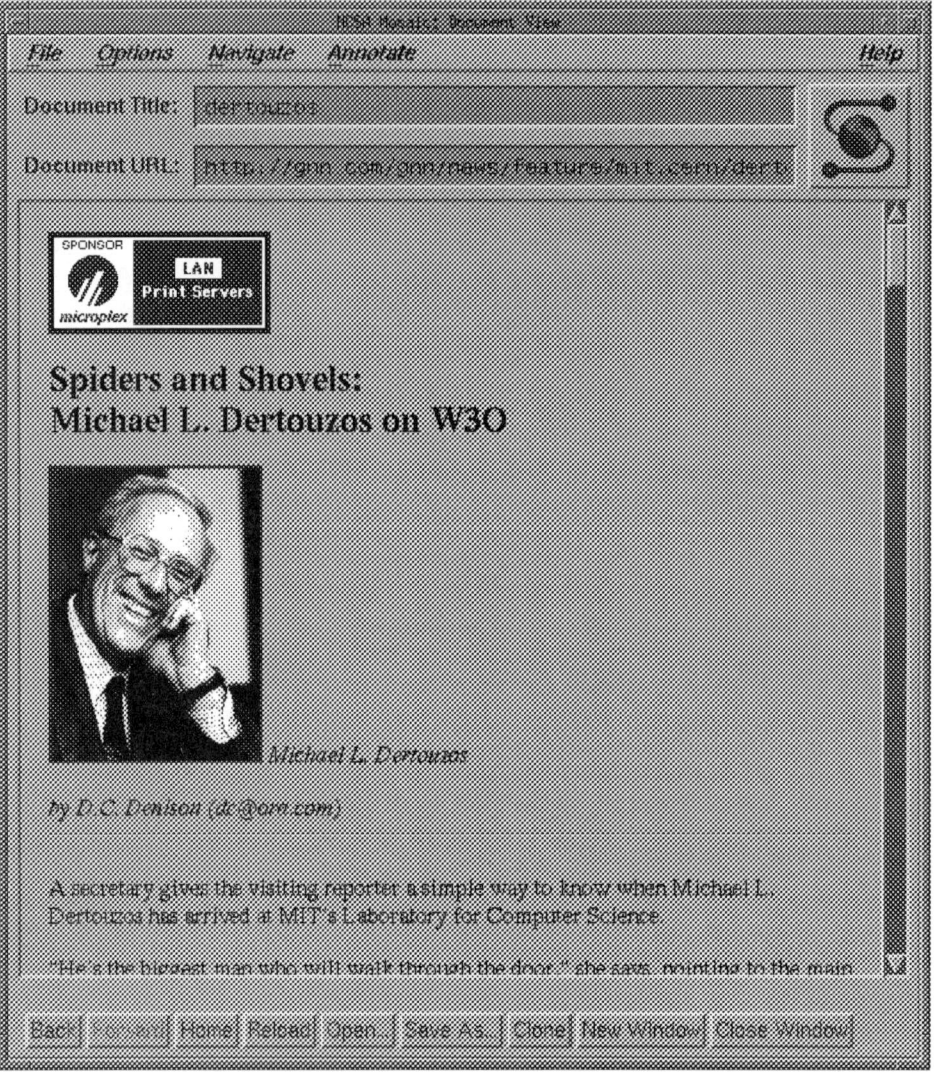

Figure 2-4. W3O Initiative Update

moving back in the order that you viewed different documents. You were looking at the pages in this order:

1. *NetNews*
2. W3O article
3. *NetNews*
4. Internet Movie of the Week

So, starting from "Internet Movie of the Week," clicking **Back** takes you to *NetNews*, then to the W3O article, then back to *NetNews* again, and then back to *GNN Home*.

The **Forward** button works the same way. From *GNN Home*, clicking the **Forward** button takes you to *NetNews*, W3O, *NetNews*, and Internet Movie of the Week.

Mosaic provides keyboard shortcuts in the form of *hot keys* for many of its commands. This is useful if you don't like mousing around. To move forward and backward from the keyboard, press the **F** and **B** keys. These two hot keys are not case sensitive, so you can also use **f** and **b**.

Hotlist

A hotlist is Mosaic's way of letting you save a list of your favorite Web sites. Once you've added a page to your hotlist, you can go right to it by selecting the entry in your hotlist. Let's take a look at how this works.

Using the **Back** and **Forward** buttons, return to the W3O article. This is a long article, so you might want to return to read it later. To make it easily accessible, you can add the article to your hotlist. Under the **Navigate** menu, you'll see the option **Add Current to Hotlist**. Choosing this option adds the article to your hotlist.

Now let's take a look at the hotlist. Again under the **Navigate** menu, select **Hotlist**. (You can also use the **H** hot key.) As you can see in Figure 2-5, the only document in the hotlist is the one we just added. As you add more documents to your hotlist, they will appear in the list window. To go to a document on your hotlist, select the title and click on **Go To**. You can also double-click on the document title.

The **Hotlist** dialog also has several options for managing your hotlist. **Add Current** does the same thing as **Add Current to Hotlist** on the **Navigate** menu. **Delete** removes documents from the list. You can also edit the title of a selected entry, using the **Edit Title** command. With **W3O** selected, click on the **Edit Title** button. Another dialog box will appear with a field for the document title. If you want, you can change the title of the document here.

Note that this dialog does not allow you to edit the URL. The only reason you would want to edit the URL is if a document's URL changes. Usually the server will maintain a document at the old URL, which points to the new document. If the URL changes, add the new document to your hotlist and delete the old one.

Next is the **Mail To** button. This lets you email your hotlist to another person. The hotlist is sent as an HTML document, so the user can save the message and create a Web document on her system that contains hypertext links to all the documents in your hotlist. This is the perfect way to share your hotlist with your friends. You can also use this feature to keep multiple hotlists. Here's how:

1. Navigate around *NetNews*, adding interesting documents to your hotlist as you desire.

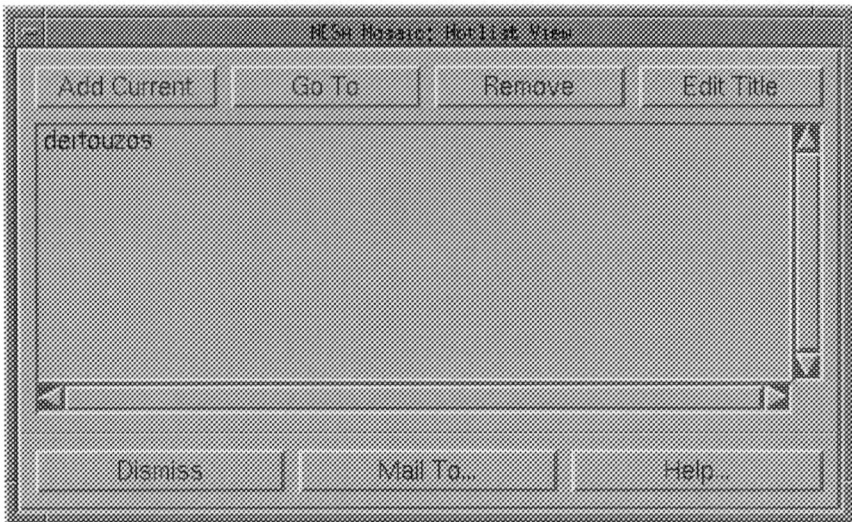

Figure 2–5. Hotlist

2. Now go back to the **Hotlist** dialog and mail the hotlist to yourself. Use your email program to save the message, giving the file a name with an *.html* extension, such as *news.html*.

3. Use **Open Local** on the **File** menu to display your new hotlist page. Figure 2-6 shows a sample hotlist document.

4. Choose **Add Current to Hotlist**. You can now open your hotlist page from the **Hotlist** dialog.

Window History

By the time you've read some of the articles in *NetNews* and visited some of *GNN*'s metacenters, you've been to quite a few places. You probably didn't add to your hotlist all of the documents you might want to look at again. But you don't have to retrace your steps from scratch in order to find those documents. (In fact, the links to some of those documents might disappear.) You can use the **Window History** feature to revisit places you've been.

If you want to go back to the W3O article, for instance, just choose the **Window History** option from the **Navigate** menu. (The hot key **h** also works.) Double-click on **W3O**, and Mosaic displays that document. The **Window History** dialog box, shown in Figure 2-7, contains all the documents you've ever visited, not just the ones you visited in the current session. That makes it quite a powerful tool because you don't have to worry about getting back to a document you saw a week ago.

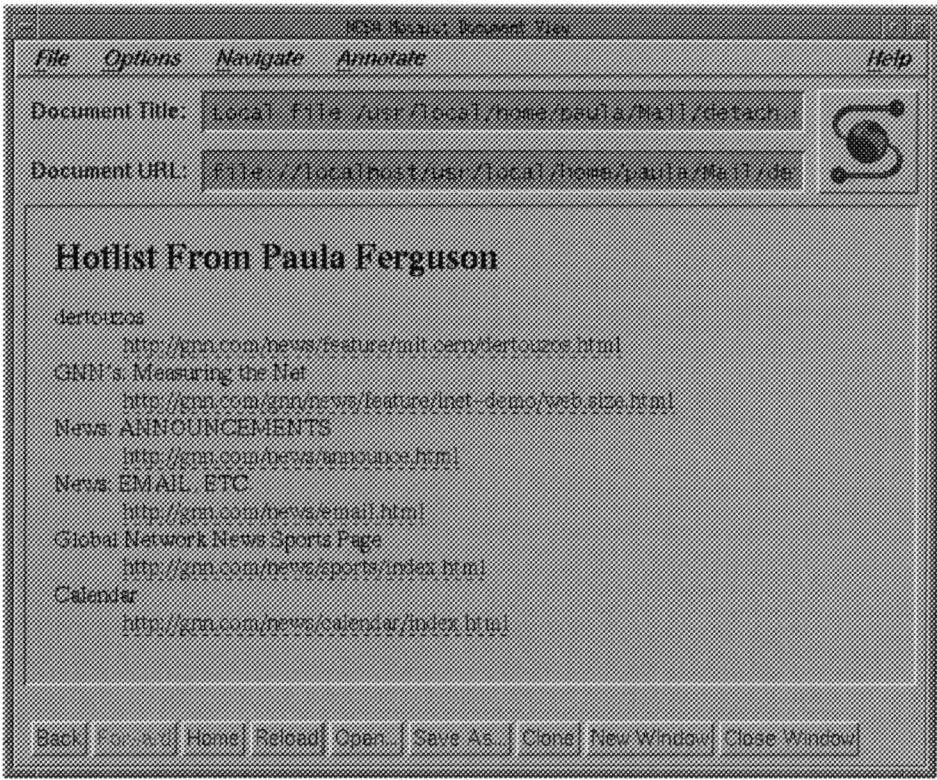

Figure 2-6. Hotlist as a document

On the other hand, it won't take long before your history list is quite unwieldy. You can't remove individual documents from your history list, but you can clear the entire history list by selecting **Clear Global History** on the **Options** menu.

Home

As you travel the Internet with Mosaic, you can get quite far from where you started. Fortunately, if you want to get back to the Home Page at any time, all you have to do is press **Home**. Mosaic stores the URL of your home page, so when you click on **Home**, Mosaic uses the URL to retrieve the document. Selecting **Home Document** on the **Navigate** menu has the same effect. With Mosaic, you can travel far and wide and still never be far from home.

Using URLs

When you know the URL of a document you want to see, you can enter it directly. Select **Open URL** from the **File** menu or press the **Open** button on the control panel to bring up the **Open Document** dialog box. (The hot keys **O** and **o** have

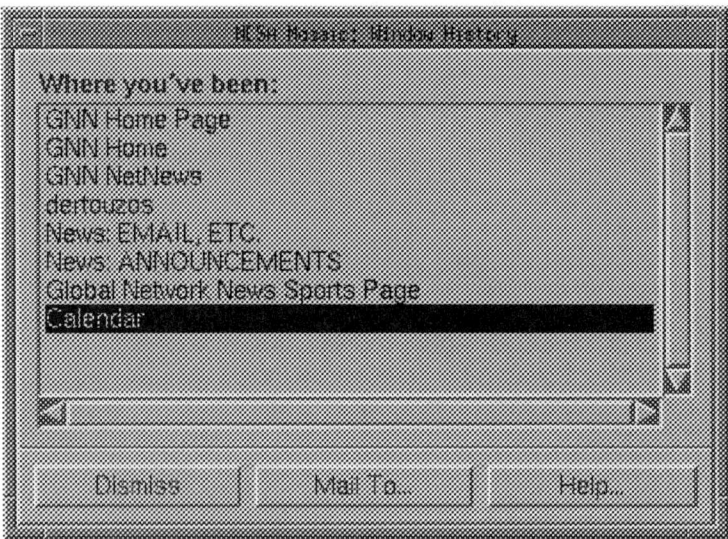

Figure 2-7. Window History

the same effect.) For instance, to get to the *GNN Home* page, you can enter the URL *http://gnn.com/GNNhome.html*, as shown in Figure 2-8. This has the same effect as clicking on a link to that document or choosing it from a hotlist or history window. All the navigation techniques do essentially the same thing—use a URL to identify a document.

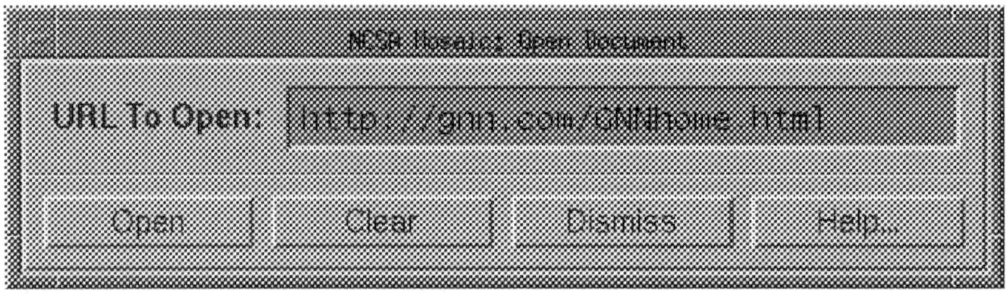

Figure 2-8. Entering a URL

You don't necessarily have to have the full URL to use **Open URL**, however. If you know the directory, you can usually get an index of it by ending the URL with a slash. For instance, try entering this URL: *http://gnn.com/meta/travel/features/*. Figure 2-9 shows the results, an index of all the files in the Travel Center *features* directory.

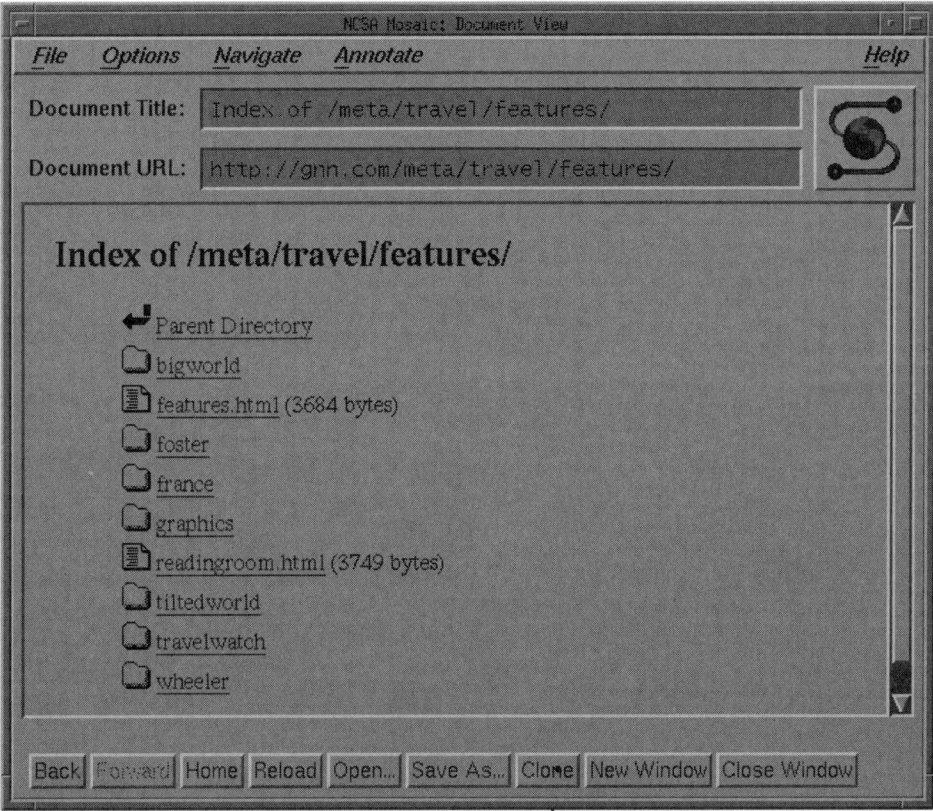

Figure 2–9. Index of the Travel Center's features directory

Finding Text

If you're looking for some specific information in a long document, you can use Mosaic's **Find in Current** command (hot keys **S** and **s**) to search for a text string. Choose **Find in Current** from the **File** menu, which brings up the window shown in Figure 2-10.

You can search forward and backward in the document, as well as use case-sensitive or case-insensitive searching by setting the options in the dialog. Type your search word or phrase into the input area and press **Find**. If Mosaic finds a match, it highlights the string and puts it in the center of the display. The **Reset** button clears the search string and returns you to the position from which you started searching.

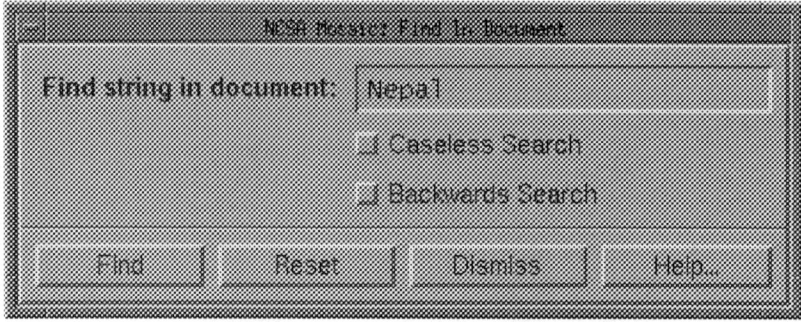

Figure 2-10. Searching a document

Saving, Printing, and Mailing Documents

Mosaic not only lets you navigate around the Net to view documents; it also lets you save documents to your system, print them, and mail them to other people. All are simple operations.

For instance, you can save the W3O article to your system, so you can read it offline. Choose **Save As** from the **File** menu (or control panel) to bring up the dialog shown in Figure 2-11.

There's a lot you can ignore in this dialog if you aren't familiar with how it works. Don't worry about the filter, or the **Directories** and **Files** lists; they supposedly make it easier to specify where the file is saved, but that's questionable. You only need to specify the name and format of the saved document. The **Format** item is a menu with four choices:

Plain Text

    Use this to save the document as a text file, but without any special attempt to format it nicely. Graphics are omitted.

Formatted Text

    This saves the document as a text file, but this time includes some rudimentary formatting. Again, no graphics are included.

PostScript

    This saves the document as a PostScript file; graphics are included in the PostScript file.

HTML

    Use this to save the document as an HTML file, which can then be read as a hypertext document by Mosaic or another World Wide Web browser. Graphics are not included when you save an HTML file.

You also have to specify a filename. The input window under **Name for saved document** shows the directory in which you started Mosaic. Move the mouse into this window and edit the path shown. If the directory that's shown is okay, just add a

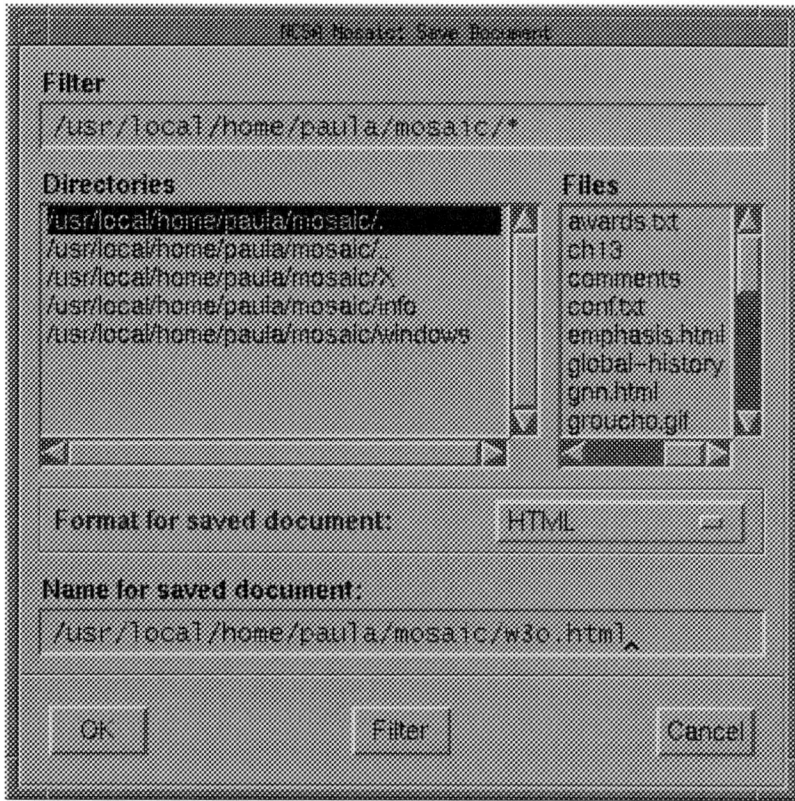

Figure 2–11. Saving a file

filename; otherwise edit the directory and add a filename to the end. If you forget to specify a filename, Mosaic will pick a filename for you, and it won't pick something reasonable.

When you're ready, click on the **OK** button to save the file. You can also press the **Cancel** button if you change your mind.

There is no easy way of saving inline graphics on your system. If you are intent on doing so, you can get the URL of the graphic from the HTML file, then enter that URL using the **Open URL** command. You can then save the file to your system. Another option would be to take a screenshot of your Mosaic window and cut and paste the graphics into separate documents.

You can view the actual HTML code for a document using the **View Source** option from the **File** menu. Figure 2-12 shows the source for the W30 article.

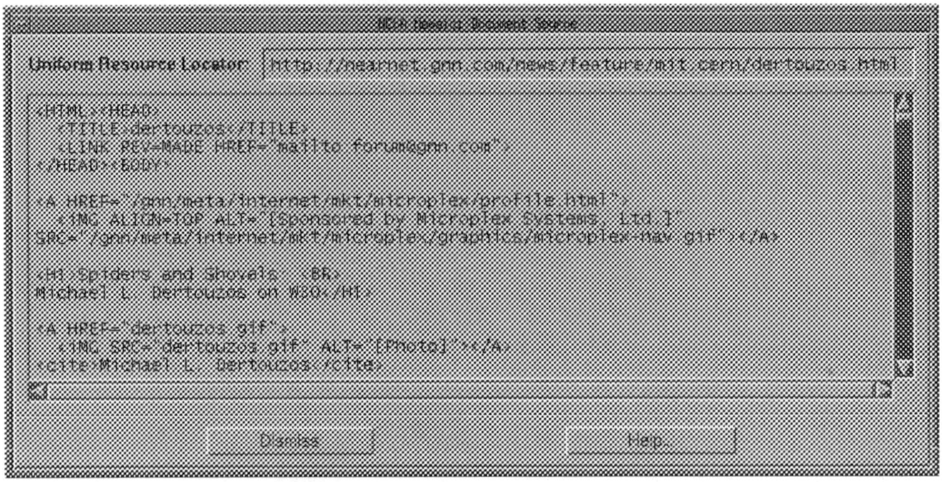

Figure 2–12. HTML document source

Whether or not you've saved a document, you can print from Mosaic by selecting the **Print** option from the **File** menu (hot keys **P** and **p**). The **Print** dialog, shown in Figure 2-13, allows you to enter the print command for your system and select the format for the printed document. The formatting options are the same as for saving documents.

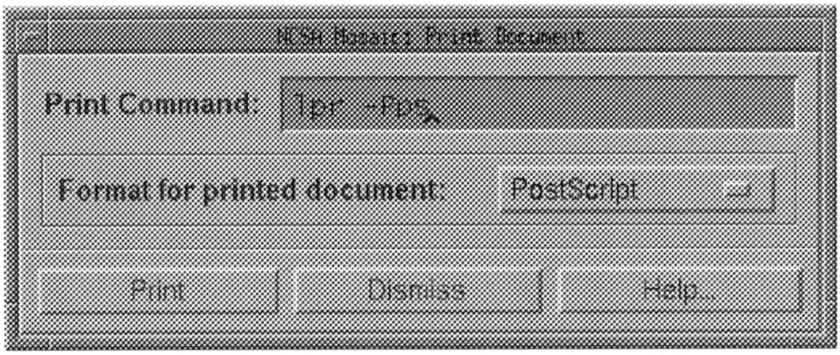

Figure 2–13. Printing a document

When you are exploring with Mosaic, you may find information that you want to share with your friends or colleagues. Select **Mail To** from the **File** menu, or use the **M** or **m** hot keys, to email a Web document to someone. Mosaic brings up the dialog box shown in Figure 2-14 to prompt you for an email address, a subject, and the document format. If you send the document as plain text, the recipient will be able to read it with a mail program. If you send it as an HTML document, however, your colleague will be able to save the message and view the document with Mosaic.

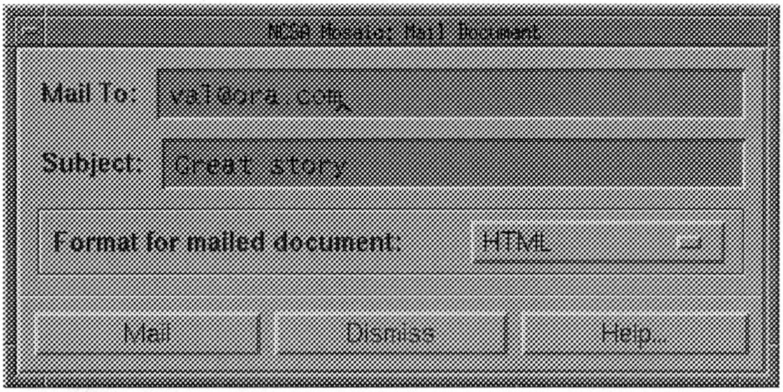

Figure 2-14. Mailing a document

The fact that you can download text and graphics brings up the subject of copyright. Remember that, even though this information is on the Net, it is someone's intellectual property and may be protected by copyright laws. If you're building your own Web documents and want to include someone else's work, it's a simple matter to include a hypertext link to the work, as described in Chapter 7, *Creating HTML Documents*.

In general, you should feel free to save or print a Web document for your own personal use. Copyright issues tend to arise when you distribute a copy of the document or make additional copies.

Making Comments

As you travel the Web, you may find that you want to make notes about the various documents you visit. Mosaic provides an annotation feature that lets you add your own private comments to any document. When you view an annotated document, Mosaic adds your comments to the end of the document as a hypertext link, as shown in Figure 2-15. To read an annotation, just click on the link and Mosaic displays your comments.

To create an annotation, select **Annotate** from the **Annotate** menu (hot keys **A** and **a**).* Figure 2-16 shows the dialox box you'll use for creating your annotation.

Type your comment in the text entry area. You can use the **Clean Slate** button to delete everything you have written. If you want to insert the contents of a file, press **Include File**. When you are done, click on **Commit** to save the annotation.

---

* **Audio Annotate** allows you to record your voice as an annotation, but it requires special hardware and software that need to be configured properly. If your system supports audio but **Audio Annotate** doesn't work, see Chapter 6 for information about configuring audio annotations.

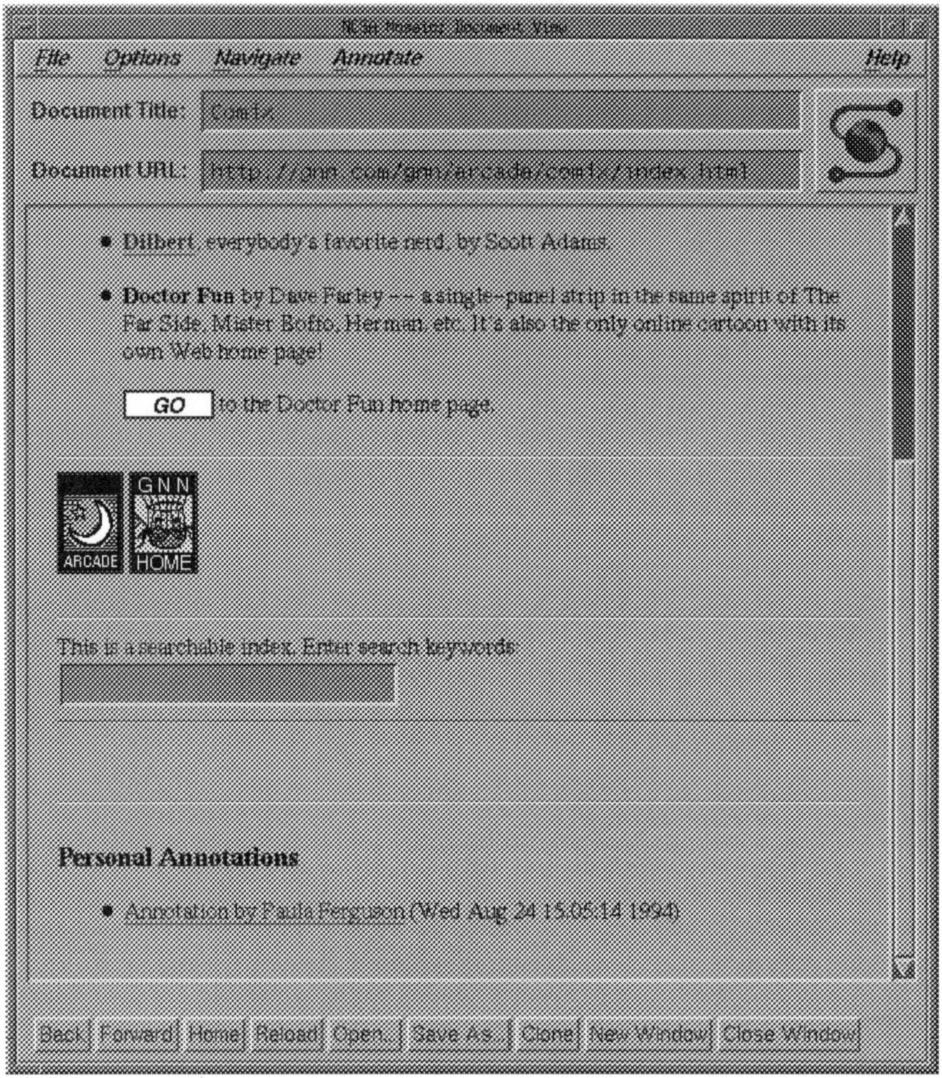

Figure 2–15. An annotated document

Once you have written an annotation, you can edit it or delete it. First, select the annotation so that it's visible on your screen. Now when you look at the **Annotate** menu, you'll see two additional options that you weren't allowed to select before: **Edit This Annotation** and **Delete This Annotation**. The **Edit** option allows you to modify your annotation using the editing window we just discussed. If you select **Delete**, Mosaic asks you for confirmation and then deletes your annotation.

The current version of Mosaic only supports personal, or private, annotations. However, there are provisions in the annotation dialog for group and public

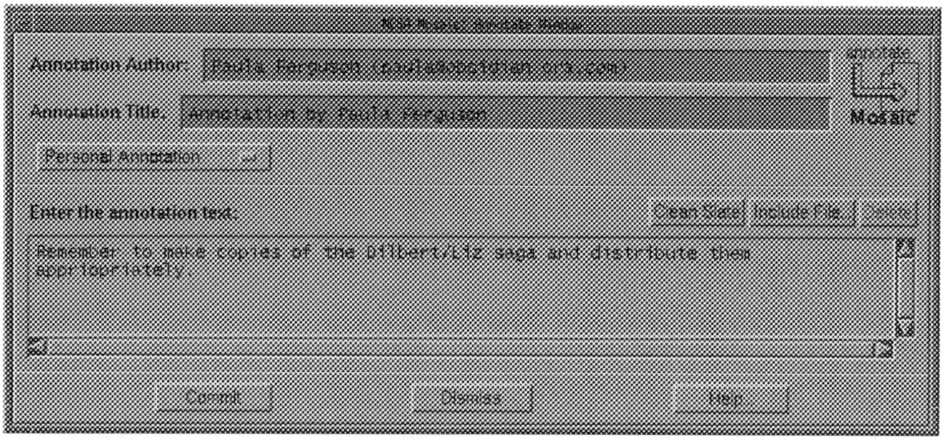

Figure 2–16. Creating an annotation

annotations. When this functionality is added, the annotation feature will be even more useful, as groups of people will be able to share comments on a document.

Adding comments to hypertext files should come naturally enough if you find the annotation feature useful. Another potential use arises when you start using Mosaic to explore other kinds of resources on the Internet. When you start accessing FTP servers and Gopher menus, as we describe in Chapter 4, *Accessing Other Internet Services*, try adding annotations. As Ed Krol comments in the Second Edition of *The Whole Internet User's Guide and Catalog*: "This may be where annotations are most useful: you can make your own notes about what you've found on any particular server, supplementing the often inadequate *README* files."

Document-based Features

Many Web servers offer features beyond simply viewing text and graphics. Two common features are the ability to search a database, and to fill out a form and send it back to the server.

Searching

As we discussed earlier, you can search an individual document using Mosaic's **Find in Current** command. But some servers offer a much more sophisticated searching function that lets you search the full text of the server. These servers use the Wide Area Information Servers (WAIS) system, described in Chapter 1, *The Wide World of Internet Services*, to provide this searching capability.

GNN offers the ability to search all the documents in *GNN* using this system. On certain pages, you will see the message "This is a searchable index" followed by a blank field. To search *GNN*, you type the words you are looking for in the field and press **Return**, as shown in Figure 2-17.

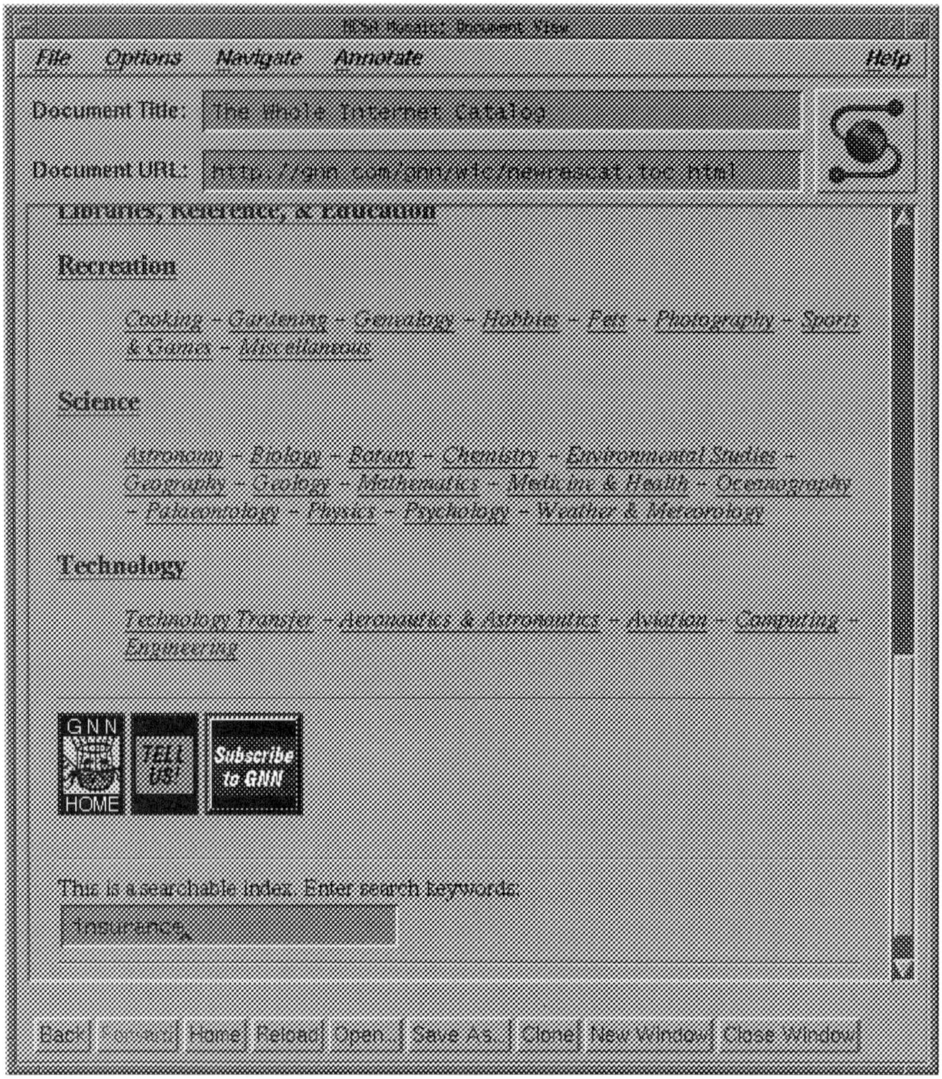

Figure 2-17. Searching the contents of GNN

Let's say you're searching for articles about insurance. Type "insurance" into the field, and in a few seconds you'll receive a list of documents that have something to do with insurance. Each item in this "hitlist," shown in Figure 2-18, is a hypertext link that you can click on to retrieve the document. The server considers this list to be in descending order of relevance. Depending on the results you get, you may beg to differ.

One important concept to remember about this kind of searching is that you are searching the full text of every document—not just descriptions of documents.

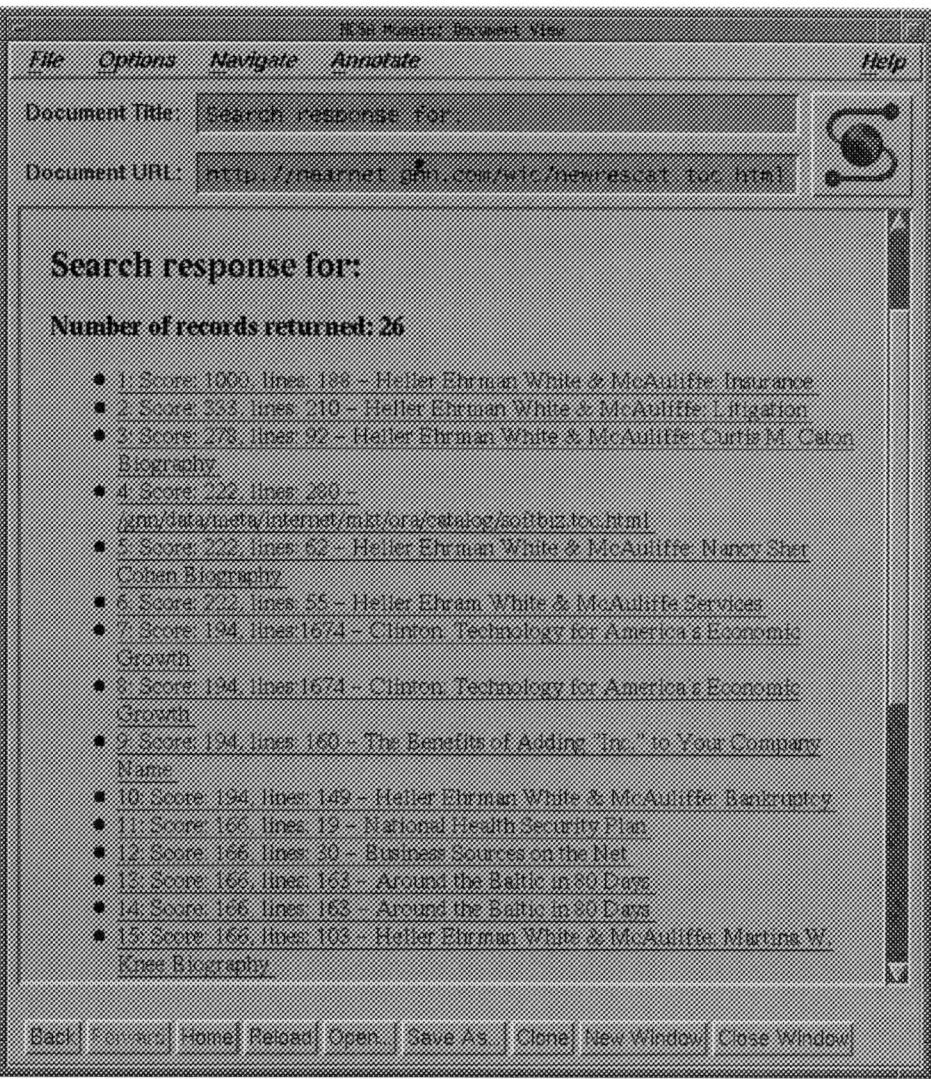

Figure 2-18. Search results are returned as a list of hypertext items

Also remember that you are searching all of *GNN*, not just the center you are in at the time.

When you're searching in *GNN*, you are only searching the contents of *GNN*. Other servers do full text searches of all Web documents. For information about servers that search the Web, see Chapter 3, *Exploring the World Wide Web*.

Filling Out Forms

Some Web documents are actually forms that you can fill out and return to the server. The *GNN* Registration Form is one of these. As you go through it, you'll notice that sometimes there are blank fields for you to fill out and sometimes you're asked to pick one of several items. Filling out forms is a fairly intuitive process, as you can see from Figure 2-19. Using your mouse to move from one field to another, fill in the appropriate text. Before you go on to Chapter 3, take the time to register your copy of Mosaic and become a registered subscriber to *GNN*. To get to the registration page, go to your Home Page and click on the **Register** link.

Understanding URLs

As we discussed earlier, Mosaic uses URLs to get the documents you ask for, whether you click on a link, enter a URL, or use Mosaic's tools like **Hotlist** and **Window History**. URLs are sort of the *lingua franca* of the Web. When you find a great new server, you can tell your friends about it by passing along the URL. In fact, there are several mailing lists devoted to announcements about new services. When we talk about Web servers and documents, we talk about their URLs. Although you can get to the servers mentioned in this book by clicking on the links in the *Mosaic Handbook Hotlist*, we also provide the URLs so you can enter them directly.

A URL consists of two main parts: the protocol and the document's location. The URL for the *GNN Home* page is *http://gnn.com/GNNhome.html*. This follows the syntax for URLs:

```
protocol://server/directory/filename
```

Table 2-1 shows the parts of a URL and the corresponding parts of the *GNN Home* page URL.

Table 2-1: Anatomy of a URL

URL	*http://gnn.com/GNNhome.html*
Protocol	*http*
Separator	*://*
Server	*gnn.com*
Directory path	*/*
File name	*GNNhome.html*

You'll notice that this URL starts with *http*. This is the protocol for the World Wide Web. Whenever you contact a Web server, the URL will start with *http*. But Mosaic also works with other Internet applications, so sometimes you'll see a URL that starts with *gopher, wais,* or *ftp*. In those cases, Mosaic is contacting one of those non-Web services and presenting the results to you in Web format. (See Chapter 4 for more about accessing other information services.)

```
┌─────────────────────────────────────────────────────────────────┐
│                    NCSA Mosaic: Document View                     │
├─────────────────────────────────────────────────────────────────┤
│  File    Options    Navigate    Annotate                   Help   │
├─────────────────────────────────────────────────────────────────┤
│  Document Title: │ GNN Registration Form                 │        │
│                                                                    │
│  Document URL: │ http://gnn.com/wel/register.html │                │
├─────────────────────────────────────────────────────────────────┤
```

GNN Registration

We appreciate your taking a few minutes to register for GNN. When you provide us with this information, we learn more about our audience.

There are three steps to the registration process.

1. Fill out the form below, pressing Register when the form is complete.
2. Get your account information and supply a password for your account.
3. Choose which GNN server is closest to you. You will get a URL (an address) for that server and you should write it down and save it to your hotlist.

To use the online registration form, you must use a browser with online form features. If there is not a place for you to type, you cannot use this form. Instead, please send mail to form@gnn.com and an email version of this form will be sent to you automatically. Or, you can save the email version to a file now.

Upon completion of the form, select the REGISTER link at the bottom to enter your subscription. We will then add you to the GNN subscriber list, and provide you with an account number. You will need this number and the GNN password you will create for a variety of GNN services.

Registration Form

    HELP

          First name
                    ┌──────────────────────────────┐
                    │   │
                    └──────────────────────────────┘

          Last name
                    ┌──────────────────────────────┐
                    │   │
                    └──────────────────────────────┘

```
Data transfer complete.
┌─────┬─────────┬──────┬────────┬──────┬─────────┬───────┬────────────┬──────────────┐
│Back │ Forward │ Home │ Reload │ Open │ Save As │ Clone │ New Window │ Close Window │
└─────┴─────────┴──────┴────────┴──────┴─────────┴───────┴────────────┴──────────────┘
```

Figure 2–19. GNN Registration Form

The characters *://* appear right after the protocol type. Their role in the URL is to separate the protocol name from the document name. When sharing Web URLs in conversation, it's customary to spell out this part of the URL: "h-t-t-p-colon-slash-slash," unwieldy as that is. *GNN* writer D.C. Denison has suggested that this URL prefix should be abbreviated to "hittip" in conversation, but that shorthand doesn't appear to have caught on.

The next part of the URL is the server name, in this case *gnn.com*. On the Internet, most names end in *.com* for commercial sites, *.edu* for educational institutions, *.gov* for government agencies, or *.net* for network providers. By checking the server's extension, you can get an idea of what kind of server you're contacting.

The server name is usually followed by a directory path; in this case, the path is simply */.* That means that the document is located in the root directory of *gnn.com*.

Next comes the actual document name (*gnn.html*). Note that the URL ends with *.html*. This is the file extension for Web documents. It stands for Hypertext Markup Language, a tagging scheme that lets authors create hypertext documents. When you see this file extension, you know you're receiving a Web page and not some other kind of file. Documents for other applications may have other file extensions. Now you know the basics of using Mosaic to navigate the Web. In the upcoming chapters, we'll talk more about customizing Mosaic, using other Internet services with Mosaic, and taking advantages of Mosaic's multimedia capabilities.

When Things Go Wrong

Sometimes when you try to open a connection, things don't go quite right. For instance, it might take a *really* long time to connect to the server. It may be that you're connecting to a distant server and it's just going to take a long time to connect. Or you may be dealing with a slow or overburdened network. If the server is actually down, you'll eventually get an error message from Mosaic that the connection failed.

If you get tired of waiting, you can cancel the current operation by clicking on the spinning-globe icon in the **Document View** window. This is also useful if you realize you've mistakenly followed the wrong link.

If Mosaic tells you that it cannot access the server you want, you can use the **Reload** button (or **Reload Current** on the **File** menu) to tell Mosaic to try again. Obviously, if the server isn't responding, trying again won't help and your best bet is to try later. But if the problem is on your end, **Reload** may help. For example, if your connection to the Internet is congested, or momentarily flaky, a retry might be all you need to set things right.

People often change the locations or names of their documents, which means, of course, that the URL has also changed. The more polite folks out there will leave a document that points to the new URL. If not, however, you'll simply get an error message that the URL couldn't be found.

You'll also get an error message if you make a mistake when entering a URL in the **Open URL** field. If this happens, check the URL and try again. Remember you can use standard X cut-and-paste techniques to avoid typing out URLs. Then, if it still doesn't work, you can go back to the person who gave you the URL and give him or her what for.

The thing to remember about Mosaic and the Web is that when things don't work out, it's hardly ever your fault. Just accept the fact that you can't get access right now, and try again later.

## CHAPTER THREE

EXPLORING THE WORLD WIDE WEB

The Ages-old Problem of Navigation
The Global Network Navigator
Mosaic Handbook Hotlist
Other Lists and Resource Guides
Searching the Web

Coming to the Internet for a new user is like arriving in a new country without a map or a guidebook. Mosaic makes it easy to get almost anywhere you want to go on the Net. However, the more difficult part is knowing what places are worth visiting and where they are located. This is especially true on the World Wide Web. Each information server has its own interface or navigational system. Some are highly structured, and others are very loosely organized. That there is such variety as you move from one server to another is one of the fascinating aspects of the Web. But navigation can be confusing, and you can get lost.

To explore the Web, you have to know where to look, and the *Global Network Navigator* is a good place to start. *GNN* provides several useful navigational guides for Mosaic users, such as *The Whole Internet Catalog.* There's also the NCSA Mosaic *What's New* page. We will start by using these guides to discover public resources that are available.

In Chapter 2, *Getting Started with Mosaic,* we used *GNN* to demonstrate how the Mosaic interface works. In this chapter, we are going to demonstrate how to use *GNN* itself. We have also organized a tour of the Internet, using selections from *GNN*'s Best of the Net award-winning sites to introduce different forms of servers. We will show examples of servers organized as online exhibits, magazines, and kiosks.

As you get more experience using Mosaic to explore the Internet, you will no doubt find your own ways to locate information sources, and you will discover you best like to navigate from one server to another. As you get out on your own, you'll want to investigate the numerous search facilities described in this chapter that index information on the Web.

The Ages-old Problem of Navigation

On the Internet, information is everywhere. Knowing where to look to find the right information is a challenge. There are thousands and thousands of servers worldwide, with hundreds being added every month. How do you find the servers that have information you are most interested in? How do you learn more about them and where they are located? How do you know when a new server comes online that might interest you? These are the basic problems of Internet navigation.

Navigation is an ages-old challenge that people must face as they enter unfamiliar territory by land or water. The problem is one that can be solved if you have good information, and throughout the ages navigational guides for all kinds of people and every form of travel have been published. One of the first books published in the American West, when Pittsburgh was on the frontier, was called *The Navigator*, by Zadok Cramer. The first edition was published in 1802, and it described how to make the journey from Pittsburgh down the Ohio River. It pointed out significant features used to measure distances between places, explained how to avoid numerous hazards, and described what to look for when buying a boat.

The Navigator was written for immigrants and traders, people new to the frontier who had never made the journey down the Ohio River. *The Navigator* brought together the experiences of those who made their living on the river, and organized them in a compact form for use by newcomers.

Just as *The Navigator* helped settlers navigate the American frontier, *GNN* is helping people find their way across the terrain of the Internet. The writers and editors of *GNN* have spent a lot of time on the Internet, probably more time than you want to spend yourself. We know where to look, and we try to keep up with the dynamic growth of information services on the Internet. *GNN* organizes access to the Internet by creating a variety of publications that will help you pursue your interests and spend your time more productively.

If you'd like to know more about significant trends and the interesting people on the Net, read *GNN NetNews*, which contains new feature stories and commentary each week. In Chapter 8, *Future Directions*, you can read a story from *GNN Net-News* that explains the new WWW organization, W3O, and has an interview with one of its organizers.

GNN's special interest areas, called metacenters, have publications aimed at specific audiences, those who enjoy travel or want to learn more about personal finance, for example. In the *GNN Travelers' Center*, you will find articles by real-world explorers who send in their dispatches to us, and we put them online.

The Internet is a new communications medium, which is one reason for all the excitement about it. What is so exciting to us, as creators of *GNN*, is that the information you need to navigate the Internet successfully can be effectively presented to you via the Internet.

The Global Network Navigator

Let's get started (finally!) by going to *GNN*. As shown in Chapter 2, you can access *GNN* by any of the following methods:

- From the Home Page, click on the link to *GNN*.

- From the **File** menu, choose **Open URL** and type in the URL for *GNN*.

  `http://gnn.com/GNNhome.html`

- From the **Documents** menu, select **GNN Home**.

You are retrieving the *GNN Home* page from one of *GNN*'s information servers on the Internet. (Just to be clear, this page is not on the CD shipped with this book, nor is it on your own system. It is out on the network, and if you can't reach the network, you will get an error because you can't retrieve this document.) The time that it takes to retrieve this page will vary depending on the speed of your connection and other factors.

When Mosaic retrieves the *GNN Home* page, you should have a document that serves as a directory to *GNN*'s publications and special-interest areas. When you choose any of the links on this page, you will download another document from the *GNN* information server. If you choose a publication, you will go to its front page.

NOTE

The figures that we use in this book may differ from what you actually see online in *GNN*. That is because *GNN* is dynamic, and there is always new information. We also restructure *GNN* periodically to accommodate new ideas or services.

One of the links on the *GNN Home* page is **What's Up in GNN**. If you click on this link, you can find an itemized summary of new things that are happening in *GNN*. An example of that page is shown in Figure 3-1. On the *What's Up* page, each item describes a feature to be found somewhere in *GNN*. You can select any of the links and go directly to a publication, for instance, or to a document in any of the publications. For now, just scroll to the bottom of the page. On the bottom, you will see a colorful icon labelled "GNN HOME," as shown in Figure 3-2. This is a navigational icon that will take you back to the *GNN Home* page, where we started. Click on it now to return to our directory of publications. (Of course, you could also use the **Back** button to return to the previous document.)

Navigational icons are but one example of how an information server can provide a system of navigation for its users. For instance, if you get lost in *GNN*, look for the navigational icons at the bottom of a page. They can take you to major sections of *GNN* or back to the home page. Similarly, if you don't see any of *GNN*'s navigational icons, then it is probable that you have retrieved a document from

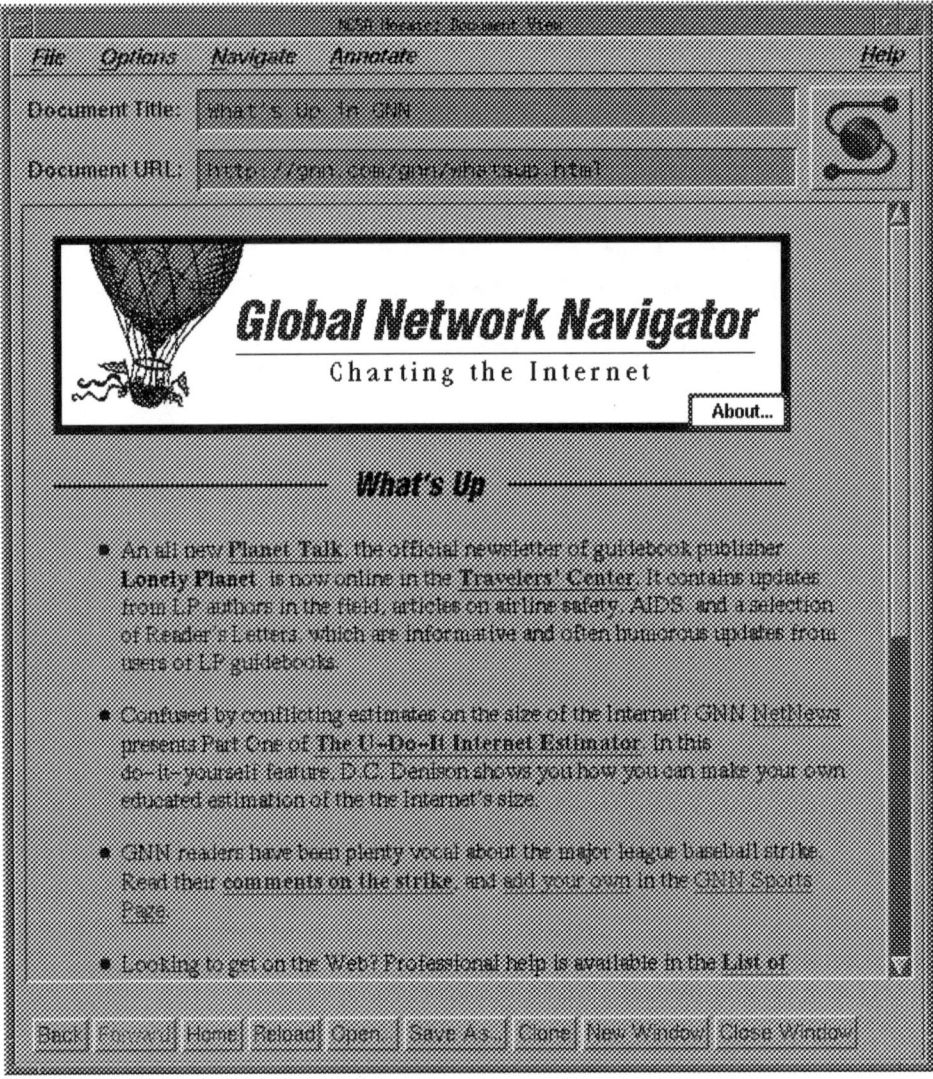

Figure 3-1. The What's Up in GNN page

another server. In *GNN*, we have explicitly labelled links that take you out of *GNN* to other servers. These are called "GO" links, and there is a **GO** button or label that you click on to traverse the link. When you link to a server outside of *GNN*, you go to another information space, and you have to figure out what the rules of navigation are for that server. You can always get back to *GNN* by using the **Back** button. You will see more examples of navigational choices as we explore *The Whole Internet Catalog.*

Figure 3-2. GNN Home navigational icon

Before beginning the next section, click on the link for **The Whole Internet** on the *GNN Home* page and open this publication.

The Whole Internet Catalog

The Whole Internet Catalog is organized by subject. It is selective rather than exhaustive in its listings of resources. We don't list absolutely every resource on the Net; instead we list the ones that we believe are the best. Our editors check out resources and evaluate them for inclusion in the *Catalog.* (We provide some pointers later in this chapter to listings that attempt to be exhaustive rather than selective.)

The Whole Internet Catalog began as a sampler of Internet resources that appeared first in print in *The Whole Internet User's Guide and Catalog* by Ed Krol. We put this catalog online and expanded it, keeping it more up-to-date than any print listing could be. Each entry in the *Catalog* describes an Internet resource and provides a link to the resource, allowing you to go there directly.

Let's look at a few examples. The front page of the *Catalog*, as shown in Figure 3-3, has a distinctive masthead followed by several links, which we'll discuss later, that give you alternative views of the catalog. The main view is a listing of subject categories. You may need to scroll down the list to see all the subject categories. You can navigate from the main subject listings or the more detailed, second-level subject categories. If you are interested in Art, click on that link. You will go to a list of information servers that specialize in Art. Here is a sample list:

```
Art

     Ansel Adams Photographs
     Architecture, etc.
     Art History in Australia
     ASCII Clipart Collection
     Black Artists at the National Museum of American Art
     Bodleian Library MSS
     The California Museum of Photography
     Computer Images & Art
     Japanese Art
     Kaleidospace
     Strange Interactions
     Krannert Art Museum
     The Ohio State University at Newark, Art Gallery
     OTIS
```

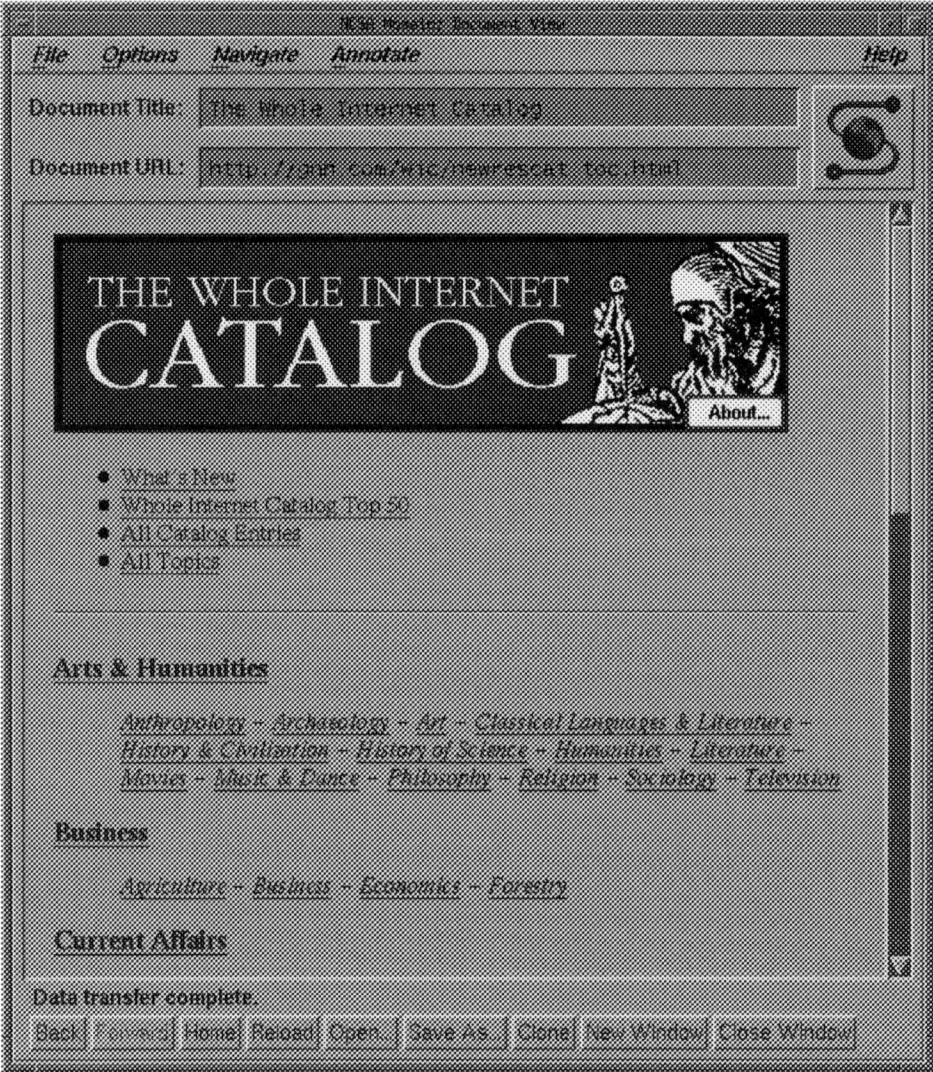

Figure 3-3. The front page of the Whole Internet Catalog

```
A Roman Palace in ex-Yugoslavia
Smithsonian Institution
Vatican Library MSS Exhibit
```

Each name in this list is a link to a catalog entry that describes the server and what it offers. These entries are like cards in a library's card catalog system, describing an online information service. Now, we will select three different servers from the *Catalog* and visit them.

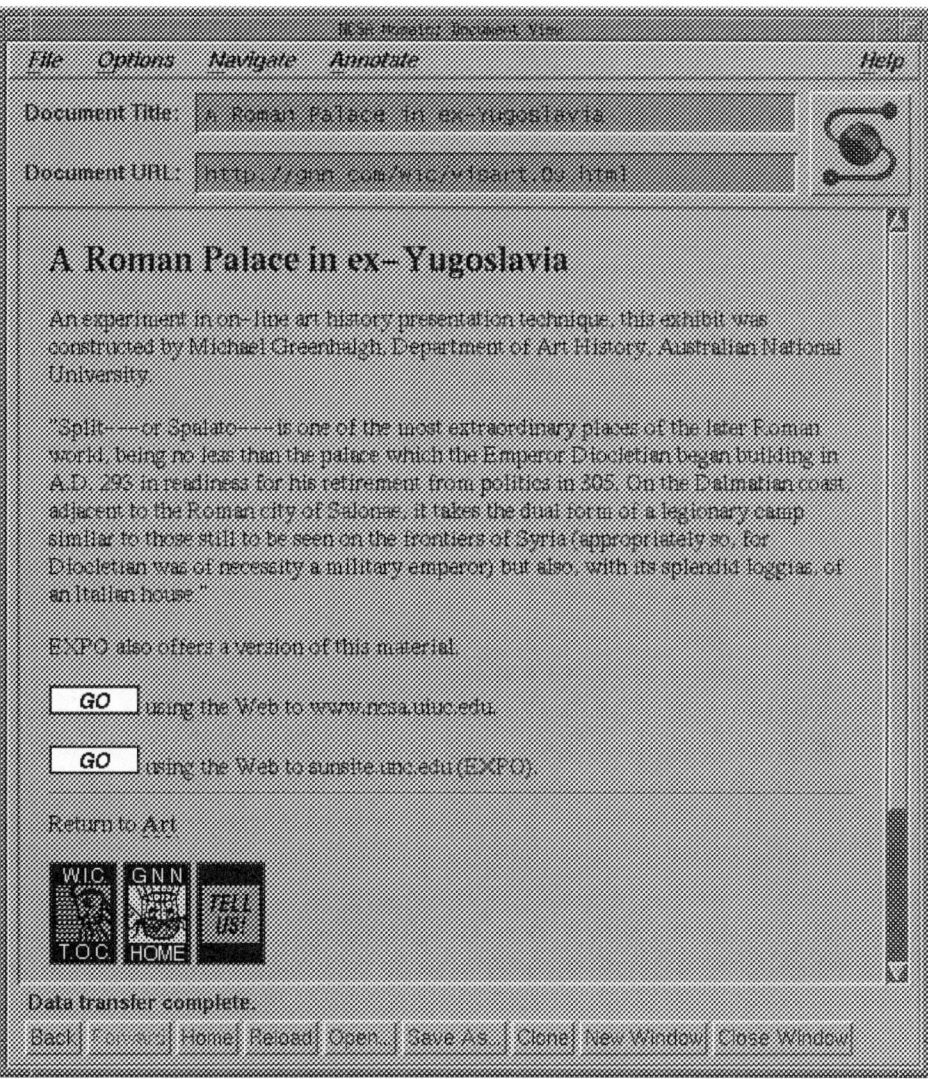

Figure 3-4. Whole Internet Catalog entry for the Palace at Split

The Palace of Diocletian at Split

Each entry contains a description of the server, as well as links that take you to it. If you choose "A Roman Palace in ex-Yugoslavia," then you go to the entry for that server, as shown in Figure 3-4. The entry for the Palace at Split shows multiple links because the information is found on several different servers. Choose the second **GO** link (the first one is to a more experimental version), and you'll go to this server to retrieve the document shown in Figure 3-5.

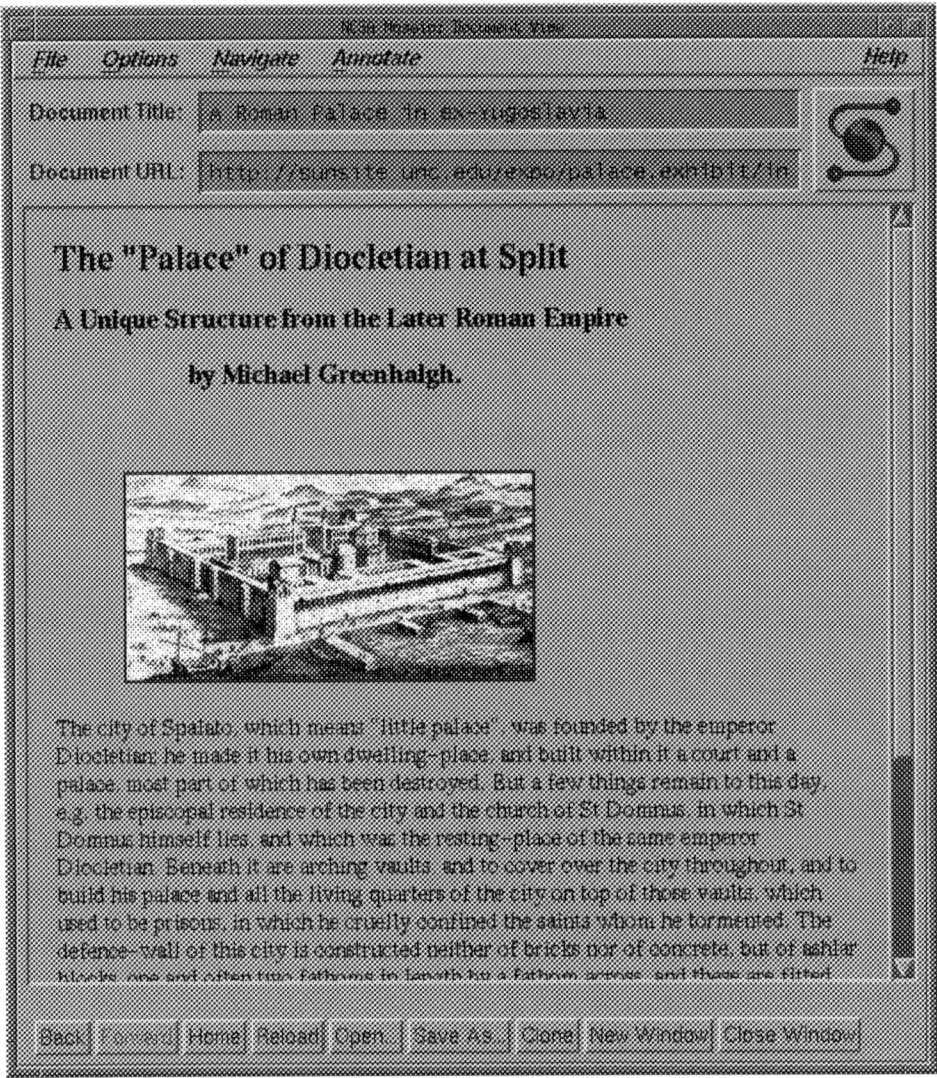

Figure 3-5. The home page for the Palace at Split exhibition

Let's make sure you understand what happened. You used *The Whole Internet Catalog* to choose an information service and traverse a link that takes you directly to that server. The document in Figure 3-5 is not part of *GNN*; it is a separate resource. This document contains lots of links to additional information, but it does not contain a link back to *GNN*.

The Palace of Diocletian at Split is an online interactive exhibit. After you have read the introductory text on this page, follow the link at the bottom of the page to the palace. This document, shown in Figure 3-6, is the main navigational document for this exhibit. An image at the top of the page contains buttons that you can click on to visit different areas of the exhibition.

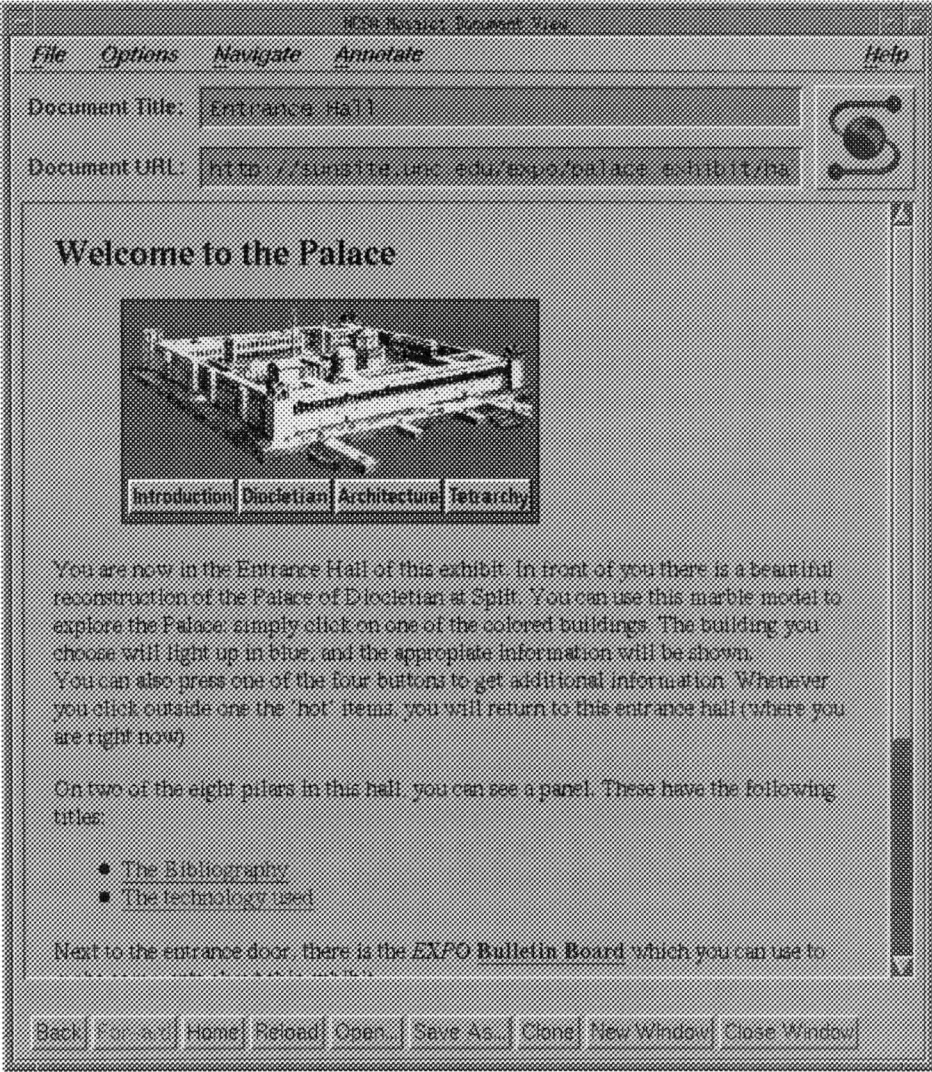

Figure 3-6. Navigational document at the Palace

You may notice a difference between the buttons found on the graphic and other buttons that you find on a page. These buttons are mapped as specific hot regions on the graphic, and when you click on one of them, the Mosaic browser sends a message to the server giving the coordinates of the region in which you clicked. It then returns a document whose URL has been mapped to that region. (Because of the HTML tag associated with this process, a navigational graphic is known as an ISMAP graphic.) You may also notice that when you move from one button to the next on this graphic, the destination URL displayed in the status area does not change.

If you click on the button labelled **Introduction**, you can begin the exhibit. At the end of the page for each document in the exhibit, you will find the same graphic, and you can use it to explore other topics.

When you are done, use the **Back** button to get back to *GNN*. Of course, if you have gone very far into the exhibit, you may find it easier to get back to *GNN* using the **Documents** menu.

If you do back up all the way to the last document you saw in *GNN*, you will return to the listing of Art resources. At this point, you can choose to visit other servers on the list. One that is very different, and definitely not classical, is OTIS, which stands for Operative Term Is Stimulate. See what today's artists are creating using all kinds of computer-based tools.

Or, if you want to choose a different subject, scroll to the bottom of the Art listings and find the navigational icon for *The Whole Internet Catalog*. If you click on it, you will go back to the *Catalog*'s front page, where the subject listings are found.

U.S. Department of Education

Let's choose another subject area—Government. Select the link for Government, then find the list for U.S. Government Agencies. On that list, you will find the U.S. Department of Education; click on that link.

As the description says, this is an information server that provides all kinds of documents generated by the U.S. Department of Education (**ed.gov**). This entry also includes **GO** links to their Web, Gopher and FTP servers. We will explain how to use the Gopher and FTP in Chapter 4, *Accessing Other Internet Services*; however, when given the choice among servers (presuming that you are using Mosaic), always choose the Web server. If you do so, you will go to this Web server's home page, as shown in Figure 3-7.

This server is fairly straightforward; it contains a listing of its contents, most of which are presented on this same page. In other words, if you click on the link near the beginning of the Contents list, you will go to a location further down in the same document. (Mosaic doesn't retrieve the document again off the Net.) This is a form of "outlining" the contents of a document using links. In long documents, it is useful to have an outline with links to the various parts of the document below. Such a list is often labelled "Contents" but another way to identify one is that the links will be displayed as though you had visited them (typically, dashed underline instead of a solid underline) because their destinations appear in the same document.

Continue, if you wish, to explore the contents of this server. Otherwise, back up to *The Whole Internet Catalog*.

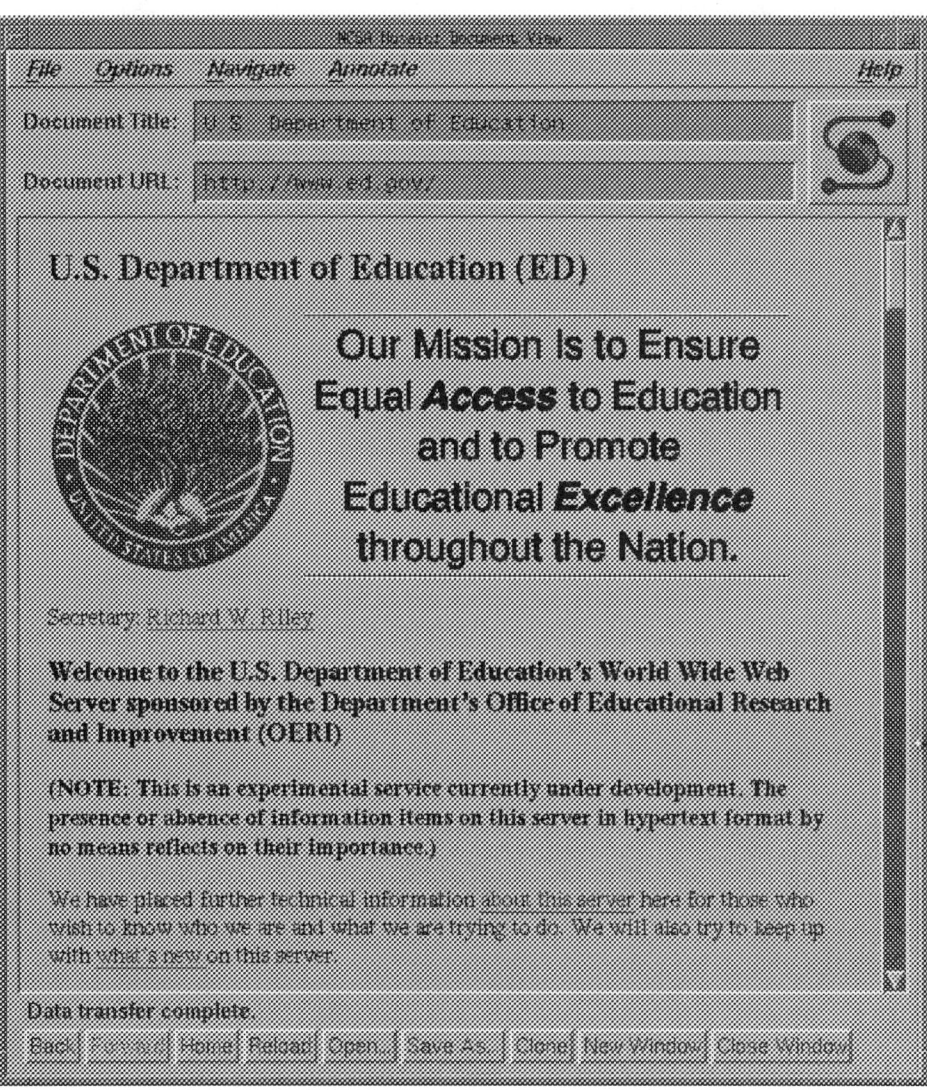

Figure 3-7. Department of Education Web server

The Paleontology Server

Let's find one more resource in a different subject area—Science. Click on the link for Science, and you will see a list of additional categories, one for each discipline. Use the scroll bar to move down through the list and find Paleontology. If you select this link, you will see a list of servers on Paleontology, such as:

```
Honolulu Community College Dinosaur Exhibit
U.C. Berkeley Museum of Paleontology Gopher
U.C. Berkeley Museum of Paleontology Public Exhibits
Paleontological Society Gopher
Palynology & Palaeoclimatology (ANU Bioinformatics Hypermedia Service)
```

Choosing the U.C. Berkeley Museum of Paleontology Public Exhibits link will take you to an entry for this server; select the **GO** link to visit it. This particular server has a well-defined but rather large graphic interface, as shown in Figure 3-8. (It is an ISMAP graphic, with the square areas defined as hotspots.) Once again, you have ventured to a new server, and you can explore it as you wish. If you find the Paleontology server interesting, you may want to add it to your hotlist so that you can go back to it very easily. A good way to use the *Catalog* is to find servers and then compile your own list of those you'd like to visit on a regular basis.

Alternative views of the Catalog

If you return to *The Whole Internet Catalog* front page, you will find several alternative ways to find information in the *Catalog*. You can look at the following:

Top 50

This document is a list of the entries most frequently accessed in *The Whole Internet Catalog*. It represents what users find most interesting in the *Catalog*.

You might use the list to check out some of the most popular servers. One server that tends to stay high up on the charts is the Web server for Recipe Archives. You can search the recipe archives when you are at work and can't consult *The Joy of Cooking*.

What's New

This document describes the most recent updates to the *Catalog*, listing new information servers or ones that have been removed for some reason.

All Catalog Entries

Click on this link and you will get an alphabetical listing of all the information servers indexed in the *Catalog*. If you select **Find in Current** from the **File** Menu, you can search this document, and perhaps find a server of interest.

Searching

As of this edition, the searching is somewhat limited. (We are working on improving it). You can search using the search text entry area at the bottom of each document. However, that currently searches all of *GNN*, not just the *Catalog*.

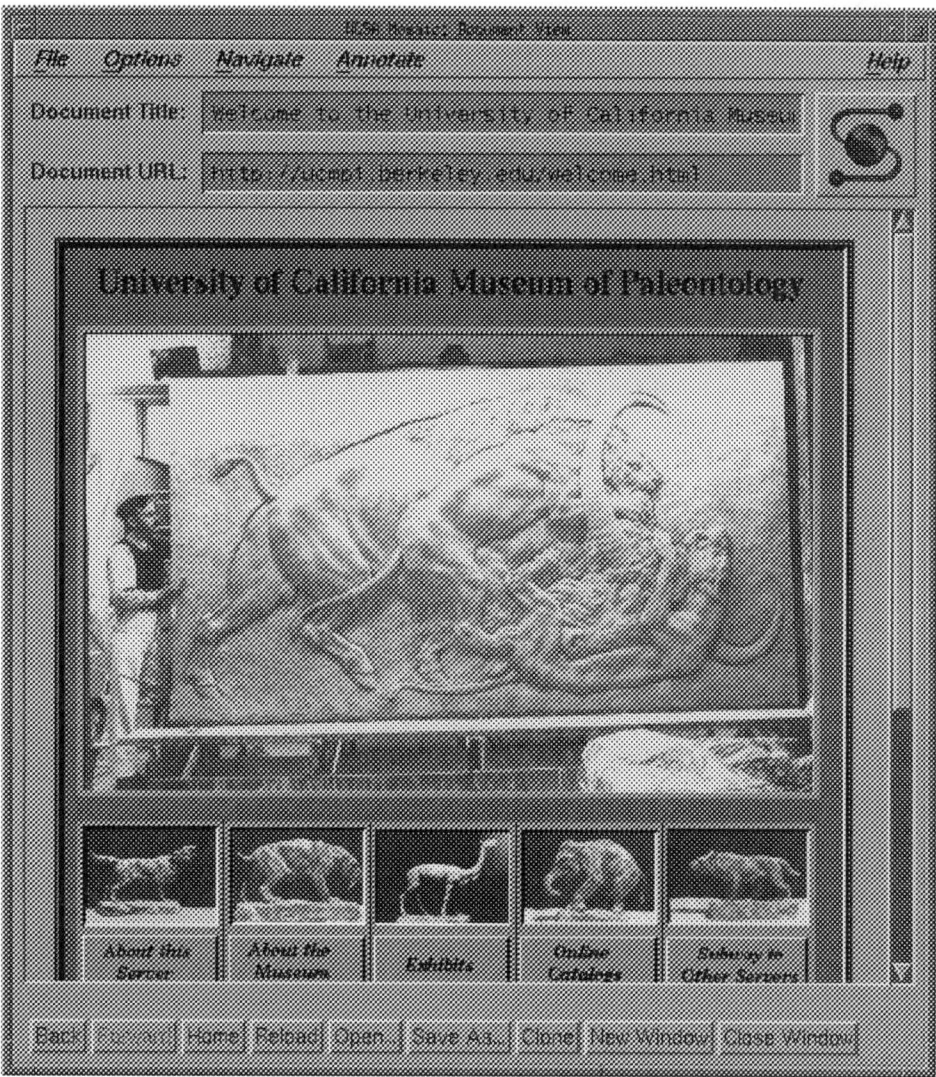

Figure 3–8. Entry for U.C Berkeley Museum of Paleontology

Mosaic Handbook Hotlist

We have created a special list of additional resources that you can use to explore the Net, and organized them as the *Mosaic Handbook Hotlist.* This *Hotlist* is on the *GNN* server, and there is a link to it on the Home Page. Choose **Chapter 3, Exploring the World Wide Web** to get a list of pointers to the servers we describe in this chapter. (This will save you having to type in the URLs to access them.) Many of the services can be found in *The Whole Internet Catalog* as well.

It is always possible that these URLs may change, so be sure to check the links on the *Mosaic Handbook Hotlist.*

NCSA Mosaic What's New

The NCSA Mosaic *What's New* page is the best place on the Internet to find out about new information servers. This page is updated several times a week, and checking it regularly will help you keep up with developments on the Web. Its URL is:

```
http://www.ncsa.uiuc.edu/SDG/Software/Mosaic/Docs/whats-new.html
```

A sample entry from this page is shown below:

Labyrinth Electronic Publishing Project
Indiana University, Bloomington, Indiana
> The Honors Division at Indiana University is proud to announce the unveiling of the Labyrinth Electronic Publishing Project, including: collections of poetry from IU faculty and students, and collections of visual art. Take a look and leave some comments on the art and poetry, or if you are feeling creative yourself, leave some noise on the Graffiti Wall.

What's New announcements are organized by date and presented as short descriptions of new resources or Net happenings. Each announcement contains links out to the sites being described.

There is also a *What's New* archive going back to June 1993. Of course, some of this information can be dated and not as useful, but you can often use it to check for a particular site.

The *What's New* page is often good reading simply because of the variety in the announcements from educational, government, and commercial sites.

FAQ Directory

Frequently Asked Questions (FAQ) are lists of questions that new users often ask, in particular, users of USENET newsgroups. As new users visit a newsgroup, they begin asking questions, and many of these questions have been asked by others before them. Eventually, someone realizes that he or she has answered "newbie" questions often enough and sets about creating a document that compiles these questions and their answers.

Don't get the idea that FAQs are answers to obvious questions; they represent the collective wisdom of the Net, and their authors take their work very seriously. You can almost regard the collection of FAQs as an online encyclopedia, they are that broad. By no means are they limited to computer or Internet-related topics. Are you interested in Games or Greek culture, Hockey or Hongkong, Magic, Model Railroads or Mexico? All have FAQs.

There's another reason that the FAQ Directory is like an encyclopedia. You might go there looking for one thing and find yourself browsing any number of subjects that you may know nothing about. That's probably true of a lot of Web servers, which is what makes exploring the Web so enjoyable.

Figure 3-9 shows the opening page for USENET FAQs, found on the Ohio State University server and compiled by Thomas Fine. Its URL is:

```
http://www.cis.ohio-state.edu/hypertext/faq/usenet/FAQ-List.html
```

You might use this directory of FAQs to find subjects that interest you and learn about a newsgroup where people discuss that subject. The first thing you should do is scroll down the page, where you will begin to see the long alphabetical list of FAQ subjects. When you select an item on the list, you get one of the following:

- a full FAQ in ASCII text

- a list of questions as hypertext links that you can follow to get the answer

- a list containing several FAQs on a subject, or parts of a single FAQ

For example, if you select "European Union" from the list, you will get a single ASCII document that explains the charter of the European Union and answers basic questions about its objectives.

If you select the Dogs FAQ, you get a list of FAQs on subjects ranging from obedience training to health. There are even more FAQs available on the next level, covering different breeds.

The FAQ server is beginning to offer different ways to access its documents. A new search facility is in the experimental stages so that you can search for an FAQ without knowing its main subject title.

Netizens

Getting to know others like yourself who are exploring the Internet can be fun. You may know people from email or from their postings in newsgroups. However, the Web has encouraged new forms of expression and users are taking advantage of it by creating their own home pages and putting them on the Net.

GNN has a publication called *Netizens* in which users list their home pages for others to view. Visit *Netizens* and see who else is out there on the Internet. Its URL is:

```
http://gnn.com/gnn/meta/internet/netizens/
```

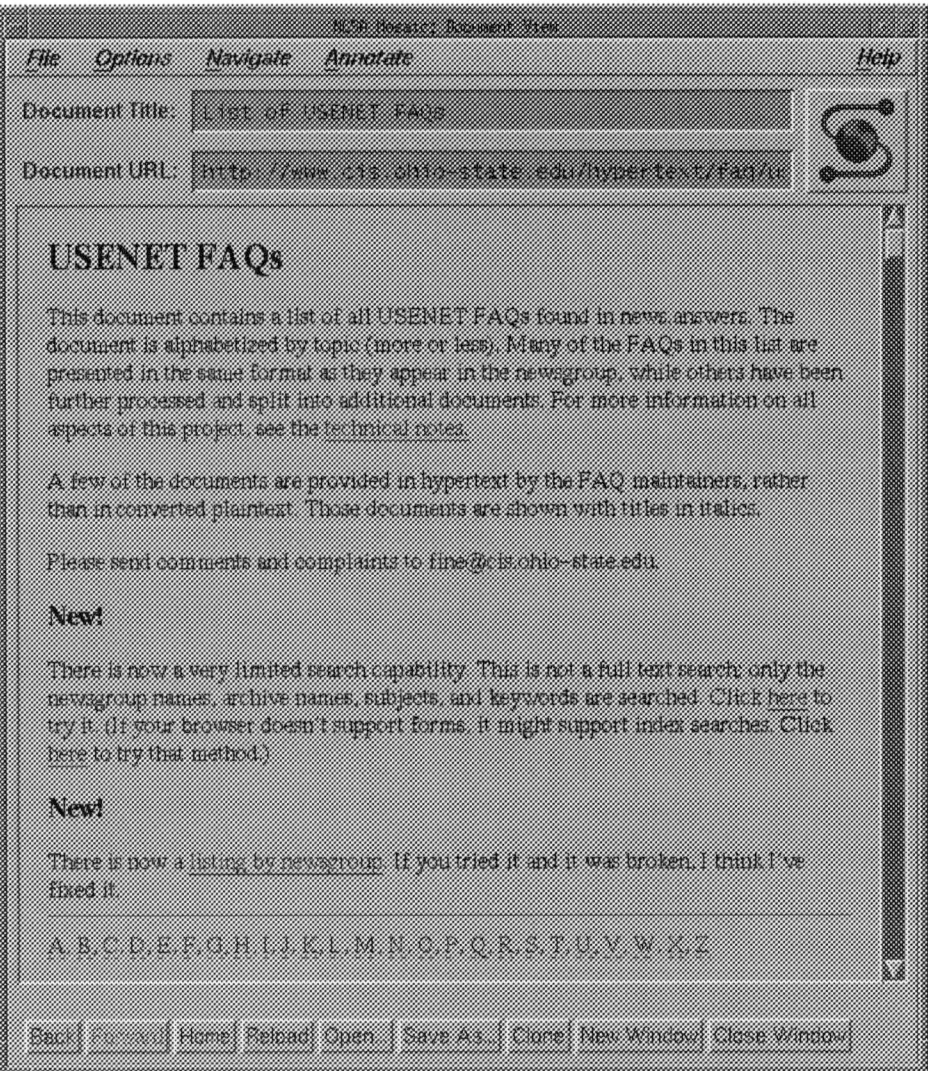

Figure 3-9. USENET FAQs

From the *Netizens* front page, shown in Figure 3-10, you can browse an alphabetical listing of names or a listing of the most recent additions.

For each user, you will find an email address, a location, and a mention of their interests. Most have supplied a link to a home page on their own server.

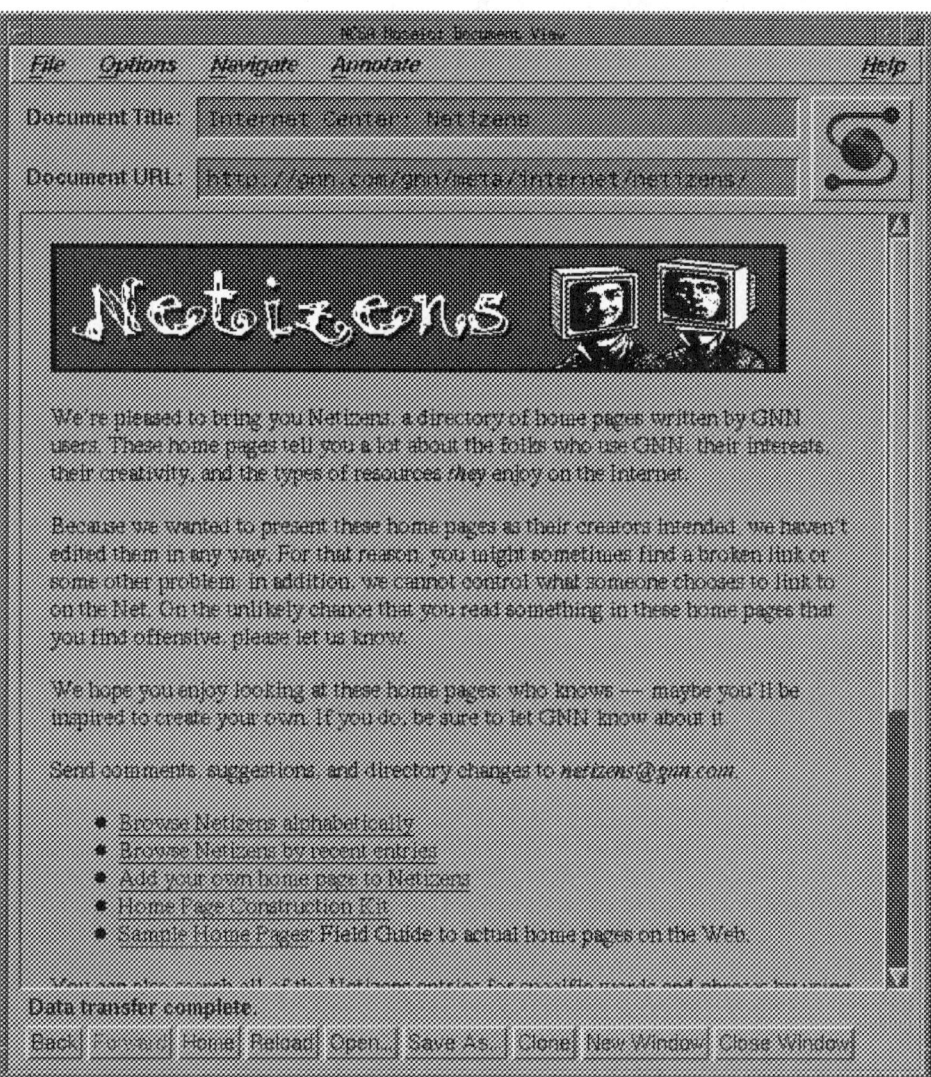

Figure 3-10. Netizens page

After you've read Chapter 7, *Creating HTML Documents*, which describes how to create your own home page in HTML, come back and add your name and become a Netizen.

Commercial Sites on the Web

If you'd like to know if a particular business has information available on the World Wide Web, the *Commercial Sites on the Web* server at MIT is a good place to look. This student-run server offers an alphabetical listing of companies by name, which are linked directly to their sites. Its URL is:

```
http://tns-www.lcs.mit.edu/commerce.html
```

The current document lists over 300 commercial sites, which is one sign of the increasing business activity on the Net. For instance, if you'd like to find out if your favorite computer company is on the Net, and offers support, look them up on this server. Remember that this server is essentially just a listing of links to other servers.

If you can't find a particular company, you may know its domain name by exchanging email with someone in that organization. The domain name for O'Reilly & Associates is **ora.com**; for IBM, it is **ibm.com**. If a company has a Web server, it often can be reached by composing an HTTP URL that prefixes "www" to the domain name. For instance,

```
http://www.ibm.com/
```

It may also work without the "www" prefix. Either way, we are guessing at the URL based on conventional practice, but this syntax is not enforced by any software. It produces an error if the company does not have a server or the server resides at a different address.

GNN also provides several ways for you to find companies that want to deliver information about products and services to Mosaic users. The *GNN Business Listings* are advertiser-paid listings that describe in brief what a company does and what information it provides online. This information is provided in a consistent format for users. You can search companies by product or service category as well as by name.

Discovering Information Services

This section gives an overview of different kinds of Web-based information services. We look at online exhibits, magazines, international kiosks, and interactive media centers.

The servers listed in this section can be accessed directly from the *Mosaic Handbook Hotlist*, but their URLs are also listed here.

Exhibits

An online exhibit organizes a collection of materials for easy access. Usually, an exhibit integrates text and graphics as a series of documents. Exhibits are usually created by universities or museums, and the number of exhibits on the Web is increasing daily.

- Artserve *http://rubens.anu.edu.au/*

Artserve from Professor Michael Greenhalgh of Australian National University is a collection of digitized art organized as an art history database. Professor Greenhalgh is also responsible for the Palace at Split that we demonstrated earlier.

- **Vatican Exhibit**
  http://sunsite.unc.edu/expo/vatican.exhibit/Vatican.exhibit.html

The *Vatican Library MSS Exhibit*, which can be found in the Art section of the *Catalog*, is a guided tour through the collections of the Vatican Library, as they were showcased at the Library of Congress. This exhibit includes some exceptionally beautiful illuminated manuscripts, which are presented as postage-stamp-size images that you can click on to retrieve an enlarged image in a separate window.

- **Dead Sea Scrolls**
  http://sunsite.unc.edu/expo/deadsea.scrolls.exhibit/intro.html

Another interesting exhibition from the Library of Congress is the *Scrolls from the Dead Sea*. This exhibit can be found in Archaeology section of the *Catalog*.

- **Hubble Space Telescope** *http://stsci.edu/top.html*

A fascinating scientific exhibit is sponsored by the *Space Telescope Science Institute* at Johns Hopkins University in Baltimore, Maryland. This resource can be found in the Astronomy section of the *Catalog*. Its home page is shown in Figure 3-11. It includes information about the Hubble Space Telescope as well as a collection of images, including some from the Shoemaker-Levy comet that impacted Jupiter in July of 1994. There are a number of collections of interest to educators and the naturally curious, including a digitized sky survey.

Magazines

When *GNN* premiered in the fall of 1993, we were the first to create a commercial Web-based magazine. Our first issue of *GNN Magazine* was about the U.S. Government's role in developing the Internet and its involvement in making more information available to the public. Our second issue was on education, and we showed many examples of how teachers are using the Internet in the classroom. Now, *GNN* has developed special-interest magazines in *Travel* and *Personal Finance*, with more to come soon.

Creating a magazine can involve more than putting the text of an article online (the most common approach used for a magazine that originates in print.) Of particular interest are online magazines that utilize the medium most effectively to create and present content. The Web will be a fascinating place for large and small publishers to create all kinds of magazines, perhaps reaching even more specialized audiences. In a few years the Internet will have more magazines than your local newstand. Here are some examples you can find today.

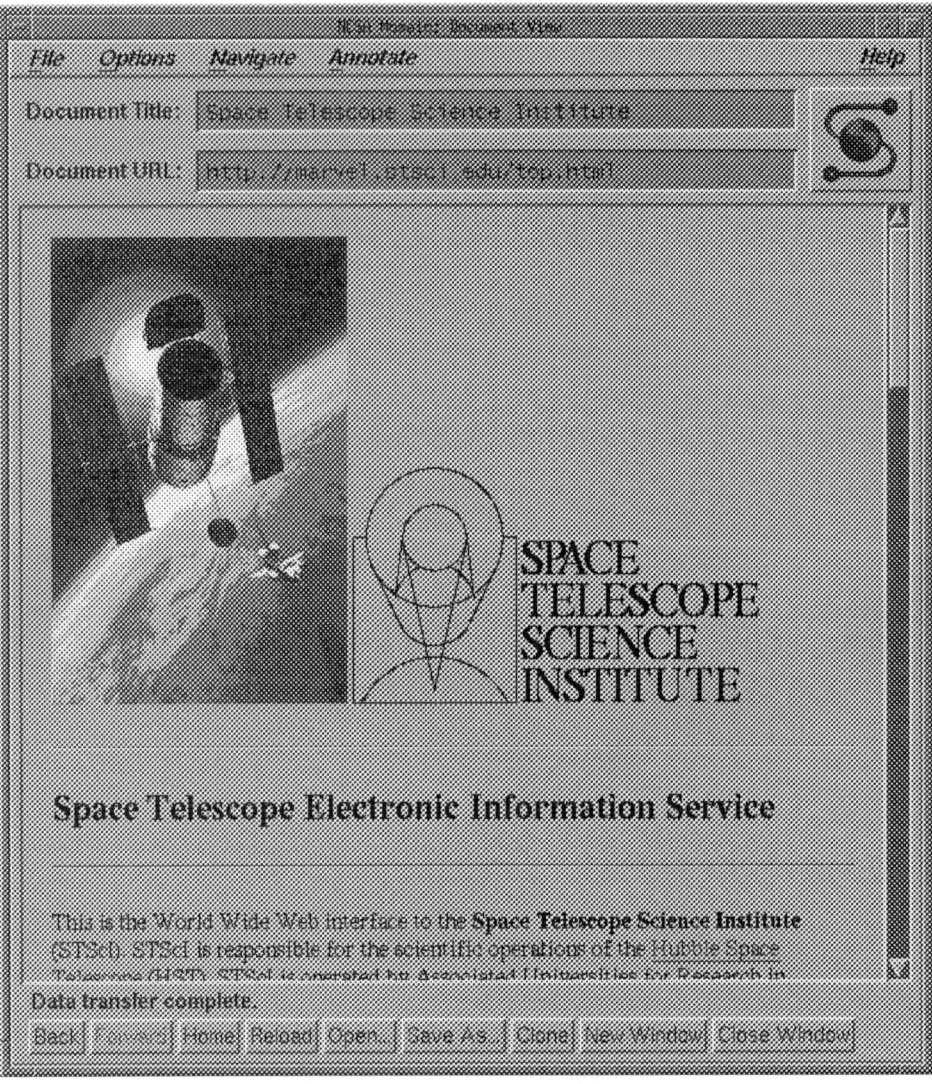

Figure 3–11. Home page for the Space Telescope Science Institute

- International Teletimes
  http://www.wimsey.com/teletimes.root/teletimes_home_page.html

International Teletimes is published in Vancouver, Canada, as a general-interest magazine. It is representative of many new magazines that are original to the Internet and have no print counterpart. Some are more sophisticated than others, and you'll also find that many of the online magazines or *'zines* are very personal in nature, and can be narrowly focused or broadly defined.

- **Zines** *http://www.ora.com:8080/johnl/e-zine-list/*

GNN Technical Services Manager John Labovitz maintains a 'zines list. This is a reasonably comprehensive list of electronic magazines published on the Net. Many of the 'zines are ASCII-text only, but there are a wide range of formats. Editorially, they are usually idiosyncratic, rather like fanzines and underground newspapers.

- **Wired** *http://www.wired.com/*

Wired is a magazine oriented toward technology and culture, with an attitude. Its Web server contains sample articles and other information. If you enjoy *Wired*, but find its page layout distracting, reading it online can be a much more pleasant experience. They have announced plans to create a HotWired online service based on Web technology.

- **Mother Jones** *http://www.mojones.com/motherjones.html*

Mother Jones, the mother of investigative reporting, has a Web server at **mojones.com**. You will find a cover image and articles for its bimonthly issues. A sample article from the July/August 1994 issue is "The Cry of the Ocean" by Peter Steinhart, which leads off a special report on how the world fish population is depleted and its consequences not only for the fishing industry but for all of us. The special report ends with an article "Fishing in the Net" that suggests a few places on the Internet where you can find related information.

International kiosks

International kiosks provide information about particular countries or states on the Net. The Regional and Cultural Interest section of *The Whole Internet Catalog* contains pointers to most countries. Some of these servers use only the native language of the country (i.e., the Norway server is in Norwegian) while others have English language materials as well. For more information on particular countries, check the listing of servers by country described later in this chapter.

- **New Zealand**
  http://www.cs.cmu.edu:8001/Web/People/mjw/NZ/MainPage.html

The *New Zealand Information* server, by Michael Witbrock, is a Best of the Net selection. This server is not located in New Zealand though, but at Carnegie-Mellon University. Even so, it has a lot of depth in its information and many unusual items.

- **Japan** *http://www.ntt.jp/japan/*

You can learn more about Japan on a *Japanese Information* Web server sponsored by Nippon Telephone and Telegraph (NTT) and produced by Takada Toshihiro. You can find Japanese language documents as well as a traveler's guide to speaking Japanese, which includes audio samples. You can hear the Japanese national anthem, *Kimigayo*, played on a recorder. You can also find a map of Japan, as well as a lot of political and cultural information.

- Iceland *http://www.rfisk.is/english/iceland/rest_of_iceland.html*

You can take a tour of *Iceland*; if you click on a map of Iceland you'll get photographs from a specific city or region.

- Germany *http://www.chemie.fu-berlin.de/adressen/brd.html*

Get more familiar with *Germany* online. This server contains geopolitical information, as well as a map of Germany. It also provides access to a German language news service.

Interactive media centers

All Web servers can be considered interactive because of the nature of hypertext. You choose what interests you and go in that direction, almost instantly. However, a number of servers have created special interactive interfaces.

- **Xerox PARC Map Viewer** *http://pubweb.parc.xerox.com/map*

The *Xerox PARC Map Viewer* is a Best of the Net selection that allows you to generate maps of specific areas that you select.

- United States Map *http://ageninfo.tamu.edu/apl-us/*

The *Digital Relief Map of the United States* is a color relief map composed of cells. If you click on a cell, Mosaic will retrieve a full-blown image of that cell. The map was created by Ray Sterner of the Applied Physics Laboratory at Johns Hopkins University, and distributed on the Web by Hal Mueller of Texas A&M University. This server can be accessed from the Geography section of the *Catalog*.

- **The Geometry Center** *http://www.geom.umn.edu/welcome.html*

The Geometry Center at the University of Minnesota, which is dedicated to "the computation and visualization of geometric structures," says that part of its mission is to help mathematicians reach the public. You will find an interesting picture archive, forums, and software, some of which only run on workstations. Be sure to check out "A Gallery of Interactive On-Line Geometry."

- Exploratorium *http://www.exploratorium.edu/*

San Francisco's innovative *Exploratorium* has a Web server called ExploraNet that is worth looking at. This hands-on science museum is taking advantage of the Net to create an interactive learning center for kids and adults.

Other Lists and Resource Guides

In addition to *GNN's The Whole Internet Catalog*, there are many subject-oriented lists and resource guides. These lists vary in completeness and timeliness. Some are organized well; others require you to scroll doggedly down a long screen (or screen after screen) of alphabetized entries. In this section, we describe a sampling of lists and guides that you might find useful.

CERN's General Overview of the Web

Overview
http://info.cern.ch/hypertext/WWW/LineMode/Defaults/default.html
Virtual Library
http://info.cern.ch/hypertext/DataSources/bySubject/Overview.html
Servers by Country
http://info.cern.ch/hypertext/DataSources/WWW/Geographical.html

The *General Overview of the Web* at CERN is a comprehensive, though less user-friendly, picture of what's available on the Web. On its *Overview* home page, it says that there is no "top" to the Web. This becomes immediately apparent when you link to the *Virtual Library*, which is a distributed subject catalog arranged alphabetically. There is no description of any of the resources in the list; instead, there is just a straight link out to the resource, so it's hard to know what to expect until you get there.

What this listing lacks in descriptiveness it makes up for in comprehensiveness. From Aeronautics and Aeronautical Engineering to Sports, pick a subject you're interested in and click on the link. What you'll get is another list of resources that relate to that subject. These lists are not arranged alphabetically; sometimes there's a brief description of the resource, sometimes there isn't.

If you're looking for information on a specific subject, you'll have to sift through a number of entries on this page before you find a link to what you're looking for—and you may not find such a link!

As with NCSA Mosaic's *What's New* page, the *WWW Virtual Library* page gets a lot of its information on new resources from readers who submit pointers to these resources. The *WWW Virtual Library* encourages readers to submit these pointers to maintainers, each of whom is responsible for a particular subject area. Updates appear to be fairly frequent.

Also available on the *General Overview of the Web* page is the *List of Servers*, which lists all registered Web servers by country. When you click on this link, you'll see links to registered WWW servers organized by continent, country, and state. It is a long, exhaustive list, and it does contain some explanatory text for some of the entries. It's a great resource if you want to know more about a particular country, especially if you wish to find information in a foreign language. Figure 3-12 shows the page that lists Web servers by country. Scroll down the list until you see South America (doing so will demonstrate that North America is most heavily represented). Click on the link for Peru. You will go to a brief description of Red Cientifica Peruana, the Internet Network of Peru. You can follow a link to their server in Peru. Offered in Spanish and (some) English, this server gives basic information about the country, and links to Latin American and Caribbean Gopher servers.

Because this list is so extensive, you might want to use the **Find in Current** feature in Mosaic to locate a particular country or state rather than scroll through the list.

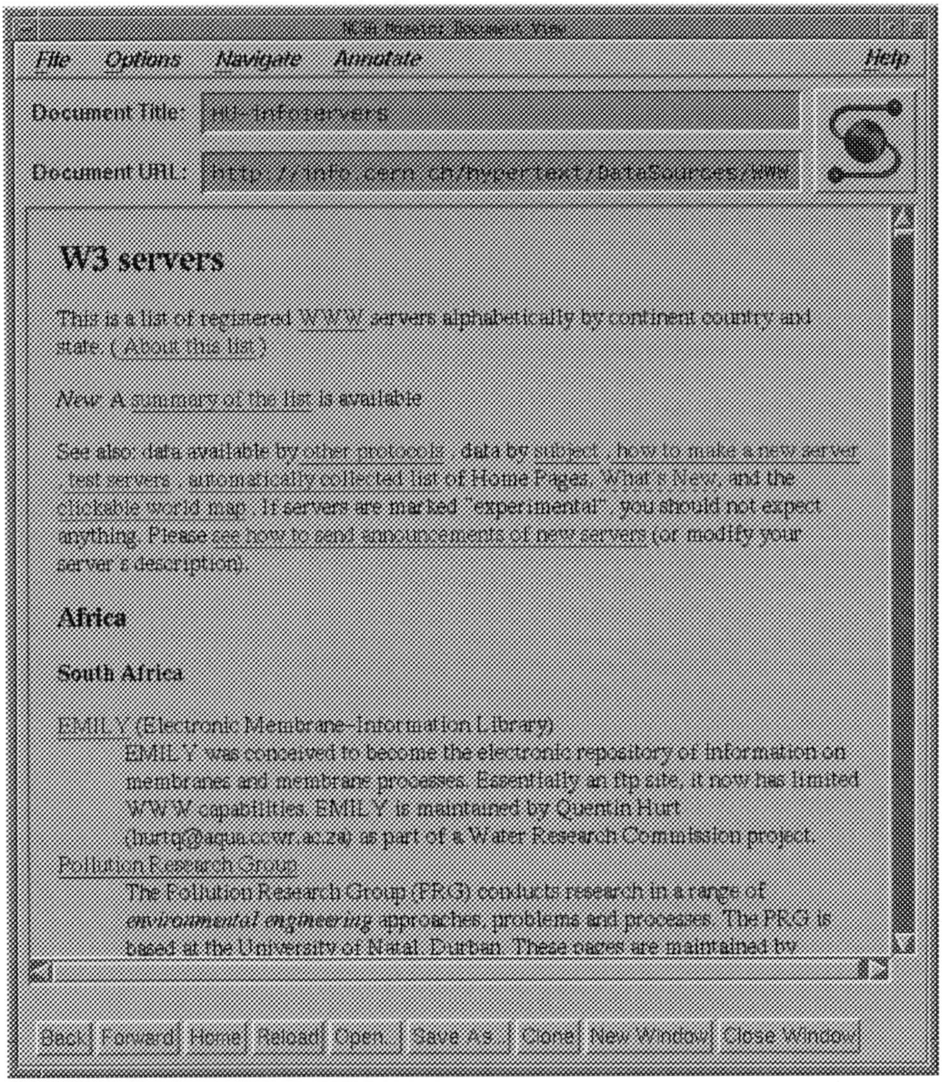

Figure 3-12. Web servers listed by country

To give you an example of how you can use this list as a point of departure for what can be a fascinating trip to almost anywhere in the world, follow the sequence of links below:

1. Find Malaysia on the list of Web servers by country and follow that link.

2. On the next document, follow the link to the University Sains Malaysia (USM) at Penang server.

3. On the USM server, follow the link to Penang Island.

This document is a tourist-information guide, describing the geography, history, and climate of the area. It lists its contents as links at the top. If you select the link labelled "Local Food," you can read about various local dishes, including Murtabak: "An Indian styled pizza filled with all the goodness of minced meat and onions and fried over a hot plate. It is eaten with a vegetarian curry."

CERN's *List of Servers* gives you an appreciation of how big the Web really is.

Special Internet Connections

http://info.cern.ch/hypertext/DataSources/Yanoff.html

Scott Yanoff offers a standard list of Internet services, which he began compiling in 1991. This exhaustive list, which is organized under broad categories such as Aviation, Law, and Travel (arranged alphabetically), contains entries and links to any kind of Internet service you can think of, from Gopher to TELNET, and everything in between. Though lengthy, the list is made up of terse entries that are not particularly descriptive of the resources they are pointing to. It is also not updated on a regular schedule.

CyberSight

http://cybersight.com/cgi-bin/cs/s?main.gmml

Terse is not the word to describe CyberSight, however. Billed as the central online "jumping off" point for alternative information seekers, CyberSight offers links to off-beat resources in a lively format. Don't approach this server with any preconceptions; just go to "The What You Want List (nutritious too!)" and choose from a few of the eclectic categories (Hot Stuff, Kitsch, Cybversive). For example, if you go to the Funky category, you'll see pointers to such unusual resources as Coke Machines, a site that helps you track the status of Coke and other vending machines around the world. Another site, Roadkill R Us ("a cornucopia of carcasses"), will give you access to more information on the truly tasteless than you ever dreamed of finding.

Searching the Web

After you've used these lists, you might decide to set out on your own to find things on the Web. You'll find several useful databases (or automated indexes), with new ones appearing all the time. Not all the searching interfaces are easy to use, and some searches will result in dead-ends or direct you to more information than you want.

The first thing to know about searching on the Web is that you are not really searching the documents on the Web itself. Rather, you are searching databases of information that have been collected from documents on the Web. These databases may include information for each document such as:

- Title

- Location (the URL)

- Documents that are linked to and from this document

- Keywords, abstracts, or brief descriptions of document contents

All this data is gathered off the Net and organized into a database, with links pointing back to the original documents. When you search for a word or phrase, you are really running a program on a remote computer that knows how to query and extract information from these databases. If your search is successful (i.e., your search words match up with words in the database), the program on the remote computer returns a Web document that contains links to the original documents.

Many of the searching databases are constructed and updated by programs called "robots" or "spiders" that continually "travel" the Net finding documents. As they encounter documents, they record information about each document, which is then used to update the database of documents.

Although robots sound like the perfect way to search the Web, there are a few problems. First, it takes a long time to search the Web, and so databases generated by robots may become out of date as documents are deleted or moved. Second, robots are generally indiscriminate about what databases they search, and a search in a robot-generated database may result in a huge number of "successful" searches, but a small number of really useful documents.

NOTE

For more information on the general design of robots and technical descriptions of robot programs on the Web, see "World Wide Web Wanderers, Spiders and Robots." (*http://web.nexor.co.uk/mak/doc/robots/robots.html*)

Most searching interfaces have a single text entry field for entering simple queries. Some interfaces are more complex, allowing you to reduce the scope of your search. Unless otherwise specified, most searchers will find any instance of a word, whether full or partial, upper or lowercase. For example, entering "zine" will match "Magazine" as well as "Zine." Below we introduce a number of these search servers for the Web.

The Wanderer

http://www.mit.edu:8001/people/mkgray/comprehensive.html

If at this point you're asking the question, "How big is the Web?," go to The Wanderer, a Perl script automaton created by Matthew Grey. The Wanderer travels the

Web searching for Web sites. It does a breadth-first search of the Web, looking for and including in a queue all the URLs contained in every document it encounters. At last count, (June 1994) the Wanderer had found more than 3000 sites on the Web. These are all listed (by numerical IP addresses, .EDU host sites, or by country); check out part or all of the list to see just how big your search can be when you search the Web.

CUSI

http://web.nexor.co.uk/susi/cusi.html

CUSI, part of the Web at Nexor (UK-based technology company) is a forms-based interface to many of the searchable indexes listed in this section, as well as other databases including catalogs, phone books, dictionaries, and technical documents. It's relatively easy to use, and you'll find it helpful to have so many of these searchers available in one document.

ALIWEB

http://web.nexor.co.uk/aliweb/doc/aliweb.html

ALIWEB ("Archie-Like Indexing for the Web") is a distributed indexing system. Because it is modelled after Archie, a program that maintains a database of software programs listed in public archives on the Net, you ask it where to find a particular program. ALIWEB's index database is generated from descriptions stored as files on the servers that contain the documents being indexed. This means that as long as publishers keep their own local descriptions up to date, ALIWEB has the potential to be of high quality. However, because it doesn't index every document on the Web, it's not a good place to look for instances of specific words or phrases.

CUI W3 Catalog

http://cui_www.unige.ch/w3catalog

The CUI searcher is a database of indexes to several popular lists and resource guides, including:

- NCSA's *What's New*
- NCSA's *Starting Points*
- CERN's W3 Virtual Library Subject Catalog and selected sub-lists
- Martijn Koster's ALIWEB—Archie-like Indexing for the Web
- Scott Yanoff's Internet Services List

- Simon Gibbs' list of Multimedia Information Sources

- John December's list of Computer-Mediated Communication Information Sources and Internet Tools Summary

Most of these resources are manually maintained subject-oriented lists (some of which are described earlier in this chapter), making the CUI catalog a good place to start if you know the topic of a search ("agriculture," for instance). Also, if a search is successful, it will return not just a list of documents, but the entry that contains the word or phrase.

WebCrawler

http://www.biotech.washington.edu/WebCrawler/WebQuery.html

WebCrawler is a robot that keeps an index of the contents of all the documents it comes across. Its interface is surprisingly simple—you type the words you're looking for into a single text entry box and click **Search**. A toggle button controls whether the words you are looking for must all be present in a document being searched (logical "AND") or whether only a subset may be present (logical "OR").

EINet Galaxy

http://www.einet.net/galaxy.html

EINet Galaxy is a combination hierarchical subject catalog and searchable database. This server, unlike the others, grabs all the documents it can find (not just HTML) and indexes them in a WAIS server. Thus you are searching the contents of the Web, and you get as many hits back as you ask for. It has a confusing interface, however, and searches often result in a large number of items returned.

The World Wide Web Worm

http://www.cs.colorado.edu/home/mcbryan/WWWW.html

The World Wide Web Worm is a database of Web document titles, URLs, and cross-references. Its power lies in the detailed level of searching that can be done: in addition to searching for words or phrases in a document title, you can also search for specific URLs or patterns within URLs. For instance, you can find documents at a particular host by searching for the hostname in the URL database. You can even search for particular types of files—searching for ".mpg" might find all the MPEG moving-image files in the database. Because WWWW keeps track of links between documents, you can supply a URL and find all the documents that link to that URL. The WWWW home page describes many such powerful search examples.

The WWWW is run weekly on selected files known to change regularly, such as the NCSA What's New page, to locate new sites and pages. In these runs, it ignores any files it has already read in a previous run. Once a month, the WWWW is run on all files, so that it rereads everything that has been previously located, in case there are changes.

Before concluding this tour of the Web, we should add that you are exploring an ever-expanding online universe. Things change every day, at every hour. This is especially important to remember if you can't find what you are looking for, or if the subject area of key interest does not have a strong set of resources on the Net. Someone may notice the deficiency one day, and the next begin putting up a lot of useful information. You may even be the person who makes that contribution!

## CHAPTER FOUR

ACCESSING OTHER INTERNET SERVICES

Mosaic and Gopher
WAIS
Mosaic and FTP
TELNET
Network News

So far, we have used Mosaic to access Web servers. However, Mosaic can access other types of Internet servers, such as Gopher, WAIS, and FTP. In Chapter 1, *The Wide World of Internet Services*, we explained that these services were available on the Internet before Web servers existed. Each service has its own distinct way of providing information to users, just as the Web does. However, Mosaic can be used not only as a Web client, but also as a Gopher client. It can be used as a client to access WAIS servers, news servers, FTP archives, and TELNET servers. Because Mosaic is such a multipurpose browser, it has become the Swiss Army knife of the Internet.

In exploring the Internet, you may be surprised when you traverse a link and you don't end up in a Web document. Instead, you'll see a list of topics, each one appearing as a link, and if you look at the URL, you will be able to identify it as a Gopher server. Similarly, you may see a list of filenames and directories. If you check the URL, you'll find that you have accessed an FTP server. In both cases, it is pretty obvious that you are not viewing a Web document.

In this chapter, we demonstrate how to use Mosaic to access these different types of servers. You don't have to learn too much about navigating to these servers. Rather, you will come to recognize the differences in the way they organize information. Knowing that a link points to a Gopher server tells you something about how the information will be presented.

Below is a list of the services covered in this chapter, along with a short description of each.

Gopher

    Gopher is a menu-based information system that allows users to browse through a hierarchical organization and select items from menus. Each item on the menu represents either a file or a directory.

WAIS

> WAIS, which stands for Wide Area Information Servers, is a search-and-retrieval system that lets users search a full-text index of all documents in a database.

FTP

> FTP, which stands for File Transfer Protocol, is an application that lets you download files from remote servers.

TELNET

> TELNET is a terminal emulation protocol that allows you log into other computer systems on the Internet.

Network news

> Network news is a system of bulletin board discussion groups covering every kind of subject from computer science to sex, pets, and surfing.

If you are interested in learning more about the Internet services discussed in this chapter and comparing other client interfaces, see *The Whole Internet User's Guide and Catalog* by Ed Krol, published by O'Reilly & Associates.

Mosaic and Gopher

Not too long ago there were a lot more Gopher servers on the Net than Web servers. There are still a lot of Gopher servers around because they are an easy way to provide information to a broad audience. What is distinctive about Gopher is that you navigate through menus, and each item on the menu is either a file or another menu with additional selections. In Mosaic, these choices are links, and you select the item you want by clicking on the link. Each choice also has an icon next to it. The two icons you'll see with Gopher servers are: a file folder, which represents a menu, and a sheet of paper with writing on it, which indicates a text file.

Figure 4-1 shows the Library of Congress Gopher as viewed in Mosaic. We begin at the top-level menu of this Gopher.

If you click on **Government Information**, Mosaic retrieves the contents of that menu, as shown in Figure 4-2.

This menu contains four links, each of which takes you to another menu as you navigate to the next level of detail in the hierarchy. Clicking on **Federal Information** takes you to a menu with more directories. On you go, tunneling through directories until you come to a menu that contains some files. Clicking on a filename displays the contents of the file.

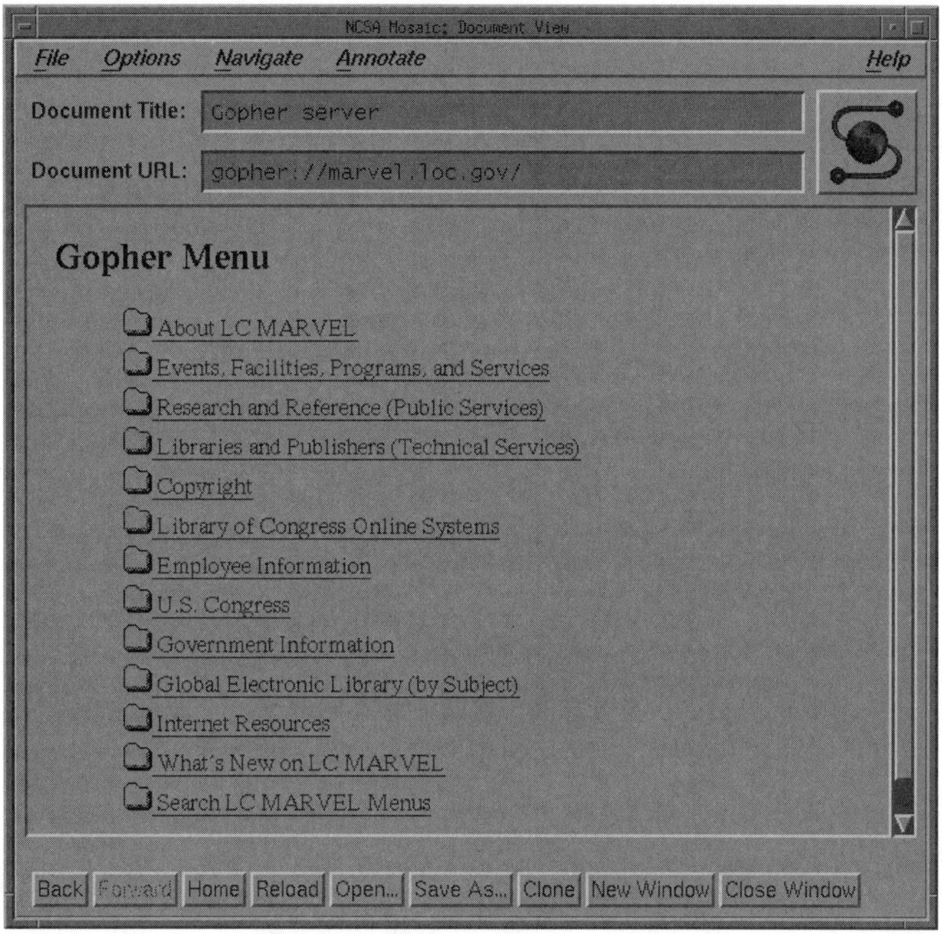

Figure 4-1. Library of Congress Gopher

Most Gopher servers deliver ASCII files that Mosaic displays in a fixed font. An example of such a file is shown in Figure 4-3. Besides letting users browse through categories of information, Gopher can transparently access information from other Gopher servers. In addition, most Gopher servers contain pointers to all the other Gopher servers in the world, so it is truly a global system.

There are some disadvantages, however. In our example, we didn't go through all the layers of menus that it took to get to a text file, but there were more than a dozen. Sometimes Gopher seems like a case study in the limitations of hierarchical filing systems. The problem is that it becomes absurd (not to mention boring) to keep selecting menu items, only to be confronted by another menu list. After padding through a dozen or so of these menus, you may lose interest in whatever you were looking for.

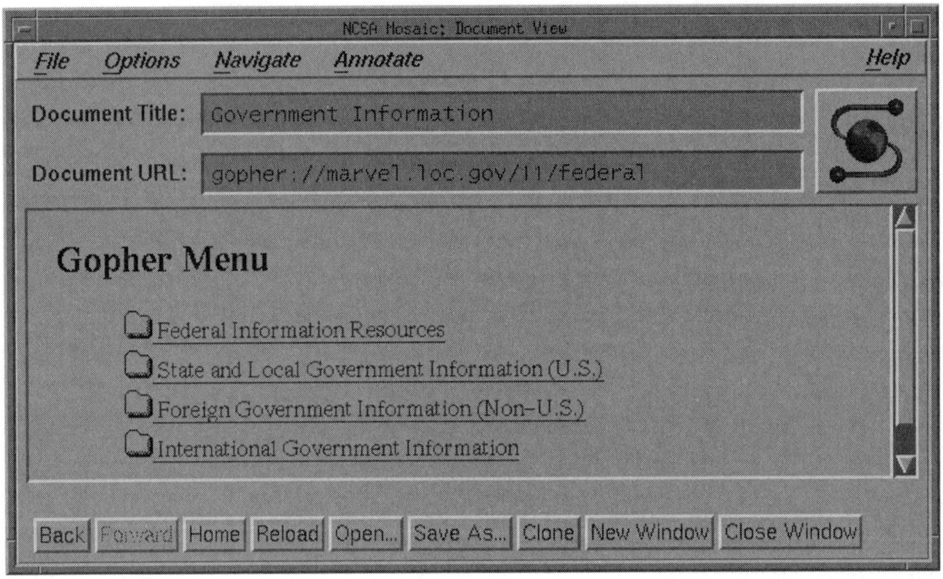

Figure 4-2. Government Information menu

Given the choice, most people would rather use a Web server than a Gopher server. However, you don't always have a choice, as some organizations may not yet be able to provide information in HTML on a Web server. You also see interesting Web/Gopher hybrids. For example, if a business already has a Gopher server, they might create a Web server with only a few original documents that serve as a high-level interface to the Gopher server. In other words, after the home page, their Web server points to information managed on the Gopher server.

That said, however, remember that lots of good information can be found in Gopher servers. *GNN*'s Whole Internet Catalog contains pointers to quite a few good Gopher servers, including:

- African National Congress Gopher

- The Bible

- Envirogopher

- CIA World Factbook

- Project Gutenberg

- The California Museum of Photography

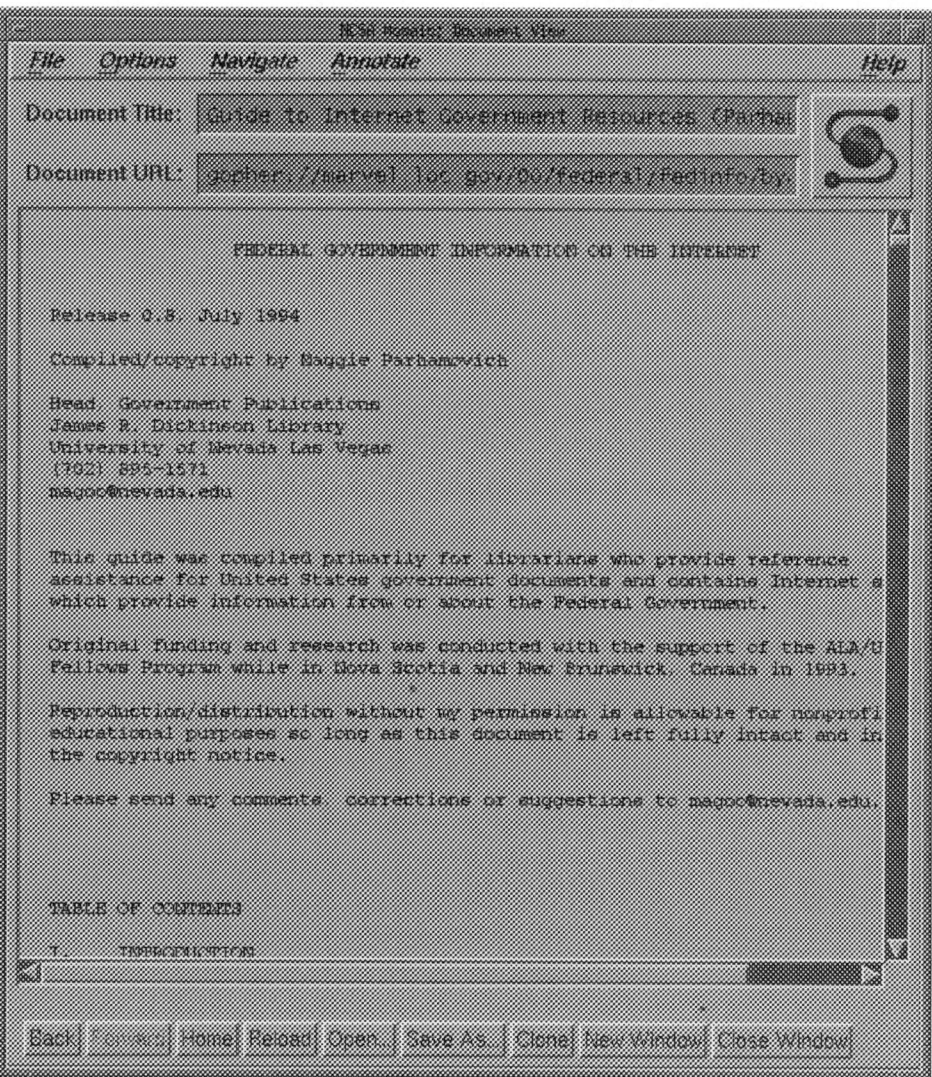

Figure 4-3. Mosaic displays ASCII file

Using the Hotlist to Manage Gophers

Since the good stuff (the documents) may be buried several layers deep in a Gopher, you'll want to use all the tools at your disposal to manage them. You can use your hotlist to create bookmarks in the Gophers you use regularly. Each menu level in Gopher can be identified by a URL. Thus when you get to the menu level that you want, you can just choose **Add Current to Hotlist** from the **Navigate** menu to add that Gopher menu to your hotlist. Of course, you can still travel up and down the menus once you're in the Gopher.

Getting Gophers with URLs

A Gopher URL is a lot like a Web URL, except that the service protocol is different, of course. Instead of HTTP, you use the Gopher protocol. So to contact the Library of Congress Gopher, select **Open URL** from the **File** menu and type:

    gopher://marvel.loc.gov

This takes you to the main menu of the server. As discussed above, it becomes pure drudgery to have to navigate through all those menus. Mosaic can help you avoid some of this awkwardness by allowing you to connect directly to a particular menu level. For instance, you can get directly to the **Federal Information** menu in the Library of Congress Gopher by typing the URL:

    gopher://marvel.loc.gov/11/federal/fedinfo

Searching Through Gopherspace

Since tunneling through menus can be a time-consuming way to find information, especially if you're looking for specific information, there are several applications for searching "gopherspace." On a Gopher menu you may see an option for searching. If you select this option, you will go to another document where you are prompted to enter a search keyword. The Gopher server then returns a menu of items matching the search criteria. Many Gopher servers also have a gateway to a WAIS server that contains a full-text index of the contents of the Gopher. We'll talk more about WAIS servers in the next section.

There are several tools that index all of gopherspace, not just a single server. You can specify a search string that will be matched against an index of words in Gopher titles or text files.

Veronica

Veronica searches all of the menu items on all Gopher servers for a string of words or characters that you enter. Follow these steps to use Veronica:

1. Log on to the Gopher server at the University of Texas at Austin by entering the following URL:

       gopher://bongo.cc.utexas.edu

   Figure 4-4 shows the top-level menu of this Gopher server.

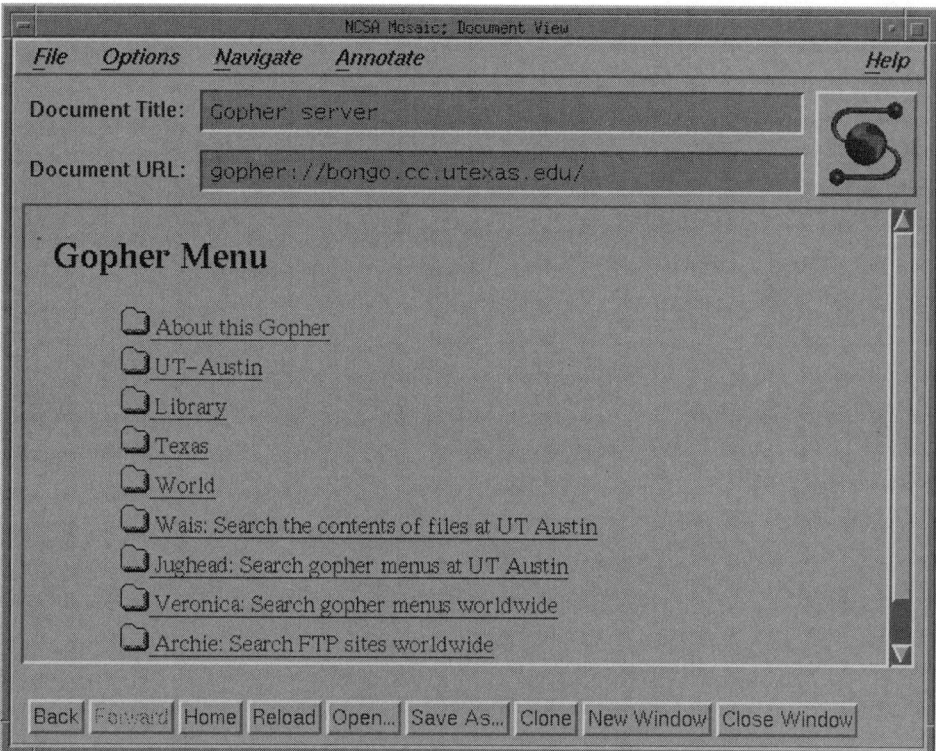

Figure 4–4. Top-level menu of the Gopher server at the University of Texas at Austin

2. Select **Veronica: Search Gopher Menus Worldwide**. This leads you to a menu where you can select a Veronica server, shown in Figure 4-5. As you can see, there are actually two types of Veronica searches—you can search the titles of all Gopher items, or you can search only for directories. If you do the first kind of search, you're likely to get a rather long list of results, so doing a directory search is usually more effective.

There are a number of different servers to choose from. As a general rule, use the server that's closest to you. Veronica servers tend to be quite busy; you may not be able to perform a search on the first server you try. In fact, don't be surprised if you have to go to Europe before you find a server that lets you perform a search.

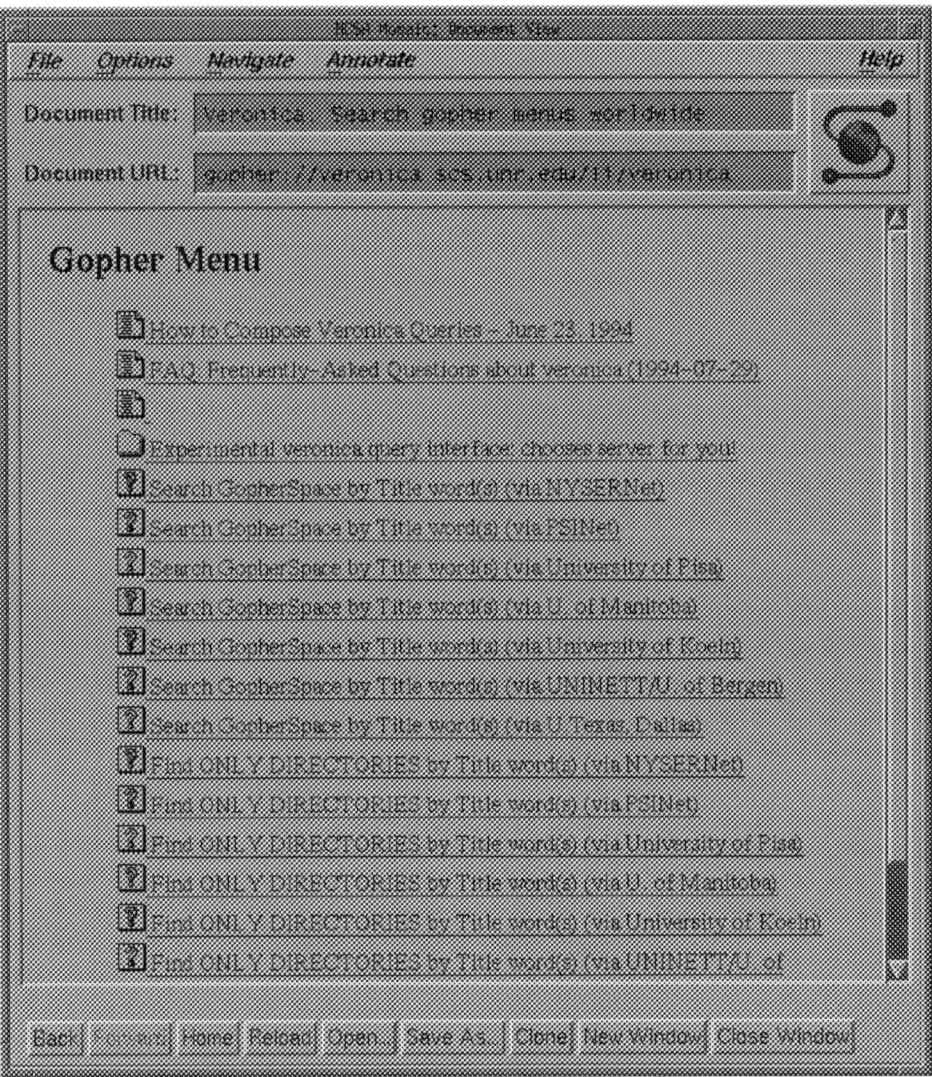

Figure 4-5. Choosing a Veronica server

3. Once you connect to a server, you will be presented with a screen that contains a text field, shown in Figure 4-6. Simply enter the text you are searching for in the field and press **Return**.

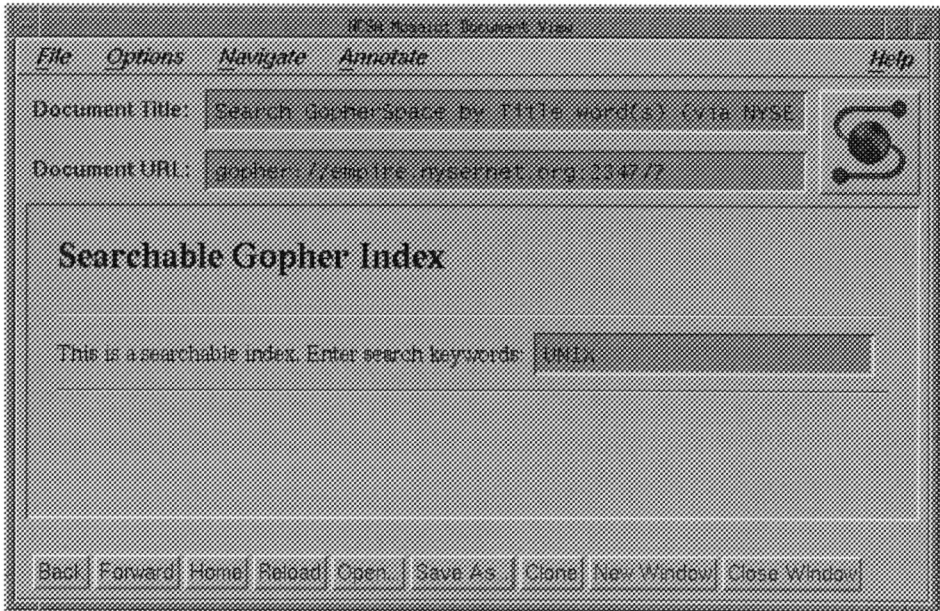

Figure 4-6. Searching Veronica for a string of text

4. The Veronica server will then search for that text and return a list of responses, as shown in Figure 4-7. If the server is too busy, it may tell you that there are too many connections, instead of performing the search. If this happens, you'll need to try another server. Each response is a hypertext link, and clicking on one brings up either a menu or the contents of a file.

Veronica searches accept "Boolean operators," words that specify conditions that must be met in order for Veronica to consider an item as matching the search. Boolean operators separate two or more strings. Veronica understands the following operators:

- AND tells Veronica that both parts of the query must be present. For instance, searching for "UNIX AND X" tells Veronica that only items that contain both "UNIX" and "X" are matches. If no Boolean operators are specified, Veronica assumes there to be an AND between words.

- OR tells Veronica that either part of the query is acceptable as a match. If the query is "UNIX OR X," any items that contain either one of those words is considered a match.

- NOT tells Veronica to search for items containing the first string but not the second. For instance, searching for "UNIX NOT X" searches for items containing "UNIX" but excludes items that refer to "X".

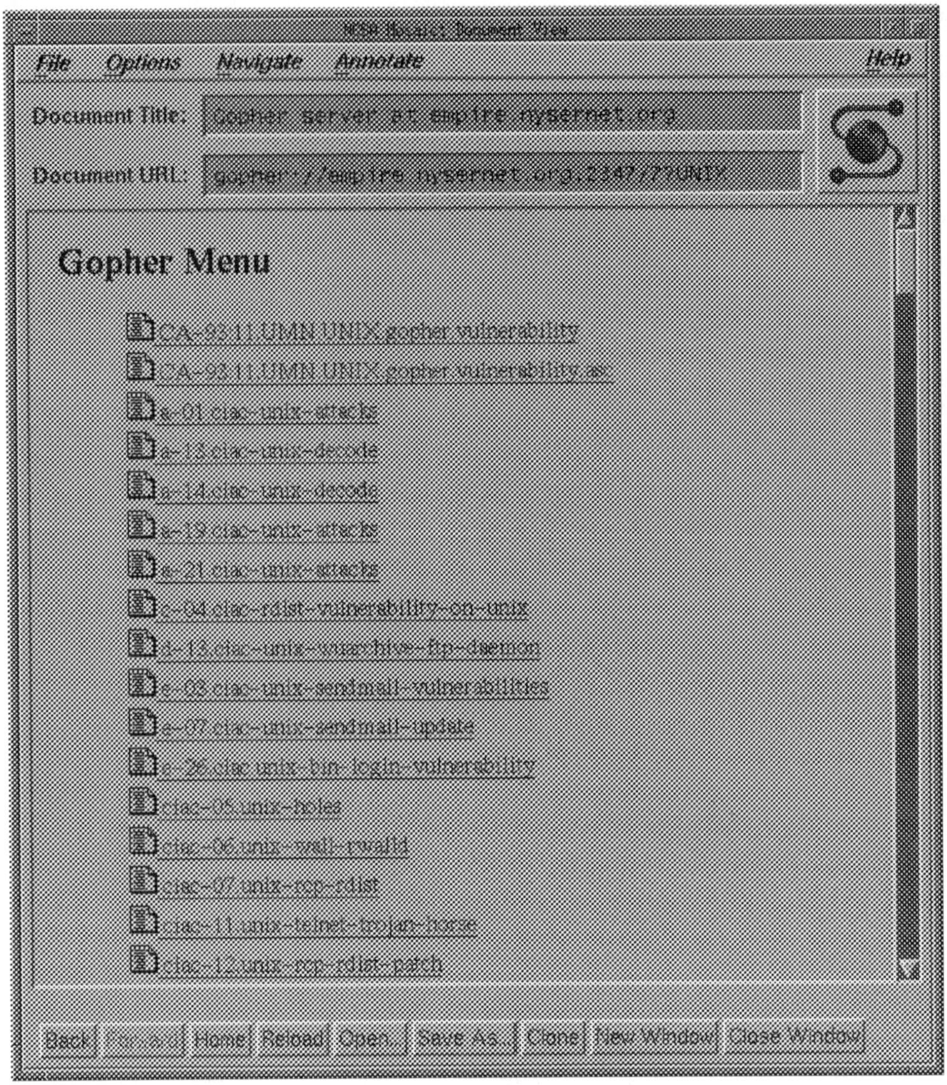

Figure 4-7. Veronica search response

You can combine Boolean operators. Veronica evaluates them from right to left, so "UNIX AND X OR CDE" searches for items with "UNIX and X" or "CDE." Veronica also accepts an asterisk as a wildcard character, which represents any combination of characters to the end of the word. For example, "shovel*" would match shovel, shovels, shoveling, shoveled, and so on.

Jughead

Sometimes you don't want to search the menus of every Gopher server in the world. If you are looking for regional or specialized information, you can use Jughead to search menu titles of Gophers at a single institution. Many colleges and universities use Gopher servers as campus-wide information systems, so students at the University of Texas at Austin can use Jughead to search for information about UTA. Or a medical researcher might use Jughead to search only the Gopher servers at Johns Hopkins University.

In most cases, you use Jughead without knowing it. While UTA's Gopher clearly identifies one menu item as **Jughead: Search Gopher menus at UT Austin**, most others simply say something like **Search Gopher menus at** ...

As with Veronica, Jughead lets you use the Boolean operators AND, OR, and NOT and the asterisk wildcard. Searches are not case-sensitive. However, Jughead only lets you search for two words at a time and doesn't support the ability to search for specific Gopher resource types.

WAIS

There are approximately 600 WAIS servers on the Internet, which let you search the full text of all the documents in a database. With Mosaic, you can access WAIS servers through either the Web or Gopher.

To use WAIS within Gopher, you can pick a WAIS server and search for a string of words. Most WAIS servers aren't terribly sophisticated when it comes to advanced searching techniques, so Boolean operators probably won't work. One good thing about WAIS, however, is that you can ask it questions in plain English , like "What information is there about Silicon Graphics, Inc.?"

Here's how to try it out:

1. Connect to the University of Minnesota Gopher at:

    `gopher://gopher.micro.umn.edu`

2. Choose **Other Gopher and Information Servers**.

3. Choose **WAIS Based Information**.

4. Choose **WAIS Databases sorted by Letter**.

5. At this point, you can either search the directory of WAIS servers or choose from an alphabetical list of servers. Since the names of WAIS databases can be a little strange, it's usually better to search the directory. To do that, choose **Directory of WAIS servers** and enter your query in the search field. For our example, we'll use the query "health insurance," shown in Figure 4-8.

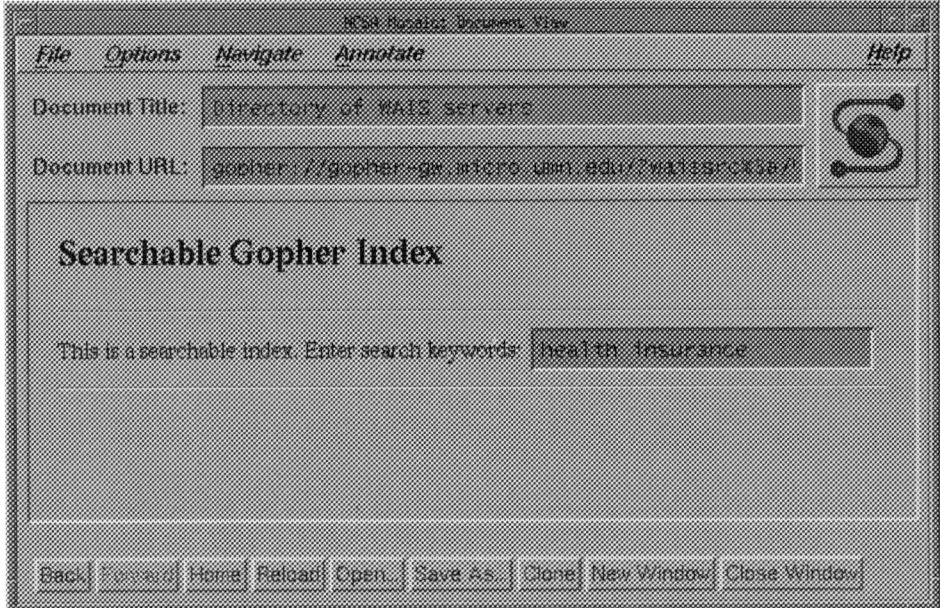

Figure 4-8. Searching the WAIS directory

6. After a little while, Mosaic will display a list of WAIS servers that say they have information about health or insurance, as shown in Figure 4-9.

7. At the top of the list is **Health-Security-Act.src**, which is a database of documents related to the health reform bill proposed by President Clinton in 1994. Click on that link to search the database. Enter your query in the search field, and the server will respond with a ranked list of headlines of documents that contain your search words.

8. To see any of these documents, click on the headline, and Mosaic will display the document. If you want to save it, use the **Save As** command.

You can also use WAIS within certain Web servers. For instance, *The Whole Internet Catalog* includes a WAIS server of the documents in *GNN*. To find documents about finance, you can simply enter "finance" in the search field, and Mosaic will return a list of description files containing that word, as shown in Figure 4-10. Clicking on one of these files will display the page that contains the link. As of this writing, this feature is only available on *GNN*'s NEARnet server, *http://nearnet.gnn.com/gnn/wic/*.

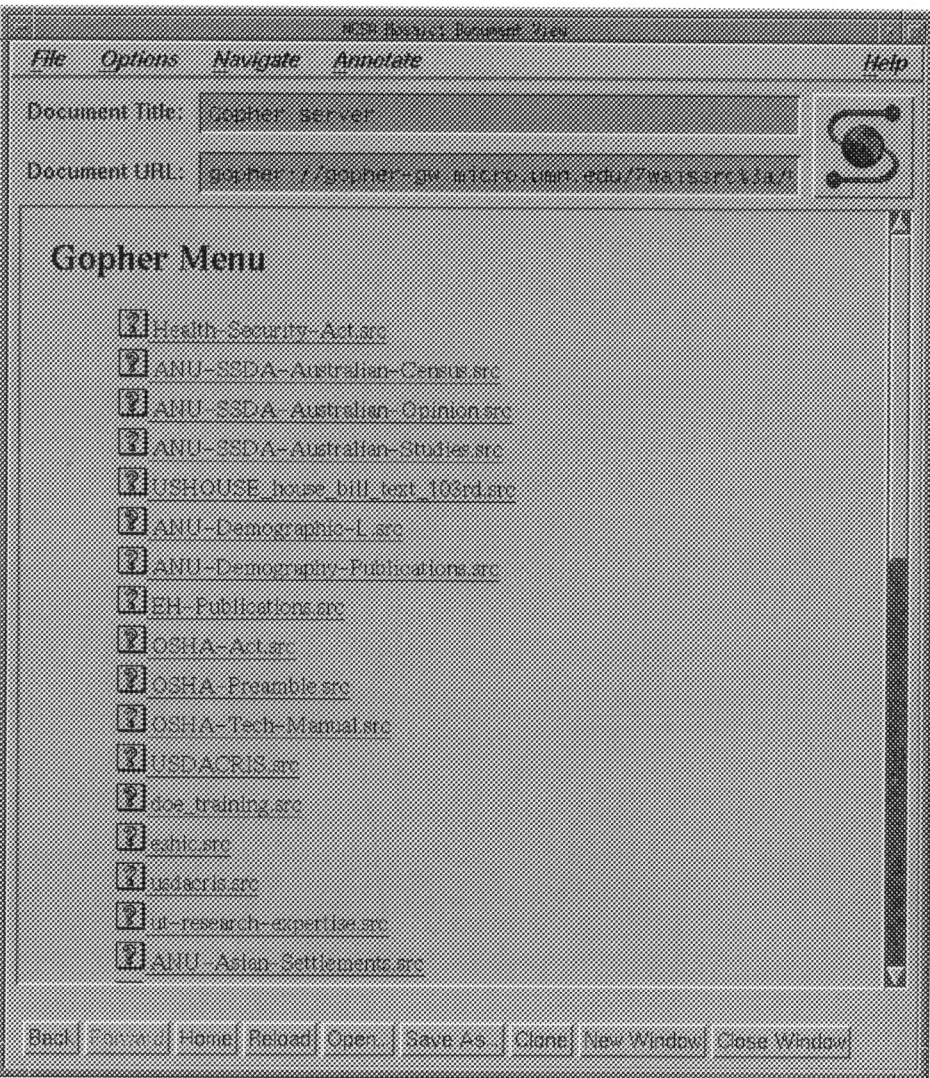

Figure 4—9. Results of WAIS directory search

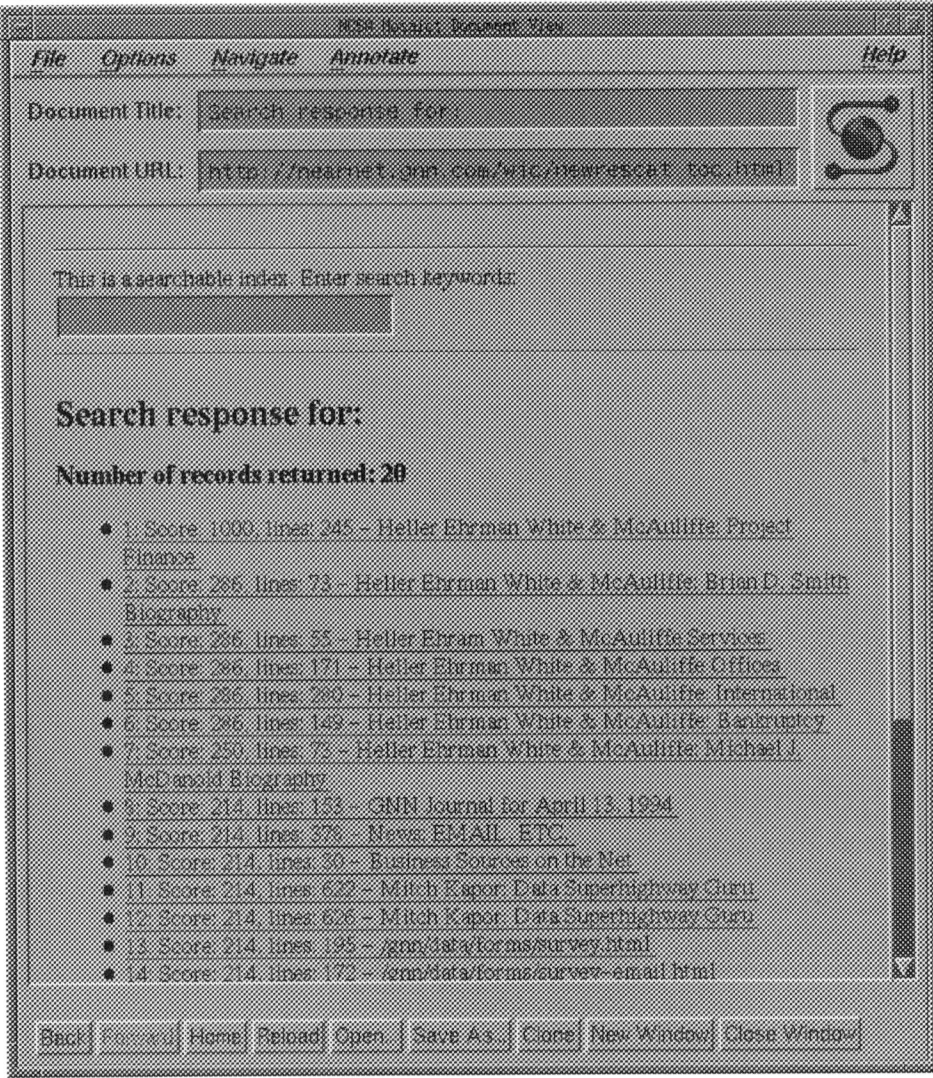

Figure 4–10. Results of searching the WIC

Mosaic and FTP

Some Web documents, such as *GNN*'s *Whole Internet Catalog*, will link you to FTP servers. While FTP collections are just about the least user-friendly things you're likely to see with Mosaic, they do hold vast amounts of information that you can download to your computer.

FTP is the Internet tool for moving files between computers. The name stands for File Transfer Protocol, which is the application protocol that handles the transfer. FTP can be a complicated program to use because files can be stored and compressed in many different ways.

There are two transfer modes available in FTP—one for ASCII (text) files and one for binary files. Binary transfer mode preserves the bit sequence of the file, so that the copy is identical to the original. ASCII mode treats the file as sets of characters so that the document will be readable on the computer receiving the file.

In addition, files are compressed using many different programs, so it's important to identify which file you can decompress and use on your system. You can usually determine this by looking at file extensions, as we'll explain shortly.

Fortunately, using Mosaic to perform FTP transfers simplifies matters quite a bit. This is because Mosaic determines whether a file should be transferred using ASCII or binary transfer mode.

One important limitation of using Mosaic as an FTP client is that it only supports anonymous FTP, a service that lets you access a public directory via an anonymous login. If you want to copy files from a computer on which you have an account, you'll need to use another FTP utility.*

Downloading Files with FTP

Now let's take a look at using Mosaic to transfer files from an FTP site. We'll start at the Whole Internet Catalog. In the Art category, the WIC has a link to the Smithsonian Institution's image server **photo1.si.edu**, shown in Figure 4-11. Clicking on the **Go** button will connect you via anonymous FTP to this server. When you click that button, Mosaic takes care of opening the connection to **photo1.si.edu** and logging you in as an anonymous user. Once connected, Mosaic displays the top-level directories of the server, as shown in Figure 4-12.

---

* This isn't quite true, as the URL syntax for FTP servers does allow you to specify a username and password. The disadvantage of this approach is that Mosaic displays your password as you type it, as well as in the URL field in the **Document View** window. For this reason, we don't recommend using Mosaic for private FTP.

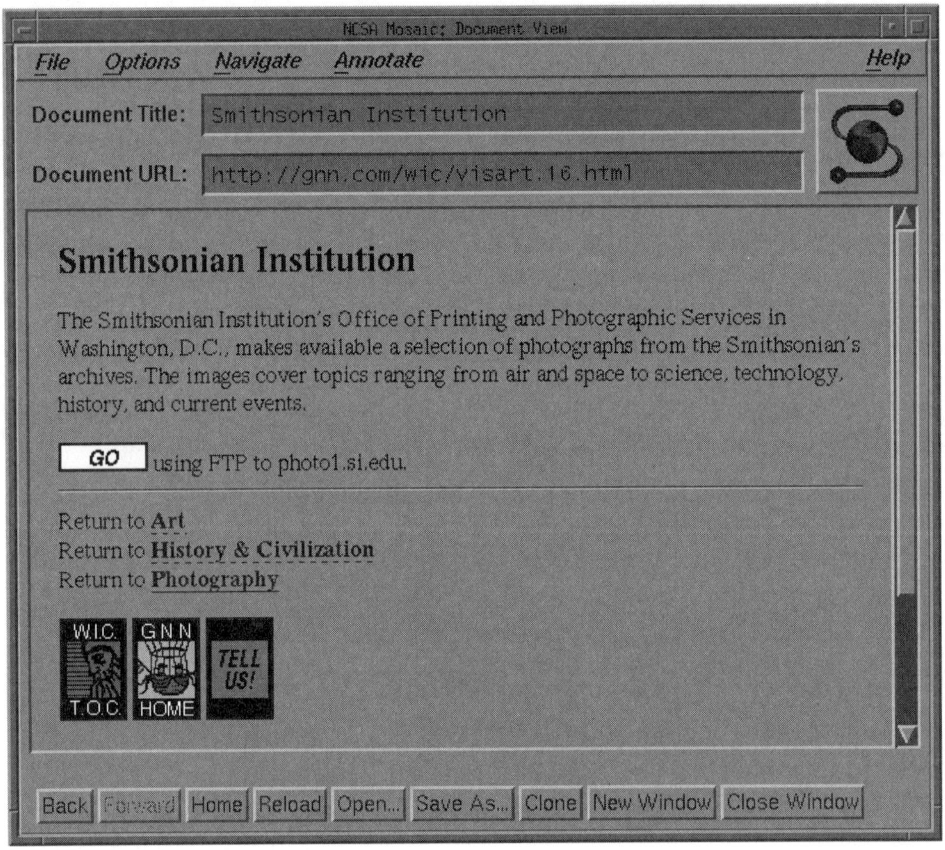

Figure 4-11. WIC description of Smithsonian image server

Now take a look at the URL for this server. The syntax should be familiar to you by now. It starts with the service protocol *ftp*, followed by the separator *://* and the name of the server. Directories and filenames can be included in the URL, just as with other services. The URL for the Smithsonian image server, then, is:

```
ftp://photo1.si.edu
```

Unlike in Gopher, FTP directory names are not particularly helpful. Remember that you are looking at a UNIX file server meant for transferring files, not browsing, so hints about content are few and far between. However, each filename has an icon next to it, telling you something about the file's contents. Table 4-1 shows the icons you'll see when you use Mosaic to access FTP servers.

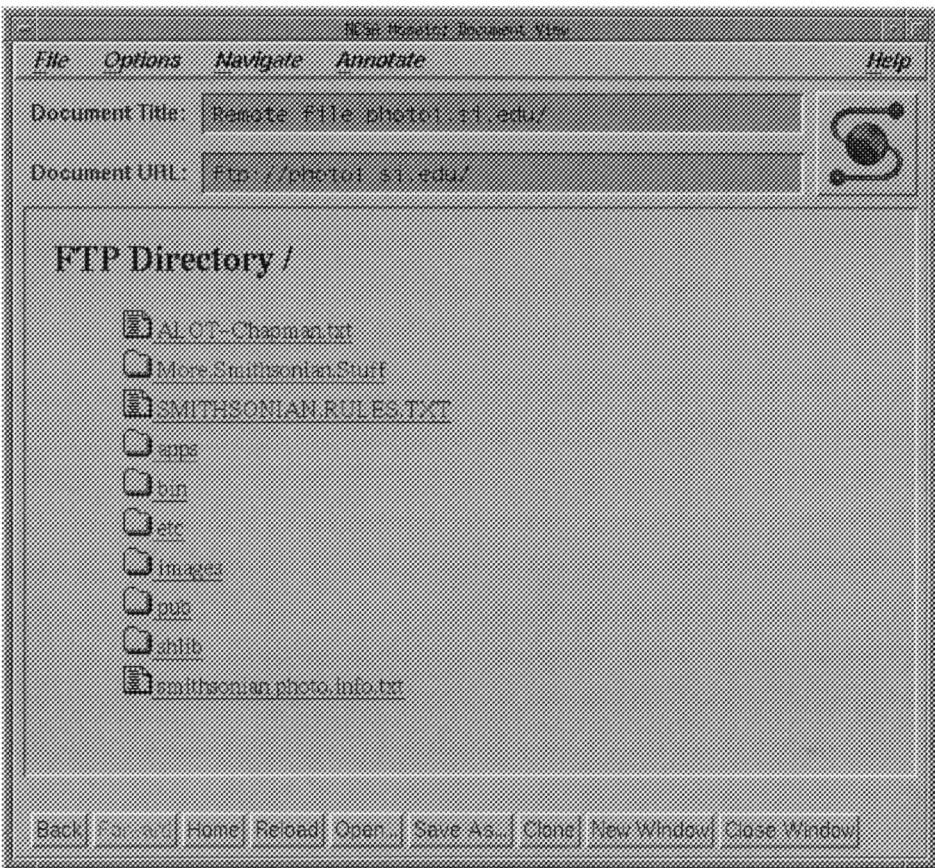

Figure 4–12. Top-level directories of photo1.si.edu

Table 4–1: Common Mosaic Icons

File type	Icon
Directory	File folder
Text file	Sheet of paper with writing
Compressed text file	Sheet of paper with writing
Binary file	Sheet of paper with zeros and ones
Picture	Sheet of paper with a pencil
Movie	Film strip
Audio	Loudspeaker
Phone books	Question mark
Veronica searches	Question mark
Searchable indexes	Question mark
TELNET services	Box with TEL inside

As you can see, each filename and directory is a hypertext link. Since this is an image server, let's look at the *images* directory. Clicking on **images** will display the contents of that directory, as shown in Figure 4-13.

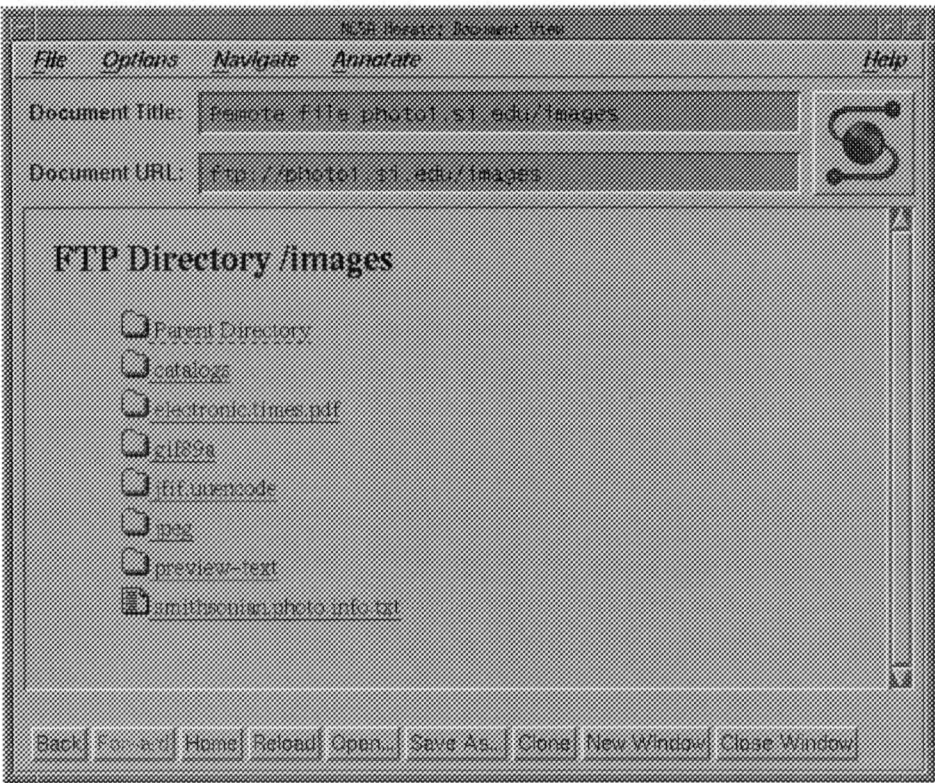

Figure 4–13. The images directory

All but one of the items here are subdirectories. Three of these—*gif89a, jfif-uuencode,* and *jpeg*—look most promising as photo archives since their names contain image file formats.

Before we dive into the image directories, let's take a look at the text file *smithsonian.photo.info.txt* to see what it tells us. To read the file, click on the filename. The file is shown in Figure 4-14. The information file explains the file and compression formats of the various files and tells us how to download appropriate software for viewing the images. To save this document for future reference, choose **Save As** from the **File** menu and choose a filename and location on your system.

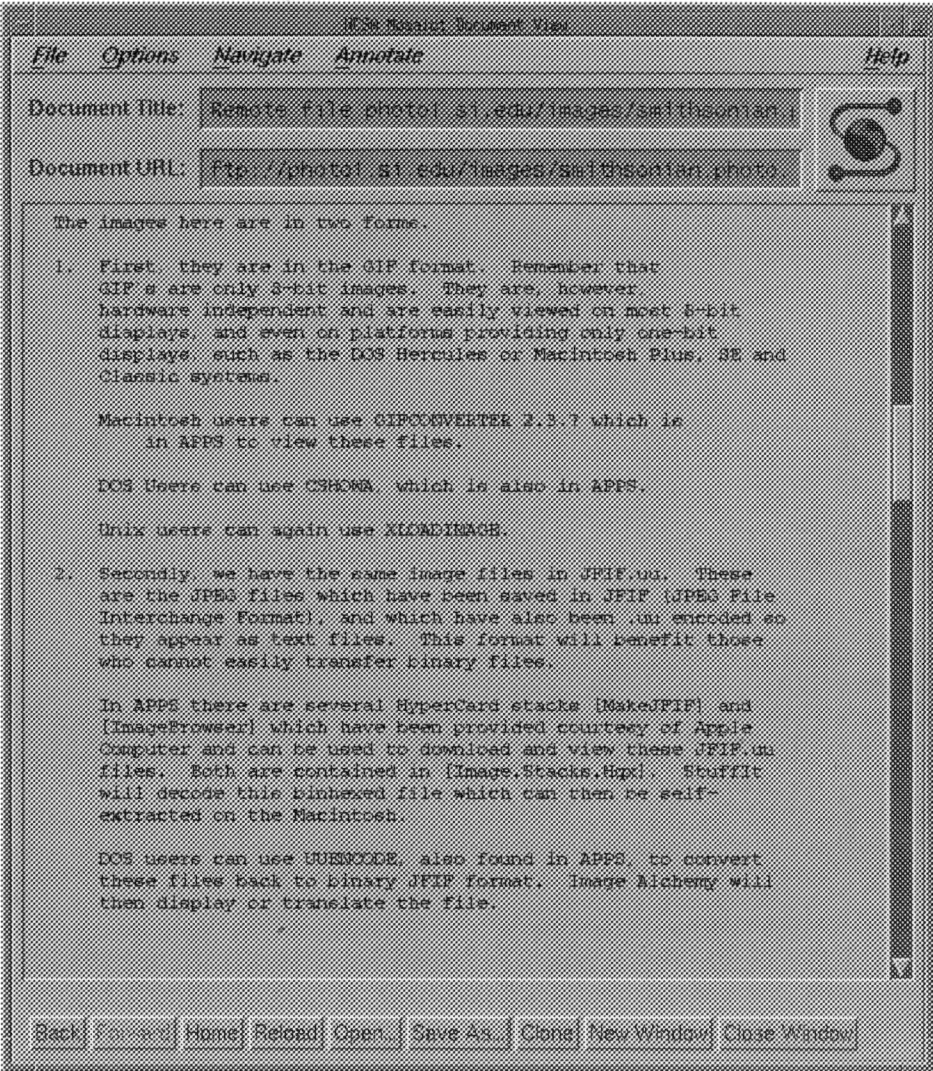

Figure 4–14. Clicking on a text file displays its contents

Now let's see what files are available. Click on the **Back** button to return to the directory listing and then click on **gif89a** to see the contents of that directory, as shown in Figure 4-15.

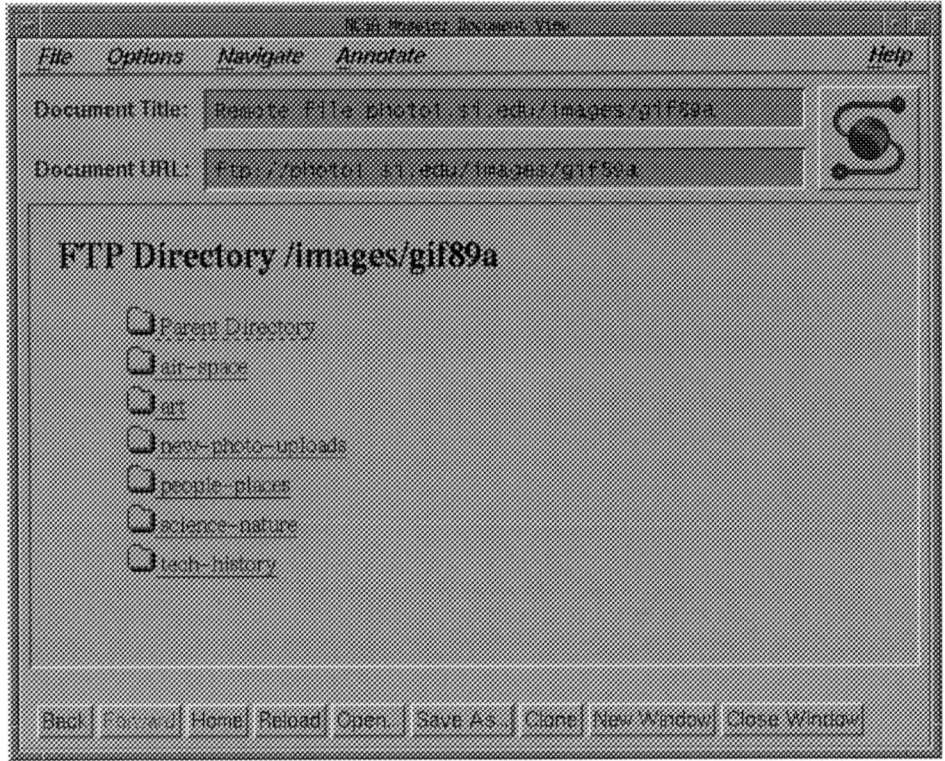

Figure 4–15. Contents of gif89a

The directory contains several subdirectories, which organize the images by category. Let's try the *air-space* directory, shown in Figure 4-16.

Finally, we've found the images. Notice that these files all end with the extension *.gif.* That tells us that they're images in the GIF format. Remember, now that you know where you're going, you can get right to this directory by entering the URL:

    ftp://photo1.si.edu/images/gif89a/air-space

Now we're ready to access an image. Let's try *APOLLO.GIF.* As we'll explain in Chapter 6, *Using Mosaic for Multimedia,* when you follow a link to an image file, Mosaic attempts to use the external viewer **xv** to display the image. If **xv** is installed on your system, when you click on the filename, Mosaic downloads the image and displays it as shown in Figure 4-17.

If, however, your system does not have **xv** installed, clicking on the filename brings up the **Save As** dialog box, which, of course, lets you specify where to save the document. You can also force Mosaic to save the image to disk, rather than display it, by selecting the **Load to Local Disk** option on the **Options** menu before you click on the filename.

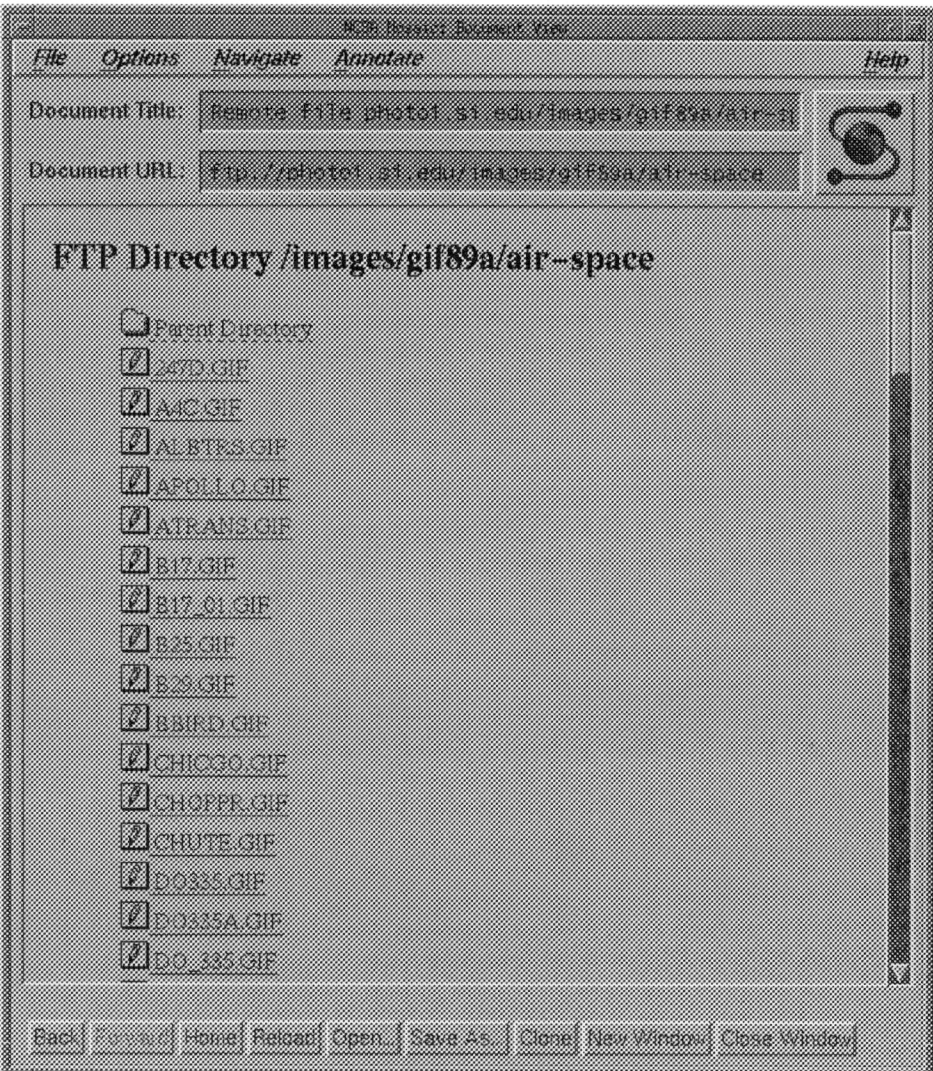

Figure 4–16. Contents of the air-space directory

When you use Mosaic to access a file on an FTP server, the program decides whether to use ASCII or binary mode to download the file. If Mosaic uses binary transfer mode, the program typically asks you to save the document, instead of just displaying it. Since Mosaic can display graphics files with an external viewer, however, these files are handled differently. Table 4-2 shows the transfer mode used for different file types.

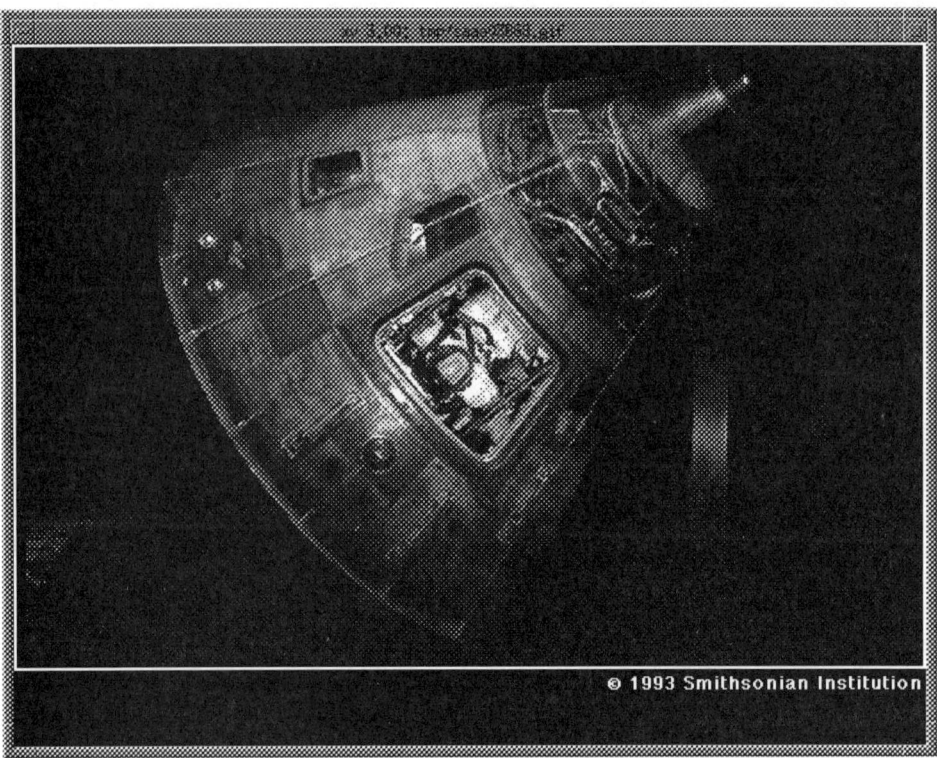

© 1993 Smithsonian Institution

Figure 4–17. APOLLO.GIF displayed with xv

Table 4–2: Common File Types and Modes

File	Mode
Text file	ASCII, by definition
Spreadsheet	Probably binary
Database file	Probably binary, possibly ASCII
Word processor file	Probably binary, possibly ASCII
Program source code	ASCII
Electronic mail messages	ASCII
UNIX shell archive	ASCII
UNIX tar file	Binary
Backup file	Binary
Compressed file	Binary
Uuencoded or binhexed file	ASCII
Executable file	Binary, but see below
PostScript (laser printer) file	ASCII, but displayed externally
Hypertext (HTML) document	ASCII
Picture files (GIF, JPEG, MPEG)	Binary, but displayed externally

Downloading a Program

The Smithsonian text file we just looked at recommends another UNIX application, called **xloadimage**, for viewing graphics files. One advantage of this program over **xv** is that **xloadimage** can display some image types that **xv** cannot. The source code for **xloadimage** is located in the *apps* directory. To get this, you can move back up to the main directory by clicking on the **Parent Directory** hyperlink, which displays the next highest directory, until you reach the main directory. (You can also use **Back** to get back to the main directory; this may be faster since Mosaic uses its document cache to display the contents, rather than accessing the FTP server across the net.) Now click on **apps**.

The *apps* directory has three subdirectories for DOS, Macintosh, and UNIX. Clicking on **unix** displays the contents of that directory, as shown in Figure 4-18.

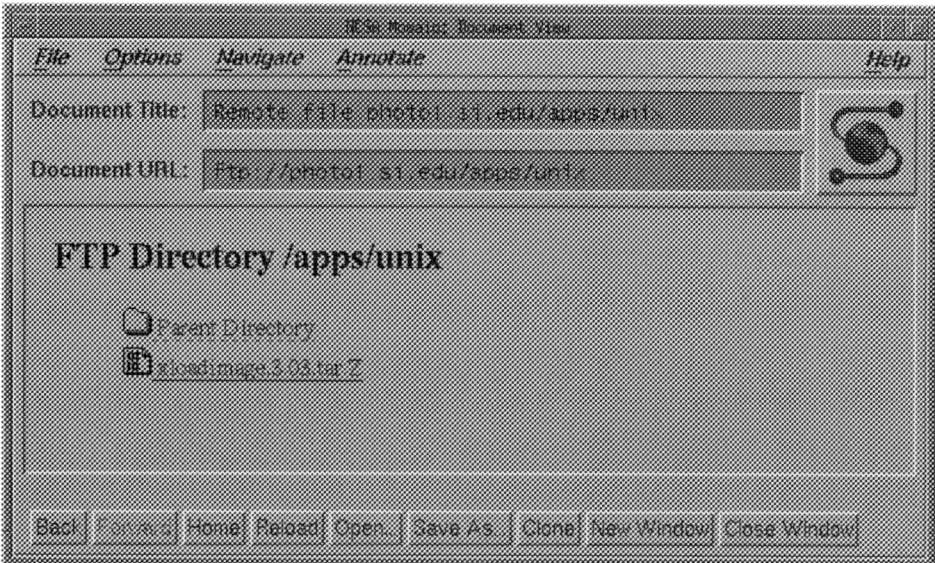

Figure 4–18. Contents of UNIX directory

Notice that the file in this directory has the extension *.Z*. This indicates that it has been compressed with a UNIX compression utility, **compress**. Other times you'll see files with other extensions, such as *.zip* or *.Sit*. Those indicate that a DOS or Macintosh compression program was used, respectively. Table 4-3 gives information about common compression extensions and the associated programs.

Table 4-3: Common Compression Programs

Compression Program	Decompression Program	Platform	File Suffix	Typical Filename
compress	uncompress	UNIX	.Z	*rfc1118.txt.Z*
gzip	gunzip	UNIX and DOS	.z or .gz	*textfile.gz*
Stuffit	unsit	Macintosh	.Sit	*program.Sit*
PackIt	unpit	Macintosh	.pit	*report.pit*
PKZIP	unzip41	DOS	.ZIP	*package.ZIP*

To download *xloadimage.3.03.tar.Z*, click on the filename. When you download a file that has been compressed with a UNIX compression utility, Mosaic decompresses the file using the appropriate decompression program if it exists on your system. Once Mosaic has downloaded the file, it brings up the **Save As** dialog. Call the file *xloadimage.3.03.tar*, since Mosaic has decompressed it. Now you have a UNIX tar archive. You can get the source code for **xloadimage** out of the archive (**tar xvf xloadimage.3.03.tar**) and build the program if you are so inclined. The directions for building the program are included in a *README* file.

Using FTP with Hypertext

Another way to use FTP in Mosaic is through hypertext links. Some servers, such as the NCSA Web server, let you download specific files via anonymous FTP by clicking on a hypertext link. This is, of course, a very simple way to get files; you don't have to wade through the FTP server—just click on a link and the file transfer process starts transparently. Here's what actually happens when you click on the link, even though the process is hidden from you.

1. Mosaic connects to the FTP server.

2. Mosaic logs you in as an anonymous user.

3. Mosaic sends an FTP request to transfer the file in binary mode.

4. The server downloads the requested file to your computer.

5. Mosaic closes the connection.

TELNET

A Web document can also contain links to TELNET servers. When you follow such a link, Mosaic creates a new window with a TELNET session running in it. Once the session starts, you can do whatever the remote computer system allows you to do. That's really all there is to TELNET access.

The Whole Internet Catalog has a link to the University of Michigan's Weather Underground service, **madlab.sprl.umich.edu**, shown in Figure 4-19. When you press the **GO** button, Mosaic creates a window and opens a TELNET connection to **madlab.sprl.umich.edu** that automatically starts the Weather Underground program.

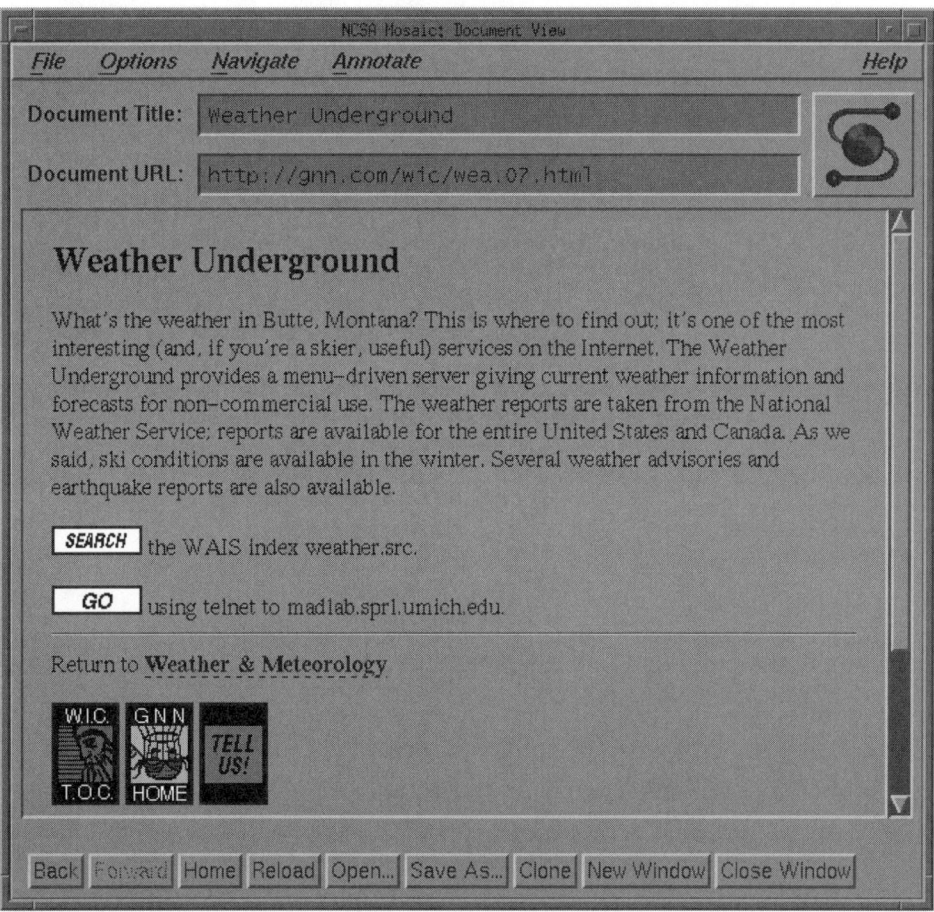

Figure 4-19. WIC description of Weather Underground server

Figure 4-20 shows the main menu for the program. When you exit the Weather Underground, Mosaic removes the **telnet** window it created. The URL for the Weather Underground is:

```
telnet://madlab.sprl.umich.edu:3000
```

The syntax is the same as for other servers; the URL starts with the service protocol *telnet*, followed by the separator *://* and the name of the server. The URL also specifies a port number (*:3000*), so **telnet** connects to the special service set up on that port, rather than the default port (*:23*). The Weather Underground uses a special port so that it can automatically start running the weather service program.

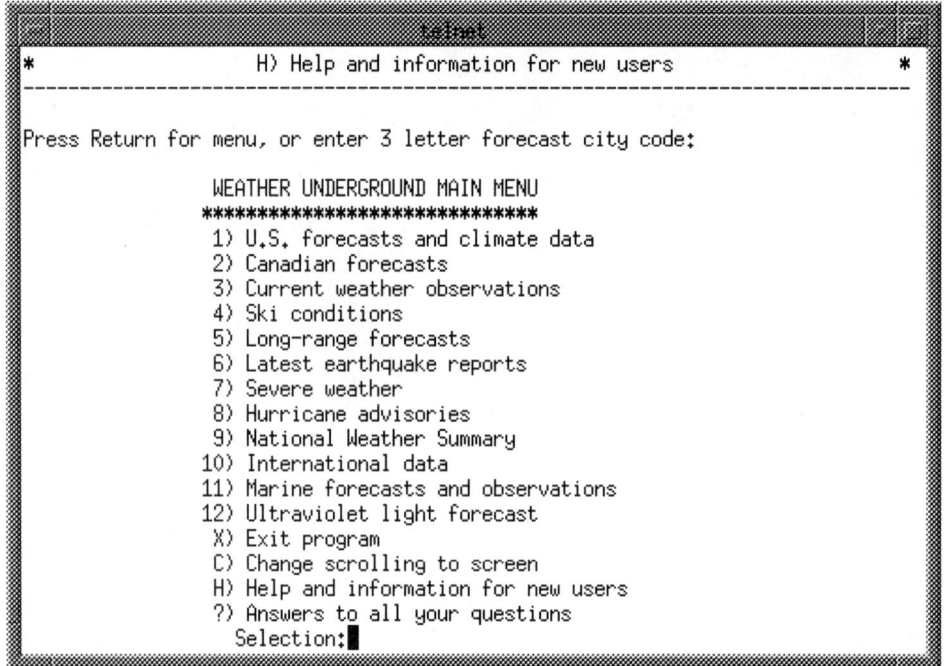

Figure 4-20. Weather Underground main menu

Network News

If the news server on your system is set up correctly, you will be able to use Mosaic as a newsreader. It's not a very full-featured newsreader, but if you don't use network news intensively, you may be happy reading news through Mosaic. If not, consider using one of the many newsreaders for UNIX, such as **nn** or **tin**.

To get started, simply enter the URL for the newsgroup in the **Open URL** dialog. The syntax is:

```
news:newsgroup-name
```

Mosaic does not allow you to specify different news hosts. The NNTPSERVER environment variable sets the news server for your system, so the URL for news does not have a hostname.

To read postings to *rec.pets.dogs*, the URL is:

```
news:rec.pets.dogs
```

Mosaic will connect to your news server and display the most recent messages, as shown in Figure 4-21.

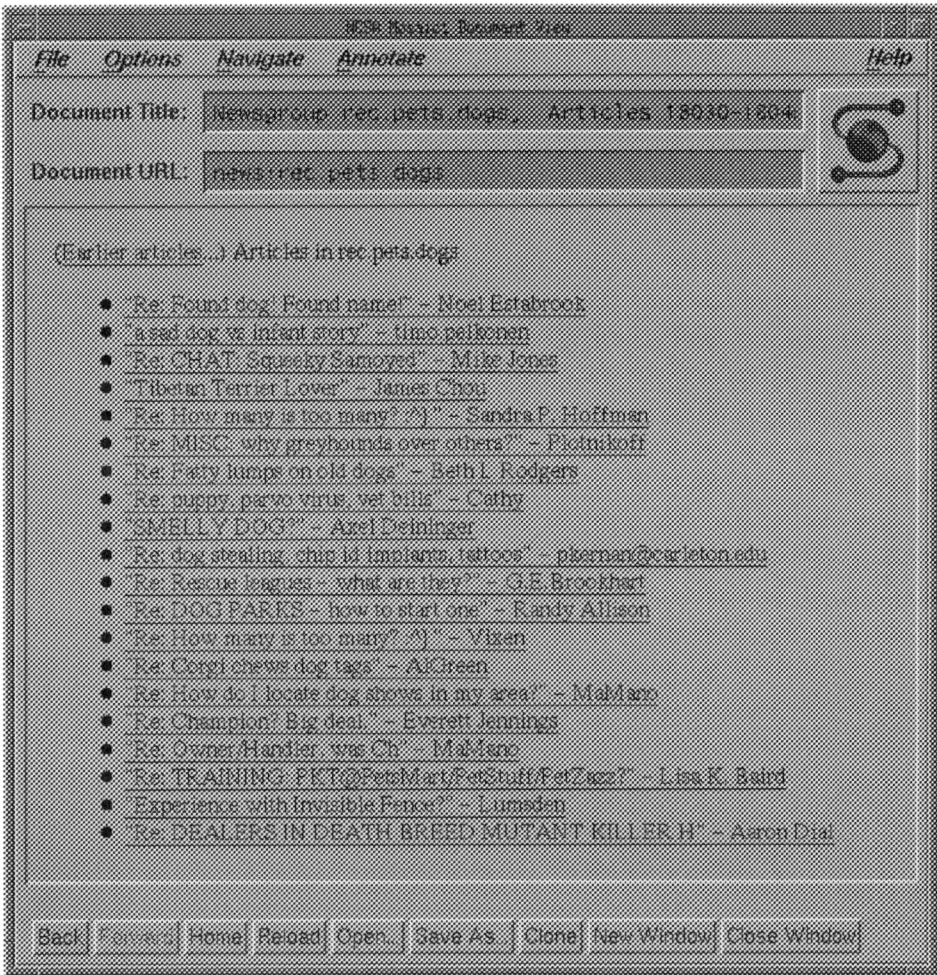

Figure 4–21. Messages in rec.pets.dogs

At the top of the screen is a link that reads **Earlier articles**. Clicking on this link displays the next most recent messages. Clicking on a message subject displays that message, as shown in Figure 4-22. The message body contains links to earlier and later messages in the thread. Clicking on these will, of course, display the linked message.

Unfortunately, after reading a message, there's not much you can do except send a personal email message to the author. Mosaic doesn't let you respond to messages

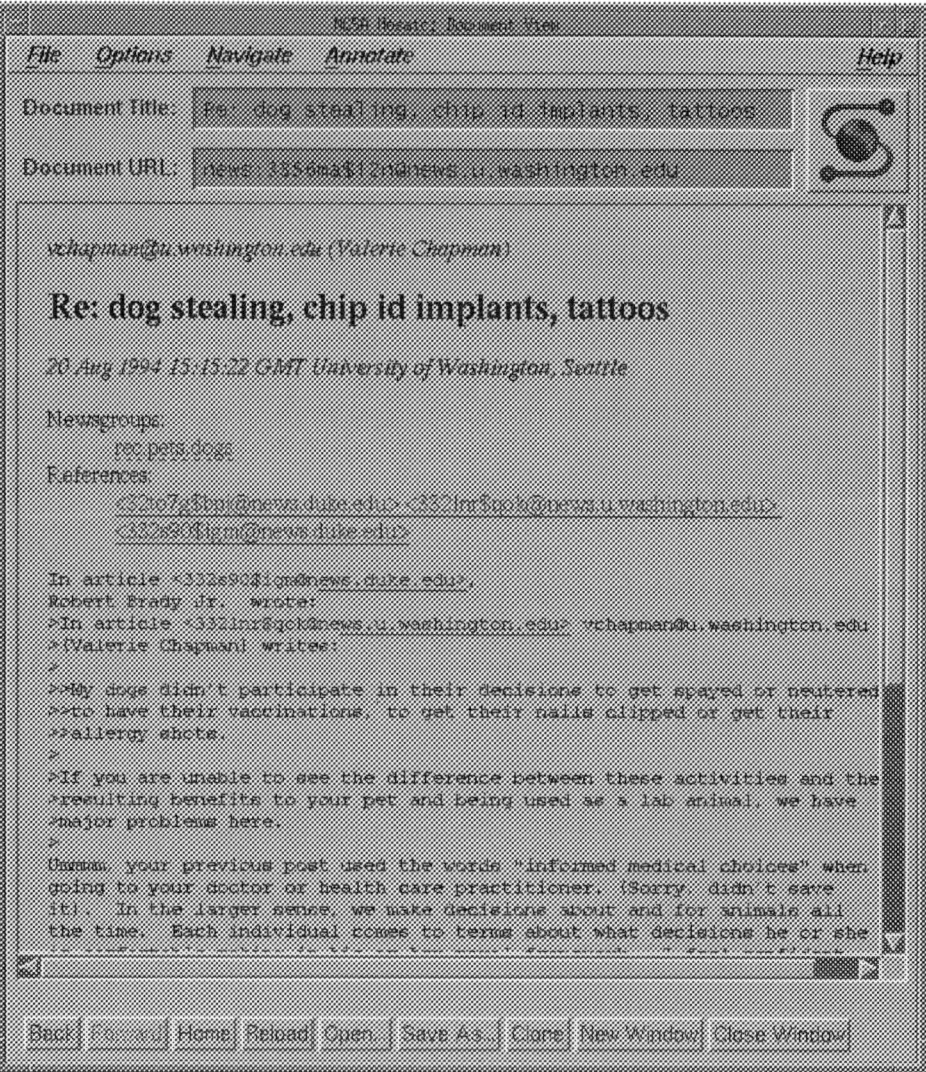

Figure 4–22. Message contents

or post new articles. In fact, there are a number of drawbacks to using Mosaic as a newsreader:

- You can't use Mosaic to browse a list of all available newsgroups. You have to know the name of the group you want to read.

- You can only access one group at a time.

- You have to enter the URL for the newsgroup or save it in your hotlist.

- Mosaic is a read-only newsreader. You can't reply to messages or start a new thread.

- While you can save messages as text file, you can't download graphics or sound files, which are included in some newgroups, such as *alt.binaries.multimedia* and *alt.pictures.find-art.graphics*.

As Mosaic continues to develop, we expect that it will improve as a client for Gopher, WAIS, FTP, news, and even perhaps email.

## CHAPTER FIVE

CUSTOMIZING MOSAIC

Changes You Really Want to Make
Specifying X Resources
Setting Behavior Preferences
Customizing the Mosaic Window
Improving Mosaic's Performance
Configuring Mosaic for Your System

M osaic is a powerful tool that allows you to explore information and the connections between information in a multimedia environment. But, as we'll see in this chapter, Mosaic is also a flexible environment that can be customized and extended in many different ways. The combination is what makes Mosaic such an exciting tool: Mosaic not only lets you view information, but also gives you control over how the information will be presented.

For example, Mosaic allows you to set your starting point for Internet exploration by specifying a "home page." You can also set various options to improve Mosaic's performance, such as using delayed image loading to reduce the network traffic involved in accessing a document. In addition to the different behaviors you can specify, certain aspects of Mosaic's appearance are configurable. You can select alternate colors and fonts for the application, for instance.

You can make certain changes by using Mosaic's **Options** menu. You can also modify some of Mosaic's behavior from the command line. You can customize most of X Mosaic's features, however, only by setting resources in an X resource file.

Before we jump into discussing the myriad customizations you can make to Mosaic, we are going to tell you about the few features that you really want to customize. After that, we spend a bit of time explaining how to set X resources. The rest of this chapter describes the resources you can use to configure Mosaic. We don't cover every resource, as some of them deal with rather obscure features. However, there is a complete list of the resources in Appendix C, *List of X Resources.*

Some of the information we present here is meant for users; other topics are targeted strictly at system administrators. We present the user-level information first, so if you don't need to know how to configure Mosaic to work on your system, you can skip the later topics.

Changes You Really Want to Make

While you can change countless aspects of Mosaic's appearance and behavior, many of these changes are rather sophisticated. They are not things that you need or even really want to do if you are a new user or someone who is content to use the default configuration. However, the few customizations we show you in this section are quite useful and easy to make—you don't have to deal with resources at all. If you don't want to know all of the details, just read this section and you'll be well on your way to becoming a Mosaic power user.

Changing Your Home Page

The home page is a wonderful navigational device that does double duty as map and safe port. Your home page—the document Mosaic retrieves and displays when you launch the program—serves first as your personal navigational map of the Web.

When you're roaming the Net, freely following links and sailing from one server to another, it is not uncommon to find yourself someplace you don't particularly want to be and with no apparent means of getting back out again. When this happens, your home page is your safe haven, a return to your familiar map. Whenever you get to a point where you'd like to start fresh, just return to your home page.

The Home Page that comes with this book has links to *GNN* and the *Mosaic Handbook Hotlist.** While this is an excellent starting point, after you've used Mosaic for a while, you may want to change your home page.

There are a number of reasons you may want to specify a different document as your home page. If you use, say, the *GNN Personal Finance* Center frequently, you may want to use the *Personal Finance Home Page* as your home page. If you have certain areas of specific interest, you may want to have a more narrowly focused home page. For example, if you're particularly interested in astrology and space, you may want to select "NASA Information Services Via the WWW" as your home page.

Or if you have discovered a number of servers you return to regularly, you may want to create your own custom map of the Web, which you can keep on your local system and update as needed. You might include URLs to your favorite sports, music, and travel servers, if those are your interests. We describe how to create your own home page in Chapter 7, *Creating HTML Documents*. On the

---

* If your system uses the public domain version of NCSA Mosaic available on the Net, you will not have this special home page. By default, the public domain version of Mosaic retrieves the NCSA Mosaic home page on the NCSA WWW server. You aren't stuck with this home page, however. One realy good reason for specifying an alternate home page is that the NCSA WWW server handles a tremendous load, so there may be times when Mosaic is unable to get the default home home page.

other hand, you might prefer to use your hotlist to navigate to your favorite servers and keep a remote server as your home page.

There are a number of different ways to specify your own home page. The simplest method is to set an alternate home page on the command line by using the following command:

```
% Mosaic -home alternate-home-page &
```

Substitute the URL of the home page you've selected for *alternate-home-page*. For example, to use the *Whole Internet Catalog*, type the following command:

```
% Mosaic -home http://gnn.com/wic/index.html &
```

This method changes your home page for this one Mosaic session. The next time you start up Mosaic, unless you again use the **-home** flag, Mosaic will use the default home page.

The home page you select can be located anywhere on the Net. However, if the home page is on your own system, you can dispense with the complicated URL syntax and just specify a filename. If you've created your own home page called *my-home.html*, you can use it as follows:

```
% Mosaic -home my-home.html &
```

To be sure that Mosaic can find the file, start Mosaic from the directory that contains the file, or specify a full pathname to it.

If you don't use the **-home** flag, Mosaic uses the specified document as the startup document, but it doesn't replace the default home page. So if you press the **Home** button, Mosaic still retrieves the Home Page we have provided for you.

You can also specify an alternate home page using the WWW_HOME environment variable:

```
% setenv WWW_HOME my-home.html
% Mosaic &
```

If you set this environment variable, the setting overrides any home page you specify with the **-home** flag on the command line. The value of WWW_HOME remains in effect until you change it, or until you log out of the session in which you set it. If you want to make the setting more permanent, you should put it in your shell start-up script.

If you start Mosaic automatically when you start your X session, you can also make your home page setting more permanent by using the **-home** flag in your X startup script. Since setting WWW_HOME overrides any command-line specification, using **-home** in this way gives you more flexibility to change your home page each time you run Mosaic.

In this discussion, we've purposefully ignored the homeDocument resource, which provides yet another way to specify your home page. We'll revisit this topic a little later, once we've explained how to set X resources. In any case, the **-home** command-line option and the WWW_HOME environment variable are completely sufficient for specifying your home page. Now all you have to do is find a suitable home page somewhere on the Net or create one of your own.

Specifying Initial Window Placement

Depending on the configuration of your window manager, Mosaic either positions the **Document View** window automatically when you start the program, or allows you to place the window yourself. In either case, Mosaic uses an initial window size of 640 by 700 pixels. You can specify an alternate size for the window, as well as set its initial location, using the **-geometry** command-line flag. The geometry option takes a single parameter that has four numerical components, two specifying the window's dimensions and two specifying its location. This standard geometry string has the following syntax:

```
% Mosaic -geometry widthxheight±xoffset±yoffset &
```

The first half of the string specifies the width and the height of the window in pixels; the second half gives the location of the window relative to the edges of the screen. The offsets can be either positive or negative. A positive x offset sets the position of the left side of the window relative to the left side of the screen, while a negative x offset positions the right side of the window relative to the right side of the display. Positive and negative y offsets function similarly, using the top and bottom sides of the window and the screen. Here's a real example of using **-geometry**:

```
% Mosaic -geometry 700x700+50+50 &
```

This command makes the initial window 60 pixels wider than it would be by default and places the window 50 pixels from the top and left edges of the screen. You can specify any or all of the components of the geometry string. If you use an incomplete specification, Mosaic fills in the missing elements with their default values. For example, to place Mosaic in the upper-right corner of the screen but keep the default window size, use the following command:

```
% Mosaic -geometry -0+0 &
```

By experimenting with various sizes and locations, you should be able to come up with a window placement that you like. The **-geometry** option is most useful in a startup file, if you start Mosaic automatically when you start your X session. Of course, you can use the option any time you run Mosaic, but you may find it cumbersome to type the geometry string repeatedly (especially given that you can move the window anywhere you want with the mouse once it is opened).

When you start Mosaic, the **Document View** window appears so that you can immediately start browsing. However, you can also start Mosaic so that the initial window appears iconified. Use the **-iconic** command-line flag to produce this effect. Again, you may want to use this feature if you are starting Mosaic in a session startup file along with a bunch of other applications. That way Mosaic does not clutter the screen until you're ready to use it.

Setting Colors

Mosaic has default settings for both color and monochrome systems. In both cases, the default scheme is designed to work with the three-dimensional appearance of the controls used by Mosaic. Mosaic tries to figure out what type of system you are running it on so that it can use the appropriate colors. However, you can force Mosaic to use the default color or monochrome settings with the **–color** and **–mono** command-line flags, respectively. To make Mosaic come up in monochrome mode, use the following command:

```
% Mosaic -mono &
```

If you have a color monitor, you can specify both the foreground and background colors. The easiest way to set Mosaic's background color is to use the **–bg** command-line options. In terms of picking a color, you can choose any predefined color name from the *rgb.txt* database, usually found in */usr/lib/X11*. For example:

```
% Mosaic -bg LightSteelBlue &
```

When you set the background color is this manner, Mosaic sets the foreground to black or white, depending on the darkness of the background. Sometimes, however, Mosaic misjudges this darkness. If you set the background color and the foreground text is difficult to read, you can set the foreground to black or white explicity using the **–fg** flag:

```
% Mosaic -bg LightSlateGray -fg White &
```

Mosaic displays all of the text in its interface using the foreground color, except for special text known as anchor text—the text that indicates hyperlinks to other documents. By default, anchor text is shaded blue. You can change the color of anchor text only by setting resources in an X resource file, but as you'll see in the next section, you can change the underlining style of this text from the **Options** menu.

Changing Text Style

Mosaic interprets and displays HTML-based documents found on the Web. Mosaic determines which font to use to display a particular block of text by interpreting the HTML tags in the document. (For more information about HTML tags, see Chapter 7.)

By default, Mosaic uses various sizes and styles of the Times Roman font for normal text and headings, and Courier for preformatted text. The easiest way to change the fonts Mosaic uses for HTML documents is to use the **Fonts** item on the **Options** menu. This item posts a submenu that allows you to choose a font family and size, as shown in Figure 5-1. The diamond-shaped indicator shows the

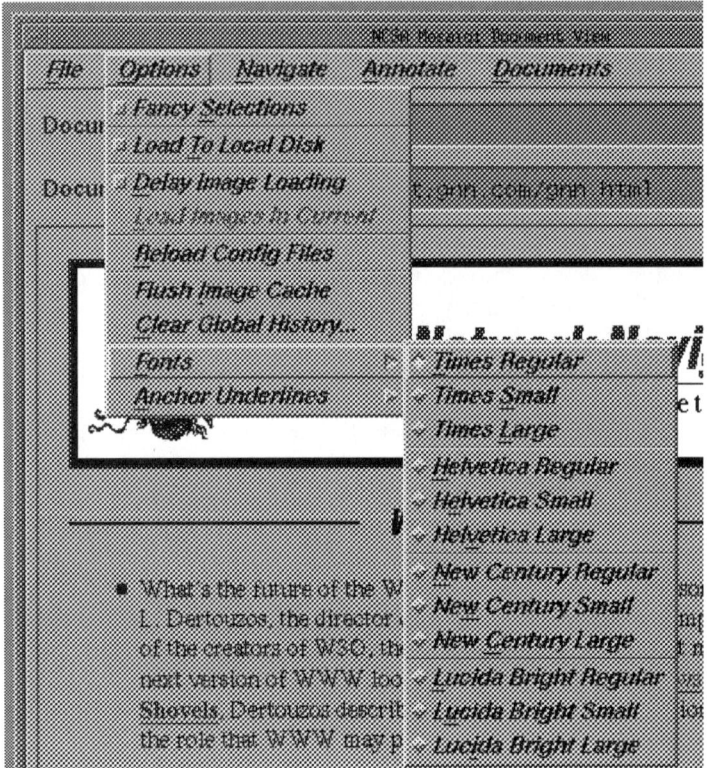

Figure 5–1. The Fonts submenu

current selection. When you use the **Fonts** menu, Mosaic changes all of the fonts consistently. Normal text and headings all use different sizes and styles of the same font family, and the sizes are set appropriately. However, if you change the fonts using the **Fonts** menu, the change only remains in effect for the current invocation of Mosaic. Later in the chapter, we'll describe how you can make the change more permanent.

Mosaic uses color and underlining to distinguish anchor text from ordinary text. Mosaic also distinguishes between hyperlinks that you have followed and those you haven't. By default, Mosaic displays visited anchors with dashed underlines and unvisited anchors with solid underlines.

The **Anchor Underlines** submenu on the **Options** menu provides a way to change the underlining style. Any change you make using an item on this submenu only remains in effect during the current session of Mosaic. **Light Underlines** is Mosaic's default style. The **Default Underlines** option also resets the underlining style to Mosaic's default style. The **Medium Underlines** option causes Mosaic to use single solid lines under both visited and unvisited anchors, while **Heavy Underlines** puts two solid lines under unvisited anchors and a single solid line under visited anchors. The final choice, **No Underlines**, turns off underlining completely.

As we mentioned before, you can only change the color of anchor text using X resources, so we'll wait on this topic until after we've covered setting resources.

Improving Performance

You can change certain features of Mosaic to improve its performance. When doing so, however, you sometimes disable some of Mosaic's nicest features. You'll have to decide for yourself whether or not better performance is worth the trade-off.

Image loading

Displaying inline graphical images can take a lot of time. You may want to suppress the display of these images if you find the delay frustrating. To prevent Mosaic from loading and drawing inline images, set the **Delay Image Loading** option on the **Options** menu. Be aware that delayed image loading only affects the display of inline images. This option does not affect images displayed using an external viewer.

Once you select this option, Mosaic does not automatically load inline images. Instead, it replaces each image with a small image icon. If the inline image also acts as a hyperlink, Mosaic adds an arrow icon to the image icon. Figure 5-2 shows these icons in a document with inline images suppressed.

If you want to display a suppressed inline image, just click on the image icon. If the image acts as a hyperlink, clicking on the arrow icon follows the link, while clicking on the image icon loads the delayed image. To view all of the delayed images in a document, select **Load Images in Current** from the **Options** menu.

If you want to configure Mosaic so that it suppresses inline images by default, you can use the **–dil** command-line flag. In this case, Mosaic starts with image loading disabled, but you can always turn it back on using the menu option.

Document tracking

[By default, Mosaic keeps track of all the documents you view. Once you view a document, it becomes part of your history. Mosaic uses this global history to distinguish visited anchors from unvisited ones.

As we'll explain later when we talk about resources, Mosaic stores the history information in a global history file. When Mosaic starts, it reads your global history file, stores all of the URLs internally, and continues to store new URLs as you follow hyperlinks. As a result, you may find that Mosaic's performance suffers when your global history gets large.

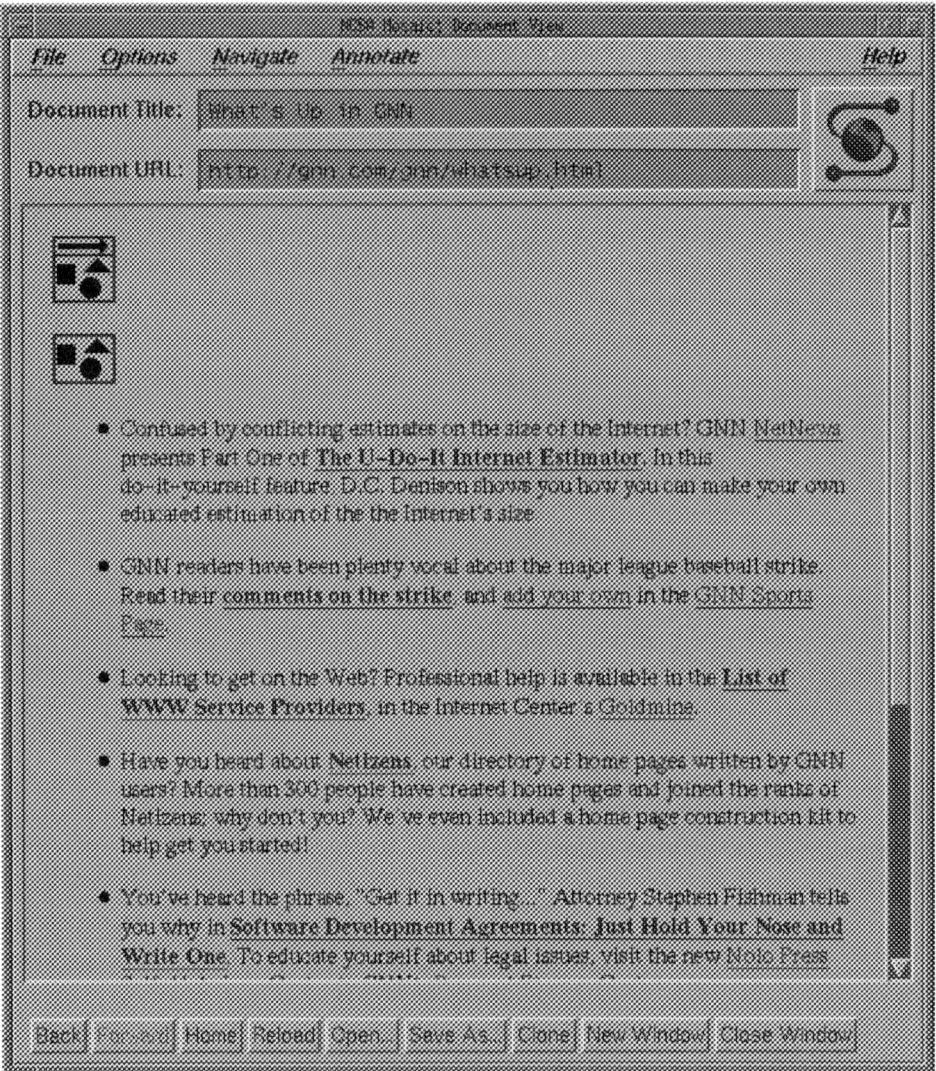

Figure 5–2. Mosaic with inline images suppressed

To keep from using an excessive amount of disk space and memory, you may want to clear your history periodically using the **Clear Global History** item on the **Options** menu. When you select this menu item, Mosaic marks as unvisited all of the hyperlinks in the documents you view until you follow the links again. You can also disable document tracking by using the **–ngh** command-line flag.

Specifying X Resources

If you're still reading at this point, that must mean you want to know more about all of the ways you can customize Mosaic. We've pretty much exhausted what is possible using Mosaic's menus and command-line options, so it's time to turn to the innumerable resources provided by Mosaic. But before we start describing the various resources, you need some general information about specifying resources.

You customize X applications by setting variables called resources; Mosaic for X is just like any other X application in this respect. The values associated with different resources control various aspects of the appearance and behavior of an application. As a user, you can override the default settings of an X application by specifying other values in a resource file. All X programs use the same mechanisms for determining resource values and the same resource specification syntax.

But that's enough abstract discussion of resources—if you want to know all the details see Volume 3, *X Window System User's Guide*, from O'Reilly & Associates. Let's discuss how Mosaic gets its resource values, and then we'll look at the resource specification syntax.

Resource Files

When Mosaic starts, it looks in two places for its resource settings. First, it looks for an application defaults file. All X applications store their application defaults files in the same directory, typically */usr/lib/X11/app-defaults*. The actual name of the application defaults file is the class name of the application; Mosaic has the class name "Mosaic," so it looks for the defaults file named *Mosaic*.* The application defaults file contains system-wide resource settings for an application. If you are a system administrator, you need to make sure this file is installed properly. If you are a user, however, all you need to know is where to find this file, so you can examine the default resource settings it contains.

If you are a system administrator who is configuring Mosaic for use at your site, you should follow the installation instructions in Appendix D, *Installing Mosaic*. When you install Mosaic from the CD, you will install an application defaults file for Mosaic. If you've already installed the public domain version of Mosaic from the Net, you will still need to install an application defaults file, as Mosaic's default installation process does not install one. You can get template application defaults files from the NCSA FTP server using the following URL:

```
ftp://ftp.ncsa.uiuc.edu/Web/Mosaic/Unix/binaries/app-defaults
```

There are three files in this directory: one for color systems, one for color SGI machines, and one for monochrome systems. Check your system's X documentation to find out where to put the defaults file. Again, the normal location is in */usr/lib/X11/app-defaults*, using the filename *Mosaic* (the capital "M" is significant).

---

* Prior to Release 2.0, the class name for Mosaic was "XMosaic" so the application defaults file was named *XMosaic*.

If Mosaic finds an application defaults file, it reads the resource settings in the file into its resource database. However, if the application defaults file does not exist, Mosaic still needs to set some default resource values to be able to function properly. In this case, the program relies on a fallback mechanism to set the default values. The only drawback to this approach is that if Mosaic finds a defaults file, it does not install the fallback resources. So if you create an empty application defaults file and then run Mosaic, you'll find that Mosaic no longer uses its default colors and fonts. The safest technique is to install an application defaults file and then modify the settings as you see fit.

After Mosaic checks for its application defaults file, it looks for any user-specified resources that are relevant to the program. Mosaic finds these specifications in a couple of places. If you use **xrdb** to load resources into your X server when you start your X session, then Mosaic reads the relevant resource settings from the server. (We'll explain how Mosaic knows which settings are relevant shortly, when we talk about resource specification syntax.) If you are not using **xrdb**, but you are running Mosaic on your local machine, Mosaic looks for an *.Xdefaults* file in your home directory. If this file exists, Mosaic reads any relevant settings in the file into its resource database.

You really should use **xrdb** to load resources because then it doesn't matter whether Mosaic is running on your local system or on a remote machine. In either case, the resources are loaded into the server so Mosaic can read them. When you run **xrdb**, you specify the resource file it reads; common names are *.Xdefaults* or *.Xresources.*

If you aren't sure how your system handles resources, your best bet is to ask someone who would know, like your system administrator. You can also poke around in your home directory and see what you find. To see if **xrdb** is being used, look in either *.xinitrc* or *.xsession* for a line of the form:

```
xrdb filename
```

or:

```
xrdb -load filename
```

If you find such a line, put any resource specifications for Mosaic in the specified file. If it doesn't look like **xrdb** is in use, see if there is an *.Xdefaults* file in your home directory. If so, add your Mosaic resource settings to the file; otherwise, create the file and put the settings in it. To simplify matters in this chapter, we are only going to refer to the *.Xdefaults* file. If you use a different file for resource settings, substitute that filename where we say *.Xdefaults.*

Resource Specification Syntax

An X application identifies its resource specifications with its class name. Since Mosaic's class name is "Mosaic," resource settings for the program are all of the form:*

```
Mosaic*resourceName: value
```

Be sure to include the colon after the resource name in the specification. If you omit the colon, Mosaic silently ignores the specification, as X does not support error messages for incorrect resource settings. Each resource specification goes on a separate line in a resource file; if the last character on a line is a backslash (\), the resource definition on that line continues on the next line. You can include a comment in a resource file or comment out a specification by starting the line with an exclamation point (!). Here's an example of a few Mosaic resources you might set in your *.Xdefaults* file:

```
! Mosaic resources

Mosaic*homeDocument: /usr/local/home/paula/mosaic/myhome.html
Mosaic*verticalScrollOnRight: False
Mosaic*confirmExit: False
```

Note the capitalization in the resource names: case is important. If you misspell a resource name or get the capitalization wrong, Mosaic ignores the specification. Every resource has a resource data type (e.g. integer, Boolean, string). When you specify a value for a resource, be sure you use a value of the appropriate type. As we describe Mosaic's resources, we'll mention the type if it isn't obvious. The list of resources in Appendix C also contains this information.

Some Mosaic resources have corresponding command-line flags. For example, the homeDocument resource can also be set using the **–home** command-line option. As we discuss the various Mosaic resources, we also describe the corresponding command-line options. However, you can also set any Mosaic resource on the command line using the **–xrm** option. This option takes the following form:

```
% Mosaic -xrm "Mosaic*resourceName: value" &
```

You can specify only one resource value with the **–xrm** option, so if you want to set multiple resources, you need to use a **–xrm** flag for each one. Setting resources on the command line provides a convenient way to to test resource specifications before you add them to a resource file. For example, you could use the following command to see if you like the effect:

```
% Mosaic -xrm "Mosaic*anchorColor: LimeGreen" &
```

Because Mosaic looks in a few different places for resource settings and you can specify resources on the command line, you may be wondering what happens if

---

* Since the class name prior to Release 2.0 was "XMosaic," old resource files need to be modified to reflect the new class name.

you set the same resource in multiple locations. Basically, Mosaic has a set of precedence rules that determines exactly which specification is used. The following list indicates the order in which resource specifications take effect, from highest to lowest:

1. A command-line specification

2. A specification in an *.Xdefaults* file (or its equivalent)

3. A resource setting in Mosaic's application defaults file

4. An internal default value

These rules are designed so that a user can override system-wide resource settings, either using a personal resource file or by specifying a command-line option.

One final bit of information about resource files is that Mosaic reads them only when the program starts. If you modify a resource file while Mosaic is running, the new specifications do not take effect until you exit and restart Mosaic. If **xrdb** loads the resources into your X server, you also need to reload the resources when you modify your *.Xdefaults* file:

```
% xrdb -load .Xdefaults
```

Now that we've covered the basics of resource specification, we can dive in and start looking at the actual resources you can use to customize Mosaic.

Setting Behavior Preferences

You can change many different aspects of Mosaic's behavior using resources. A few of these resources duplicate what you can do using command-line flags and menu options, but for the most part they tweak very specific features of Mosaic. For example, you can set your home page, specify the files Mosaic uses to keep track of your global history and hotlist, and decide whether or not the program asks for confirmation when you try to exit.

Changing Your Home Page Revisited

Earlier, we described how to specify an alternate home page using the **–home** flag and the WWW_HOME environment variable. While setting a home page on the command line is easy, unless you start Mosaic automatically from a startup script, you'll have to type out the document name each time you start the program. The best way to specify an alternate home page for all future Mosaic sessions is to set the homeDocument resource. For the version of Mosaic on the CD, we set this resource to point to the Home Page:

```
Mosaic*homeDocument: /usr/local/lib/mosaic/xbook.html
```

If you want to use a different home page and you are configuring Mosaic for your own personal use, you should specify this resource in your *.Xdefaults* file.

However, if you are setting up Mosaic for your site and you want to set a different site-wide home page, put this specification in Mosaic's application defaults file, typically */usr/lib/X11/app-defaults/Mosaic*. That way a user can override the specification by putting her own setting in her *.Xdefaults* file.

Since there are so many ways to specify a home page, it can be confusing to figure out the precedence of the different methods. Here's a precedence list, from highest to lowest, to help you sort things out:

1. A home page specified with the WWW_HOME environment variable

2. A document specified with the **–home** command-line flag

3. A resource specification for homeDocument in your *.Xdefaults* file

4. A specification for homeDocument in Mosaic's application defaults file

5. The hardcoded, default home page (the NCSA Mosaic home page)

If you specify a document URL on the command line without the -**home** flag, Mosaic uses the document as the start-up document, but it does not replace your home page. This feature is useful if you want to start a Mosaic session someplace other than your home page, but you'd still like to be able to go home.

Startup Behavior

As we discussed earlier, you can start Mosaic so that the initial window appears iconified by using the **–iconic** option. Setting resource" the initialWindowIconic resource to True provides the same effect. The autoPlaceWindows resource controls how Mosaic positions **Document View** windows. When the resource is True, as it is by default, Mosaic determines the initial position of the window. If you set the resource to False, Mosaic does not automatically place the window. However, in either case, your window manager still controls the actual positioning of the window. Depending on how you have your window manager configured, you may or may not have to position Mosaic's window.

Confirming Actions

Like any good graphical interface, Mosaic is set up to protect you from doing things that you might not mean to do. For example, when you select **Exit Program** from the **File** menu, Mosaic presents a dialog box that makes sure you really want to exit the program, as shown in Figure 5-3. Mosaic lets you turn off these confirmation dialogs. By setting confirmExit and confirmDeleteAnnotations to False, you can eliminate these precautionary devices.

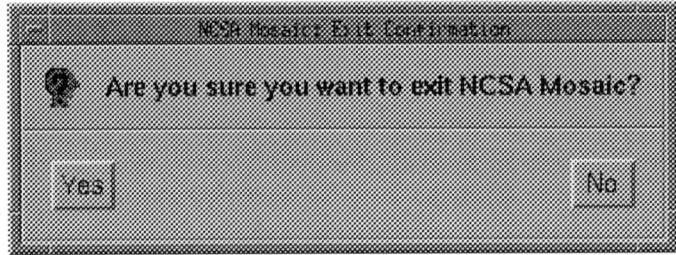

Figure 5-3. Exit confirmation dialog

Tracking Documents

The useGlobalHistory resource controls Mosaic's document tracking feature we discussed earlier. By default this resource is True; if you don't want Mosaic to keep this information, set the resource to False. If you want Mosaic to keep a global history, but not distinguish visited anchors from unvisited ones, you can set the trackVisitedAnchors resource to False and useGlobalHistory to True. Anchor tracking is the piece of the history functionality that takes the most time, so these setting may improve Mosaic's performance.

If global history is enabled, Mosaic stores the URLs of all visited documents in the file specified by globalHistoryFile. The default filename is *.mosaic-global-history*. When Mosaic starts, it looks in your home directory for this file by adding the value of the HOME environment variable to the beginning of the filename. Mosaic reads the URLs from the file and stores them in an internal hash table; while the program is running it does not use the history file. When you exit the program, Mosaic writes the visited URLs to the history file to save them.

You can specify another filename, but Mosaic always looks for the file relative to your home directory. The only real reason to change the filename is if you want keep all of Mosaic's configuration files in a separate directory. For example, if you are storing the files in a *.mosaic* subdirectory, specify globalHistoryFile as follows:

```
Mosaic*globalHistoryFile: .mosaic/.mosaic-global-history
```

Just make sure that the *.mosaic* subdirectory exists so that Mosaic can write the history file.

Mosaic also uses a file to store the URLs of the documents you have selected for your hotlist—your list of documents that you access frequently. As we discussed in Chapter 2, *Getting Started with Mosaic*, you can add documents to your hotlist, as well as make other modifications, using the **Hotlist** option on the **Navigate** menu. The defaultHotlistFile resource specifies the filename; the default value is .mosaic-hotlist-default. Mosaic looks in your home directory for this file.

Again, to store configuration files in a *.mosaic* subdirectory, put the following in your *.Xdefaults* file:

```
Mosaic*defaultHotlistFile: .mosaic/.mosaic-hotlist-default
```

When you move the pointer over a hyperlink, Mosaic displays the URL of the linked document in the status area. You can turn off this behavior by setting `trackPointerMotion` to `False`. This may improve Mosaic's performance over a slow network connection. Setting this resource to `False`, however, causes Mosaic to remove the status area completely, so you no longer get status information as the program retrieves documents.

If you keep pointer tracking enabled, you can set `trackFullURLs` to `False` to get Mosaic to present more useful, human-readable information about linked documents. The program attempts to figure out the format of the document, and it displays that information in the status area along with the location of the document and information about how it would be accessed, as shown in Figure 5-4.

Document titles are more useful than URLs in terms of identifying WWW documents, so Mosaic displays document titles in all of its document lists, like the hotlist and the window history list. To see URLs instead, so you can know exactly which documents you are dealing with, set `displayURLsNotTitles` to `True`.

Controlling Annotations

In Chapter 2, we discussed Mosaic's annotation feature. For annotations to work, Mosaic needs a place to store annotation information. The `personalAnnotationDirectory` resource specifies the name of the directory where Mosaic stores personal annotations, as well as the log file of all such annotations. The default directory is *.mosaic-personal-annotations*; Mosaic looks for this directory in your home directory by adding the value of HOME to the beginning of the directory name.

You can specify an alternate directory by setting `personalAnnotationDirectory` in your file. If the specified directory does not exist, Mosaic creates it, but Mosaic does not create any intermediate directories. To keep all of Mosaic's configuration information in a separate *.mosaic* directory, use the following specification:

```
Mosaic*personalAnnotationDirectory: .mosaic/.mosaic-personal-annotations
```

You can also set the location of annotations in the browsing area. When `annotationsOnTop` is `False`, as it is by default, annotation hyperlinks are displayed at the bottom of documents. If you set this resource to `True`, however, annotations are displayed at the beginning of documents. Where you want annotations to appear is really a matter of personal preference.

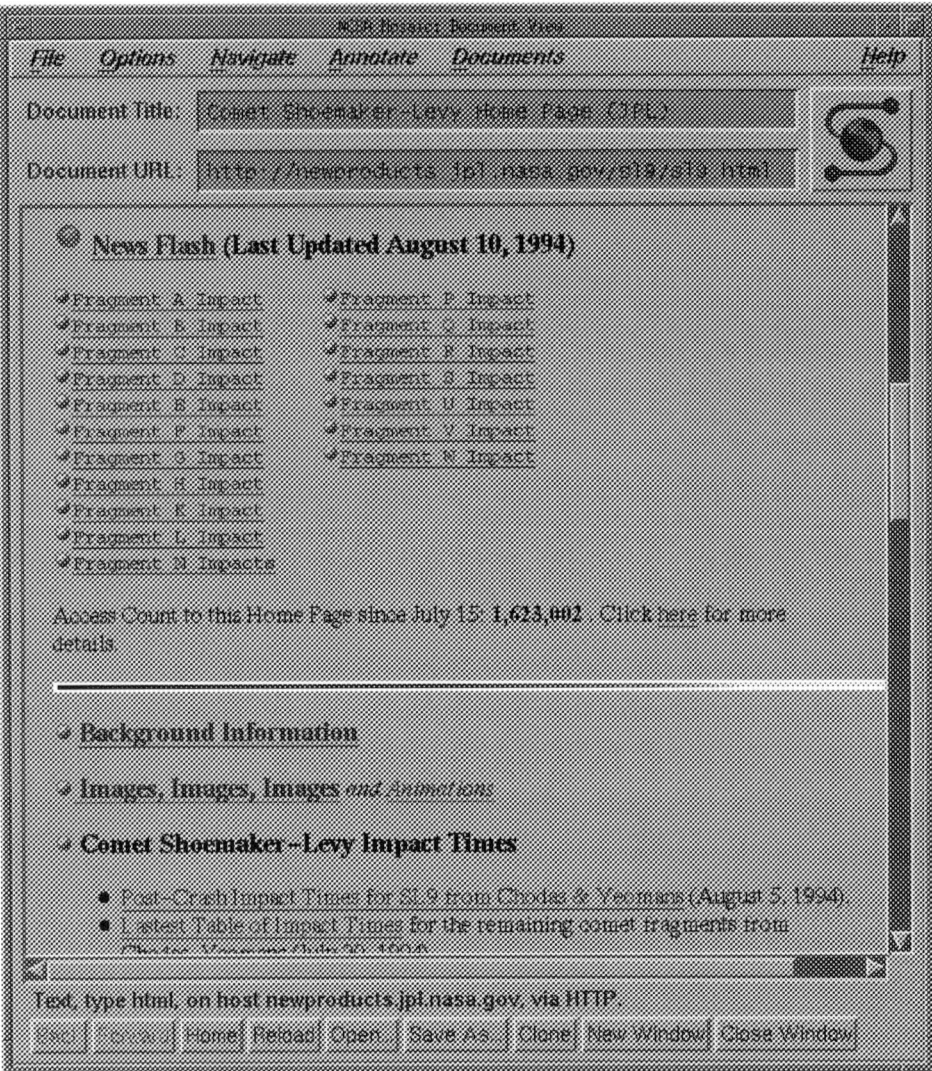

Figure 5-4. Linked document information in the status area

When you annotate a document, Mosaic presents a dialog box that you fill in with the comments you want to make about the document, as shown in Figure 5-5. The dialog also contains fields that specify the author and title of the annotation; this information is included as part of the annotation. By default, the value of defaultAuthorName is used in the author field. The default value of this resource is NULL, which causes Mosaic to get your name from the system password file. You can override this behavior by setting the resource to any string you like.

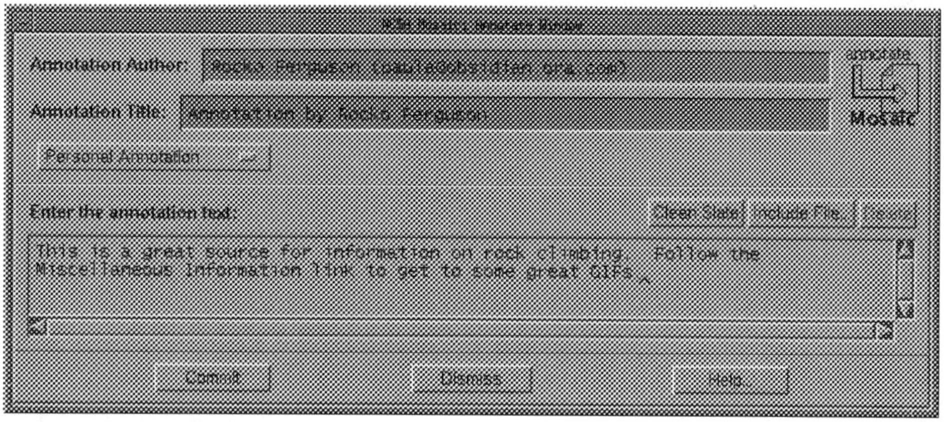

Figure 5-5. Annotation dialog

Displaying Images

Normally, Mosaic loads inline images so that they are displayed as intended in a document. However, if you are running Mosaic over a slow network connection, you may want to use the **-dil** command-line flag to set the delayImageLoads resource to True.

When Mosaic displays an inline image, it only allocates up to a certain number of colors for the image. The number of unique colors is controlled by colorsPerIn-linedImage; the default value is 50. If an image uses more than this maximum number of colors, Mosaic reprocesses it to reduce its color usage. This limit has no effect on images passed to an external viewer, though. For the majority of images that are inline in HTML documents, 50 colors provides sufficient clarity. However, if you are going to use Mosaic to look at the Comet Shoemaker-Levy home page (**http://newproducts.jpl.nasa.gov/sl9/sl9.html**), you may want to use a larger value for colorsPerInlinedImage to get the full effect of the inline images.

Sometimes the colors in inline X Bitmap (XBM) images are reversed because of inconsistencies between different X servers. If this appears to be the case, you should set reverseInlinedBitmapColors to True so that Mosaic can reverse the foreground and background colors in these images and correct the problem.

As of Version 2.0, versions of Mosaic for some platforms include internal support for viewing data files that use NCSA's Hierarchical Data Format (HDF). HDF is a multi-object file format that supports the transfer of graphical and numerical data between various machines and operating systems. For more information on HDF, use the following URL:

```
http://www.ncsa.uiuc.edu/SDG/Software/HDF/HDFIntro.html
```

Mosaic uses a few X resources to control certain aspects of the HDF browsing capabilities:

hdfMaxImageDimension
> This resource specifies the maximum size in pixels of an inline HDF image; the default value is 400. If an image is larger than the specified maximum, it is scaled down for display and the original dimension is noted in the text description next to the image.

hdfMaxDisplayedDatasets
> This resource controls the maximum number of datasets that are displayed for an inline HDF image. The default is 15 datasets. If there are more datasets than this maximum, Mosaic displays the image in "brief mode."

hdfMaxDisplayedAttributes
> This resource sets the maximum number of attributes displayed for an inline HDF image; the default value is 10. If there are additional attributes, the image is shown in brief mode.

hdfPowerUser
> If this resource is set to True, HDF images are displayed in "expert mode," which means that Mosaic does not display much of the supporting text in an HDF file. By default, the resource is False.

For more general information on the HDF browsing support in Mosaic, see:

    http://www.ncsa.uiuc.edu/SDG/Software/Mosaic/Docs/hdf-browsing.html

Making Selections

The browsing area of the **Document View** window supports cut and paste, as it should to be a good citizen in the X world. You can select some text using the first mouse button and then paste the text in another application, such as a text editor, with the second mouse button. Because the text in the browsing area is formatted, Mosaic gives you the option of having the text you paste retain some of the formatting. By default, this mechanism is disabled, but you can turn it on by setting the fancySelections resource to True. The **Fancy Selections** item on the **Options** menu also controls this functionality, so you can turn it on and off on a per-window basis while Mosaic is running.

Figure 5-6 shows a Mosaic window with text selected. If you turn **Fancy Selections** off, when you paste the text to another application it appears as follows:

    The NCSA Mosaic client

        Introduction to NCSA Mosaic for the X Window System
        Installation Guide
        Using NCSA Mosaic
        Configuration Resources and Command-Line Flags
        Technical Information and Specifications

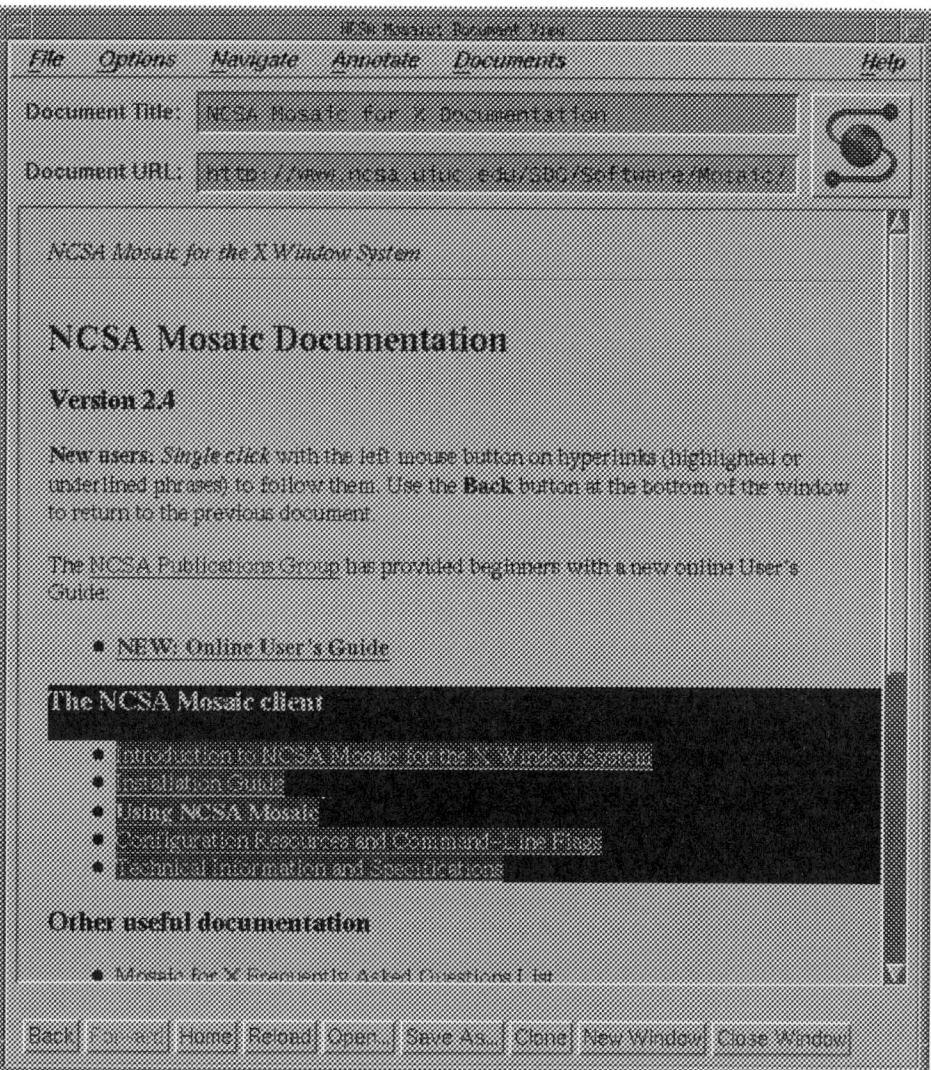

Figure 5–6. Selecting text in Mosaic's browsing area

Although the indentation is maintained, the pasted text does not preserve any other aspects of the format. However, if you use fancy selections, the pasted text contains underlined headers and bulleted lists, as shown here:

```
The NCSA Mosaic client
========================

  o Introduction to NCSA Mosaic for the X Window System
  o Installation Guide
  o Using NCSA Mosaic
```

o Configuration Resources and Command-Line Flags
o Technical Information and Specifications

If you are going to use cut and paste to transfer text to other applications that don't provide any formatting, you probably want to enable fancy selections to improve the appearance of the text.

Working with Other Services

As you saw in Chapter 4, *Accessing Other Internet Services*, one of the most powerful features of Mosaic is its ability to function as a interface for a number of Internet services. There are a couple of resources that control how Mosaic handles other services. When you are using Mosaic to access WAIS resources on the Net, you may want to set the `maxWaisResponse` resource. This resource specifies the maximum number of matches Mosaic retrieves from a WAIS server; the default is 200.

Mosaic also has a `tweakGopherTypes` resource that controls how it interprets Gopher documents. By default, this resource is `True`, which means that Mosaic uses its own mechanism to determine the file types of Gopher documents. If you set this resource to `False`, Mosaic instead uses the Gopher typing mechanism, which may be more familiar if you are accustomed to using a standard **gopher** client.

Customizing the Mosaic Window

Like most X applications, Mosaic gives you broad control over the appearance of the Mosaic window and its various components. You can, for example, select the colors of Mosaic's window components. You can also specify the typefaces that are used for different textual elements. And you can define the characteristics of anchor text—the text that indicates hyperlinks to other documents.

General Appearance

Mosaic provides a few resources that control its general appearance. For example, you can set the `defaultWidth` and `defaultHeight` resources to control the initial size of the Mosaic **Document View** window. The default width and height are 640 and 700 pixels, respectively; these defaults create a reasonably-sized window. However, if you find yourself constantly resizing the Mosaic window, maybe to accomodate large documents, you may want to reset these resources. You can also specify the default size and position of the Mosaic window using the `geometry` resource. This resource works exactly like the the **-geometry** command-line option we described earlier. Use a standard geometry string to set this resource:

```
Mosaic*geometry: 700x700+50+50
```

The `simpleInterface` resource controls whether Mosaic presents its full set of controls or a pared down version. The default value is `False`, which means that

Mosaic provides the menu items and buttons you saw in Chapter 2. If you set this resource to True, Mosaic provides a minimal set of command buttons and menu items, as shown in Figure 5-7.

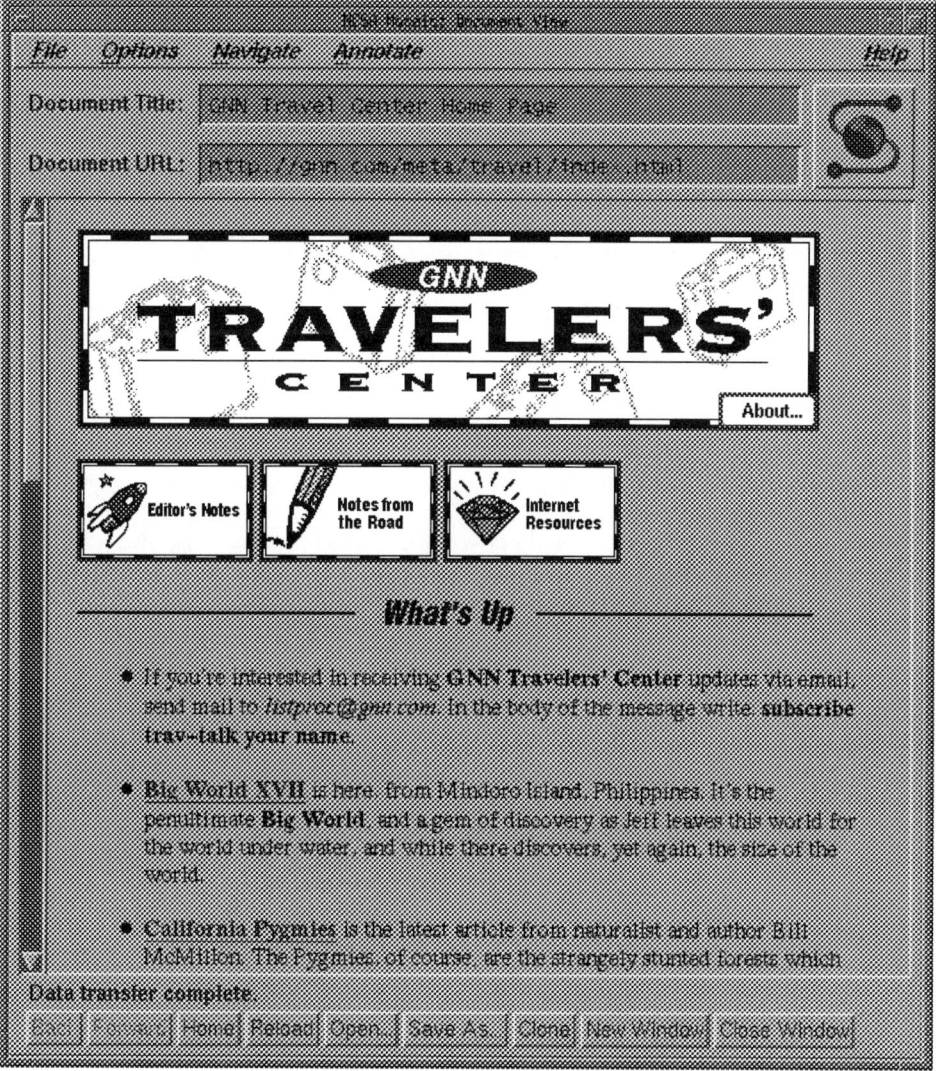

Figure 5-7. A simple Mosaic window with the scroll bar on the left

One other resource that affects Mosaic's general appearance is the vertical-ScrollOnRight resource. When this resource is True, as it is by default, the scroll bar in the **Document View** window appears on the right side of the window. Set the resource to False to place the scroll bar on the left side of the window; you may find this convenient if you are a left-handed mouser. Figure 5-7 shows the Mosaic window that results from the following resource settings:

```
Mosaic*simpleInterface: True
Mosaic*verticalScrollOnRight: False
```

Color

The user interface for Mosaic is built with the Motif widget set, a collection of interface components, called widgets, that have a 3D appearance. Motif uses top and bottom shadow borders around various components to make them appear either recessed into the screen or raised out of it. Mosaic sets its default colors in the program code, but you can override these settings using resources.

Unlike other customizations, modifying the colors Mosaic uses involves setting actual Motif widget resources, instead of Mosaic resources. The syntax of widget resource settings is complicated; the full details go beyond the scope of this book. For more information on specifying colors, see Volume 3, *X Window System User's Guide, Motif Edition*; or Volume 6A, *Motif Programming Manual*, from O'Reilly & Associates.

If you simply want to change the background color used by Mosaic, you don't need to understand the gory details. You can use the **–bg** command-line option to set Mosaic's background, as we've already explained, or you can use the following specification in your *.Xdefaults* file: color via"

```
Mosaic*Background: your-favorite-background-color
```

As with the **–bg** command-line option, you can choose any predefined color name from the *rgb.txt* database, which is usually found in */usr/lib/X11*. For example:

```
Mosaic*Background: LightSteelBlue
```

You can also specify the red, green and blue (RGB) values of a color using hexadecimal notation; this technique is most useful if you are using a color editor, such as **xcoloredit**, that outputs the RGB values of colors. (For more information on color editors, see *X User Tools* from O'Reilly & Associates.) The following specification sets the background to a light purple color:

```
Mosaic*Background: #cdcd9696cdcd
```

When you set the background color, the Motif toolkit sets a number of other colors based on that background. For example, the top and bottom shadow colors that create the 3D effect are set to lighter and darker shades of the background. Motif also sets the foreground to black or white, depending on how dark the background is. The algorithms that Motif uses are fairly smart, so you shouldn't need to set these colors explicitly. However, there are some background colors that fool the foreground color selection mechanism. If you set the background color and the foreground text is difficult to read, set the foreground to black or white explicitly, as follows:

```
Mosaic*Foreground: black-or-white
```

The **-fg** flag has the same effect as this resource specification.

If you look in Mosaic's color application defaults file, you'll see a slew of hexadecimal-style color resource specifications:

```
Mosaic*Foreground:                        #000000000000
Mosaic*XmScrollBar*Foreground:            #bfbfbfbfbfbf
Mosaic*XmLabel*Foreground:                #1d1d15155b5b
Mosaic*XmToggleButton*Foreground:         #1d1d15155b5b
Mosaic*XmPushButton*Foreground:           #5b5b00000000
Mosaic*logo*Foreground:                   #1d1d15155b5b

Mosaic*Background:                        #bfbfbfbfbfbf

Mosaic*XmList*Background:                  #bfbfbfbfbfbf
Mosaic*XmText*Background:                  #bfbfbfbfbfbf
Mosaic*XmSelectionBox*Background:          #bfbfbfbfbfbf
Mosaic*XmMessageBox*Background:            #bfbfbfbfbfbf
Mosaic*XmTextField*Background:             #9c9c9c9c9c9c

Mosaic*TopShadowColor:                     #e7e7e7e7e7e7
Mosaic*XmList*TopShadowColor:              #e7e7e7e7e7e7
Mosaic*XmText*TopShadowColor:              #e7e7e7e7e7e7
Mosaic*XmSelectionBox*TopShadowColor:      #e7e7e7e7e7e7
Mosaic*XmMessageBox*TopShadowColor:        #e7e7e7e7e7e7

Mosaic*TroughColor:                        #646464646464
Mosaic*SelectColor:                        #ffffffff0000
Mosaic*HighlightColor:                     #bfbfbfbfbfbf
```

Many of these colors are various shades of gray—the settings tweak various colors to make the Mosaic interface appear just so. In most cases, if you just set the background color, all of the other colors will take care of themselves. However, if you would like to mimic the default settings, you can copy these lines from the application defaults file to your and modify the colors to suit your tastes.

Text Style

Mosaic allows you to specify the fonts used to display text. Mosaic distinguishes a number of different textual elements in HTML documents; you can specify a distinct typeface for each of these elements. Mosaic also provides a way to control the fonts used for labels on buttons and other interface components. Mosaic has an additional textual element, anchor text, that is unique to hypertext browsers. Anchor text is used to indicate hypertext links, so it must be visually distinct from ordinary text. Mosaic provides a number of resources that control the visual characteristics of anchor text.

HTML documents

When Mosaic processes an HTML document, it decides which font to use for a particular block of text based on how that text is coded in the document. Mosaic provides a number of font resources for specifying the actual typefaces used for the various types of text. Mosaic recognizes the following types, which we will explain more fully in Chapter 7:

Normal text

> Normal text is not specially coded within an HTML document. The `font` resource specifies the typeface used to display this text. Even though text within lists is specially coded, it is displayed using the font assigned to normal text. Quotations formatted with the `<BLOCKQUOTE>` tag are also considered normal text. Individual words or sentences of normal text can be tagged so they are displayed using different styles, such as bold, italic, or fixed-width fonts. The `italicFont` and `boldFont` resources control the fonts used to display italic and bold normal text, respectively. Fixed-width text can be plain, bold, or italic, so Mosaic has `fixedFont`, `fixedboldFont`, and `fixeditalic-Font` resources to handle these cases.

Headings

> HTML supports six different levels of headings, `<H1>` through `<H6>`, with `<H1>` being the highest level of heading. Mosaic provides a font resource for each type of heading: `heading1Font` through `heading6Font`. Headings should be displayed with larger, bolder fonts than normal text.

Preformatted text

> This text corresponds to the HTML `<PRE>` tag. Documents use this tag for text that has already been formatted and must be displayed as is, such as program listings, so the text should be displayed with a fixed-width font. The `plain-Font` resource specifies the typeface used for preformatted text. Preformatted text can be tagged as bold or italic, so Mosaic also provides `plainboldFont` and `plainitalicFont` resources.

Listings

> HTML also supports a `<LISTING>` tag for computer listings, so Mosaic has a `listingFont` resource to handle this case.

Addresses

> The HTML `<ADDRESS>` tag indicates the author of a document, along with an email address. The `addressFont` resource specifies the font used for this tag.

Mosaic treats anchor text as part of the text in which it is embedded, so anchor text is rendered using the same font. However, as we'll discuss shortly, other visual characteristics of anchor text, such as its color, can be modified to distinguish it from regular text.

The default configuration of Mosaic uses various sizes and styles of the Times Roman font for normal text and headings, and Courier for preformatted text and other fixed-width styles. As we described earlier, the **Fonts** submenu on the

Options menu provides the easiest way to change the fonts Mosaic uses for HTML documents. Unfortunately, if you change the fonts using the **Fonts** menu, the change only remains in effect for your current Mosaic session.* To make the change more permanent, you have to set the various font resources in a resource file. The application defaults file for Mosaic contains the following font specifications:

```
Mosaic*Font: -adobe-times-medium-r-normal-*-17-*-*-*-*-*-iso8859-1
Mosaic*ItalicFont: -adobe-times-medium-i-normal-*-17-*-*-*-*-*-iso8859-1
Mosaic*BoldFont: -adobe-times-bold-r-normal-*-17-*-*-*-*-*-iso8859-1
Mosaic*FixedFont: -adobe-courier-medium-r-normal-*-17-*-*-*-*-*-iso8859-1
Mosaic*FixedboldFont: -adobe-courier-bold-r-normal-*-17-*-*-*-*-*-iso8859-1
Mosaic*FixeditalicFont: -adobe-courier-medium-o-normal-*-17-*-*-*-*-*-iso8859-1
Mosaic*Header1Font: -adobe-times-bold-r-normal-*-24-*-*-*-*-*-iso8859-1
Mosaic*Header2Font: -adobe-times-bold-r-normal-*-18-*-*-*-*-*-iso8859-1
Mosaic*Header3Font: -adobe-times-bold-r-normal-*-17-*-*-*-*-*-iso8859-1
Mosaic*Header4Font: -adobe-times-bold-r-normal-*-14-*-*-*-*-*-iso8859-1
Mosaic*Header5Font: -adobe-times-bold-r-normal-*-12-*-*-*-*-*-iso8859-1
Mosaic*Header6Font: -adobe-times-bold-r-normal-*-10-*-*-*-*-*-iso8859-1
Mosaic*AddressFont: -adobe-times-medium-i-normal-*-17-*-*-*-*-*-iso8859-1
Mosaic*PlainFont: -adobe-courier-medium-r-normal-*-14-*-*-*-*-*-iso8859-1
Mosaic*PlainboldFont: -adobe-courier-bold-r-normal-*-14-*-*-*-*-*-iso8859-1
Mosaic*PlainitalicFont: -adobe-courier-medium-o-normal-*-14-*-*-*-*-*-iso8859-1
Mosaic*ListingFont: -adobe-courier-medium-r-normal-*-12-*-*-*-*-*-iso8859-1
```

As you can see, specifying fonts in an X resource file is no easy task—the font name syntax is quite arcane. However, if you are going to set the font resources, you will want the various sizes and styles to work well together. You need to have a basic understanding of the naming syntax to pick reasonable fonts; we'll cover the bare minimum here. For more details on font name syntax, see Volume 3, *X Window System User's Guide*, or *X User Tools*.

The components of an X font name allow for the complete specification of all of the characteristics of a font. Fortunately, you really only need to specify a few of these components to get the font you want; you can wildcard the rest of the font name. The **xlsfonts** program lists the names of all of the fonts available on your system. Use this program, a standard X client, to get an idea of the fonts you have to choose from.† One of the first few fonts listed by **xlsfonts** is:

```
-adobe-courier-bold-o-normal--12-120-75-75-m-70-iso8859-1
```

This is a fully-specified font name. Using wildcards, you can specify the same font as follows:

```
*courier-bold-o*120*
```

To use wildcarding successfully, you need to specify four font characteristics: the font family, the weight, the slant, and the point size, in that order. The

---

* This limitation will probably be corrected in a future version of Mosaic.
† If you have the **xfontsel** client on your system, you can use it to preview fonts and pick the ones you like.

punctuation is important—make sure you use the asterisks and dashes as shown above. Use the output from **xlsfonts** to find out what font families and point sizes you have available. Your choices for font weight are "medium," "bold," and "demi-bold." As for the slant component, "r" stands for roman, "i" is for italic, and "o" means oblique.

In general, proportional fonts such as Times Roman or Helvetica work best for normal text and headings. Be sure to use a monospaced font for all of the fixed-width textual elements so that any formatting comes out looking right. Once you have selected the fonts that you want to use for the various HTML elements, you should copy the font resource lines from Mosaic's application defaults file to your *.Xdefaults* file. Now all you have to do is edit the file and specify the fonts using the appropriate wildcarded names.

Interface text

Because Mosaic is built using the Motif widget set, you can control the fonts used to display text for the different components in the user interface. For example, you can specify the fonts used for menu items, buttons, and text entry areas. As with the color settings we discussed earlier, these fonts are specified with Motif widget resources. Since the details of setting widget resources are beyond the scope of this book, we recommend that you use Mosaic's application defaults file to guide you if you want to set these font resources. You may also want to consult Volume 3, *X Window System User's Guide, Motif Edition*; or Volume 6A, *Motif Programming Manual*, to keep from getting in over your head. Wrestling with widget resources is not for the faint of heart; in our opinion, you're probably better off using the defaults and leaving well enough alone.

If you look in the the defaults file, you'll see a number of specifications like the following one:

```
Mosaic*XmLabel*fontList: -*-helvetica-bold-r-normal-*-14-*-*-*-*-*-iso8859-1
```

Basically, every Motif widget has a `fontList` resource that controls the font it uses to display text. The `fontList` specifications in Mosaic's application defaults file ensure that the different widgets use fonts that look good together. By default, all of the labels in Mosaic's interface use a bold Helvetica font, buttons use a normal Helvetica font, and menu items use a bold, oblique Helvetica font. The only components that don't use a Helvetica font are text entry areas—they use a fixed-width Lucidetypewriter font.

Just as with specifying colors, if you want to change the fonts that Mosaic uses, you should copy the relevant lines from the application defaults file to your *.Xdefaults* file and then make the changes. As before, use **xlsfonts** to determine the fonts that are available and wildcard the font names to avoid typing the entire names.

Anchor text

Anchor text must be clearly distinct from ordinary text, so Mosaic provides a number of resources that control the visual attributes of hyperlinks. Mosaic distinguishes between hyperlinks that you have followed and those you haven't. By default, Mosaic displays visited anchors using a different style than anchors that have not been visited.

Mosaic allows you to define the color of anchor text explicitly with the anchorColor resource. By default, anchor text is shaded blue. Once an anchor has been visited, if anchor tracking is enabled, it is displayed using the color specified by the visitedAnchorColor resource. The default value of this resource is a blue-violet color. Using two distinct colors for these resources makes it easy to distinguish between links you have followed and ones you haven't. As with the color resources we discussed earlier, you can specify a predefined color name from the *rgb.txt* database or specify RGB values using hexadecimal notation.

When you click on anchor text, Mosaic follows the link; this process is called activating the anchor. While the anchor is being activated, Mosaic changes the foreground and background of the anchor text to the colors specified by activeAnchorFG and activeAnchorBG, respectively. By default, the foreground of an active anchor is red and the background is the same shade of gray as Mosaic's default background.

Anchor text can also be distinguished by underlines using the anchorUnderlines resource. The value of this resource specifies the number of lines Mosaic draws underneath unvisited anchors, while XX "visitedAnchorUnderlines resource" \&visitedAnchorUnderlines controls the number of lines drawn under visited anchors. Both of these resources can take the values 0, 1, 2, or 3. By default, they are both set to 1.

The dashedAnchorUnderlines and dashedVisitedAnchorUnderlines resources provide yet another means of differentiating between visited and unvisited hyperlinks. Their resources take Boolean values. By default, dashedAnchorUnderlines is False, and dashedVisitedAnchorUnderlines is True, which means that unvisited anchors have solid underlines and visited anchors have dashed underlines.

Although you can set these resources in a resource file, the easiest way to change Mosaic's underlining style is to use the **Anchor Underlines** submenu. We discussed this menu earlier, but one thing we glossed over is just how the **Default Underlines** option works. This item resets the values of the various underlining resources to their default values—either Mosaic's internal defaults or the default values you have set in a resource file.

Improving Mosaic's Performance

The Internet is a decentralized network that spans tens of thousands of miles and may connect hundreds of thousands of users. As a result, it is not surprising that bottlenecks occur, and that the Internet's response time may seem unsatisfactory. Since Mosaic is designed above all as a hypermedia browser for the Internet, attempting to fine-tune Mosaic's performance necessarily means looking for areas in which Mosaic can access a faster device (like your computer's memory or its disk) instead of the comparatively slower network.

Mosaic offers a few different techniques for reducing its need to access the Internet, as well as some other methods for improving performance. However, these performance improvements are not without a cost, as they require turning off some of Mosaic's best features. As we describe the different techniques, we'll also explain the tradeoffs involved, so you can experiment and decide whether or not the improved performance is worth the cost.

A Local Home Page

If you find that it takes Mosaic a long time to retrieve and display your home page located on the Internet, you may want to use a local home page instead. The best approach is to download a home page and use it as a template to create your own. While this approach requires learning a little bit about HTML, it really isn't that difficult, and you get to decide exactly what's on your home page. You can create your own images, say exactly what you want, and provide links to all of your favorite Web documents. You'll learn how to create a home page in Chapter 7.

All you have to do to download a home page is select **Save As** from the **File** menu when you are viewing the home page. Be sure to set HTML as the format of the saved document and pick an appropriate filename with a file extension of *.html*. Once you've modified the home page to look like you want and contain links to your favorite documents, you can use any of the methods we've already described to specify the location of your new home page. Be sure to specify a full pathname to the document, so that Mosaic can find it regardless of your current directory when you run Mosaic. For example:

```
Mosaic*homeDocument: /usr/local/home/paula/mosaic/my-home.html
```

Image Loading and Caching

As we discussed earlier in the chapter, Mosaic supports delayed image loading. Enabling this feature reduces the amount of data Mosaic has to retrieve from across the network. You can set the `delayImageLoads` resource to **True** to turn on delayed image loading. If you set the resource to **True**, you can still turn off the behavior using the **Delay Image Loading** menu option we described earlier.

One thing we didn't mention in our earlier discussion of image loading is that Mosaic uses an internal image cache to speed up its handling of inline images. Mosaic stores the inline images from your most recently viewed documents in the cache, so that if you view a document again, Mosaic does not have to retrieve the images again. If you've experimented with delayed image loading, you may have noticed that once you load a delayed image, Mosaic continues to display the image each time you come back to the document that contains it. The image cache is responsible for this behavior.

The `imageCacheSize` resource controls the size of the cache; the default size is 2058 kilobytes. Once the image cache is full, Mosaic makes room for the current images by flushing the least recently viewed images. Even if the images in the current document exceed the size of the cache, Mosaic temporarily caches them all while you are on that page. If your system has a lot of memory, you could increase the size of the cache to improve Mosaic's image handling even further. Either set the `imageCacheSize` resource in your resource via" file, or use the **-ics** command-line flag.

You can also clear out the image cache by selecting **Flush Image Cache** from the **Options** menu. This feature is mostly useful if you are working on an HTML document that contains inline images and using Mosaic to view the document. If you don't flush the cache, Mosaic uses the cached images each time you display the document, so you won't see any changes you may have made to the inline images. If you are using Mosaic for this purpose, you may want to set `reload-ReloadsImages` to `True`. This setting causes Mosaic to remove the cached images for the current document before reloading the document, which means that the images are reloaded as well.

Document Tracking

We've already discussed Mosaic's global history mechanism a couple of times, so we're not going to repeat that information here. The important point in terms of performance is that tracking visited anchors requires a fair bit of processing. If Mosaic's performance seems to be sluggish, you can experiment with turning off this tracking by setting `trackVisitedAnchors` to `False`. The drawback here is that now you don't get any feedback as to the documents you've already viewed. Alternatively, you can clear your global history periodically using the **Clear Global History** menu option. You can also tell Mosaic not to use the global history mechanism by using the **-ngh** flag or setting `useGlobalHistory` to `False`.

Configuring Mosaic for Your System

Certain aspects of Mosaic's behavior as a networked hypermedia browser rely on the existence of external programs and other system services. Mosaic for X is designed to work on different machines and operating systems, so various mechanisms may need to be configured to work properly on a particular system. A site may also want to customize Mosaic to allow easy access to frequently-used documents. Mosaic provides a number of resources that handle these configurations.

If you are simply a Mosaic user, you don't need to worry about these resources, provided that Mosaic has been installed properly. You may still want to read this section out of curiosity, though. If you are a system administrator, however, you need to understand these resources so that you can make sure Mosaic is configured properly for your site.

Defining a Documents Menu

The menus provided by Mosaic (the **File**, **Options**, **Navigate**, **Annotate**, and **Help** menus) are all defined internally and cannot be modified. You can set the `simpleInterface` resource to `True`, which causes Mosaic to display pared-down menus, but other than that there is no way to control the contents of these menus. The simple interface is useful if you are configuring Mosaic to be used bulletin-board style, as the pared-down version does not allow users to open documents other than those linked to the startup document.

However, Mosaic does provide a way for a site to create its own customized **Documents** menu.* The **Documents** menu should be set up site-wide by the system administrator to provide easy access to frequently-used documents. The version of Mosaic we have provided on the CD uses a **Documents** menu to provide access to *GNN* publications. If an individual user wants to set up quick access to other documents, he can add the documents to his hotlist, or even better, create a local home page as discussed in Chapter 7.

Mosaic uses the `documentsMenuSpecfile` resource to specify the file that contains the description of the **Documents** menu. The default filename is */usr/local/lib/mosaic/documents.menu*. In the specification file, you list pairs of document titles and URLs, where each title and each URL is on a separate line. Mosaic displays the document title in the menu; when a user selects the item, Mosaic accesses the corresponding URL. Putting a line containing two or more dashes ("--") between title/URL pairs causes Mosaic to display a separator in the menu. The specification file can contain up to 80 title/URL pairs.

We use the following specification file to set the **Documents** menu on the CD:

```
GNN Home
http://gnn.com/GNNhome.html
Whole Internet Catalog
http://gnn.com/wic/index.html
Business Pages
http://gnn.com/bus/index.html
NCSA What's New
```

---

* If you used version 1.2 of Mosaic, you may be wondering what happened to the **Documents** and **Manuals** menus. These menus have been removed from the menu bar as of Version 2.0. The **Internet Starting Points** and **Internet Resources Meta-Index** items on the **Navigate** menu provide similar functionality to the old menus.

```
http://www.ncsa.uiuc.edu/SDG/Software/Mosaic/Docs/whats-new.html
GNN NetNews
http://gnn.com/news/index.html
Special Interests
http://gnn.com/pubs.html
--
Registration
http://gnn.com/index.html
```

This specification creates the **Documents** menu shown in Figure 5-8.

Figure 5-8. An example Documents menu

Defining Multimedia Viewers

As we will explain in detail in Chapter 6, *Using Mosaic for Multimedia*, Mosaic uses a variety of external viewers to display images, sounds, and other types of documents that are not HTML or plain text documents. By default, Mosaic is configured to use certain viewers for particular document types, as well as to recognize various document types based on file extensions.

The useDefaultExtensionMap resource controls whether or not Mosaic uses its default mappings of file extensions to document types. useDefaultTypeMap controls the use of the default mapping of document types to external viewers. The default value of each of these resources is True. We recommend that you leave it that way, as it is easy to override the defaults using the techniques discussed in Chapter 6.

Modifications to the default external viewer configuration can either be made system-wide or on a individual basis. The globalExtensionMap and globalTypeMap resources specify the filenames of the system-wide extension map and mailcap configuration files, respectively. The default extension map filename is */usr/local/lib/mosaic/mime.types*, and the default mailcap filename is */usr/local/lib/mosaic/mailcap*. Mosaic does not provide default mapping files, as the program sets its defaults internally. If you want to alter the default configuration, you need to create these files for your system. You can also specify alternate filenames if that is appropriate. For example, if you have installed Mosaic someplace other than */usr/local*, you should use filenames that are appropriate for the installed location.

For personal modifications, the relevant filenames are set by the `personalExtensionMap` and `personalTypeMap` resources. In both cases, Mosaic checks for the specified filenames relative to a user's home directory. By default, Mosaic looks for a user's personal extension mapping in *.mime.types* and a personal mailcap file in *.mailcap*. If your system is set up so that Mosaic's personal configuration files are kept in a *.mosaic* subdirectory of a user's home directory, you should set `personalExtensionMap` and `personalTypeMap` accordingly.

If you change any of the mappings in these files while Mosaic is running, you can get Mosaic to load the new configuration by selecting **Reload Config Files** from the **Options** menu. However, if you change the actual filenames of the configuration files, you have to restart Mosaic to get the changes to take effect.

The `recordCommandLocation` and `recordCommand` resources also specify an external program used for recording audio annotations. The `recordCommandLocation` resource defines the full pathname of a program for recording audio files. The default value is */usr/sbin/recordaiff* on SGI machines, */usr/demo/SOUND/record* on Sun's, and */usr/audio/bin/srecorder* on HP's. If Mosaic cannot find the specified program when it starts, Mosaic disables audio annotations. The `recordCommand` resource sets the full command for recording, where the first word of the command is the program specified by `recordCommandLocation`. The default value is **recordaiff -n 1 -s 8 -r 8000** on SGI machines, **record** on Sun's, and **srecorder -au** on HP's. The command needs to take an additional filename argument and the program needs to stop recording correctly when sent a SIGINT signal.

System Commands

When Mosaic encounters a compressed file, it looks for an appropriate utility to uncompress the file. The `uncompressCommand` resource specifies the command used to uncompress files with a *.Z* file extension. The default value of this resource is `uncompress`. If a compressed file has the extension *.gz* or *.z*, Mosaic uses the command specified by `gunzipCommand` to uncompress the file. The default command is `gunzip -n -f`. This command requires Version 1.2.4 or higher of **gzip** and **gunzip**. These programs can be obtained from the following URL:

```
ftp://prep.ai.mit.edu/pub/gnu
```

When a user selects **Print** from the **File** menu, Mosaic uses the value of `printCommand` to print the file. Mosaic expects this command to take a single filename argument. The default command is `lpr`. You should set this resource appropriately for your system. A user can also change the print command using the **Print Document** dialog box that appears when **Print** is selected.

Hostname Problems

Some Sun machines have a problem when they call the `gethostbyname()` routine to get their full hostname. If you are running Mosaic on a Sun that coredumps when you start the program, you should set the `gethostbynameIsEvil` resource to `True`. This setting tells Mosaic not to use `gethostbyname()`. Alternately, using the **-ghbnie** command-line option has the same effect. If you have to set `gethostbynameIsEvil` to `True`, you should also set the `fullHostname` resource to the fully-qualified hostname for your system.

Other Problems

The `catchPriorAndNext` resource is also designed to work around a problem that can occur on some machines. The **PageUp** (prior) and **PageDown** (next) keys are supposed to move the scroll bar in the **Document View** window up and down by page increments. If you find that these keys are not working, set `catchPriorAndNext` to `True` to correct the problem.

## CHAPTER SIX

USING MOSAIC FOR MULTIMEDIA

What You'll Need
Getting the Big Picture
Digital Drive-In
Sound Waves
Formatted Documents
Extending Multimedia Support
Recording Audio

Multimedia on the Internet can be one of the most exciting uses of Mosaic. You can play movies and music, look at full-color images of space or great artwork, run scientific animations and models, display 3D graphics, and more.

But Internet multimedia can sometimes be frustrating and is almost always time-consuming. The problem is that these files can be quite large. A one-minute MPEG movie can be a megabyte or more, a three-minute song might be four or five megabytes, large full-color graphics are typically half a megabyte or so.

How long it takes to download a file depends on the kind of network connection you have, how far away the server is, and how busy the network is. If you connect to the Internet over a modem, downloading large files will quietly drive you insane if you sit and stare at Mosaic's spinning globe. So, when you start downloading movie and sound files, be prepared to take a break or work in another application.

Even so, using multimedia files on the Net can be worth the pain because the results can be stunning, perhaps even more so because it takes so long to get the files. When you bring up that full-screen version of the Mona Lisa, or sit back and play a four-minute track from an unsigned band, or fly through a computer-generated fractal environment . . . in short, when you sit back, stare at your screen, and say, "Wow!" that's when you'll appreciate the full power of Mosaic.

What You'll Need

You won't have much of a multimedia experience if you can't hear sounds or see color. You'll want a monitor capable of displaying at least 256 colors. For sound you'll need a machine that has speakers. The hardware setup is just one part of the puzzle, though; you'll also need software programs capable of displaying various kinds of files. "Wait a minute," you may be saying, "I have Mosaic. What other software do I need?"

Mosaic cannot directly display all types of files you might want to use. Instead it relies on other programs that are designed to handle specific kinds of files. There are different programs for graphics files, audio files, video files, and so on. When you download a file that Mosaic can't display by itself (basically, anything except HTML and text), it launches one of these programs (referred to as "external viewers" because they are external to Mosaic), which then displays the file.

These viewers give Mosaic its power as a multimedia application; they make it possible for Mosaic to display the diversity of digital media on the Internet. The default configuration of Mosaic assumes the presence of certain viewers. In this chapter, we'll show you how to view full-color images, watch movies, and listen to sounds using the default viewers. These viewers may already be installed on your system; if not, we'll tell you where you can find them on the Net. We'll also cover configuring Mosaic to specify alternate viewers and to define additional file types and corresponding viewers.

The Default Configuration

When you click on a link to a document that isn't HTML or plain text, like an image or a sound file, Mosaic tries to use an external program to display the image or play the sound. The default configuration of Mosaic expects to find the programs shown in Table 6-1.

Mosaic searches for these programs based on the value of the PATH environment variable. If Mosaic cannot find the program it is looking for, it prints an error message stating that it cannot find the viewer. If this happens even though you know the program is on your system, make sure that the appropriate directory is in your PATH.

There's nothing special about the default viewer applications; you can use any X application as a viewer for the file types that program handles. Since the main purpose of external viewers is simply to display files, rather than to do a lot of editing, it's best to use small programs that launch quickly and don't require a lot of memory. Later in the chaper we'll explain how to configure Mosaic to use different viewers.

Table 6–1: Default External Viewers

Program	Purpose
xv	Display graphical images
showaudio*	Play audio files
mpeg_play†	Display movies
ghostview	Display PostScript files
xdvi	Display DVI files
xwud	Display X window dumps
metamail	Display RFC822 messages

* The current version of **showaudio** works only on Sun and Sony workstations. On an SGI machine, Mosaic uses the program **sfplay** to play audio files, while on a DEC Alpha, it uses **aplay**.

† On SGI machines, Mosaic also supports the quicktime and sgi-movie formats using the **movieplayer** program.

Installing a Viewer

Before we jump into exploring the power of multimedia, let's spend a few minutes talking about viewer installation. Chances are, if you are using Mosaic at work or at school, your system administrator has installed the external viewers and configured Mosaic appropriately, so you can skip ahead to next section. If things don't work as we describe, you'll want to bug your sys admin to set up Mosaic correctly.

If you manage your own workstation, however, you'll probably need to download and install the various viewer programs. Table 6-2 shows the URL where you can get the source code for each of the default viewers.

Table 6–2: URLs for External Viewers

Program	URL
xv	*ftp://ftp.cis.upenn.edu/pub/xv*
showaudio	*ftp://thumper.bellcore.com/pub/nsb*
mpeg_play	*ftp://tr-ftp.cs.berkeley.edu/pub/multimedia/mpeg*
ghostview	*ftp://ftp.cs.wisc.edu/pub/ghost*
xdvi	*ftp://ftp.x.org/contrib/applications*
metamail	*ftp://thumper.bellcore.com/pub/nsb*

These URLs are also on the *Mosaic Handbook Hotlist* in *GNN*. As shown in Figure 6-1, the Other Mosaic/WWW Software page of the NCSA Mosaic Frequently Asked Questions page also provides pointers to the source for the default viewers. The URL for this page is:

```
http://www.ncsa.uiuc.edu/SDG/Software/Mosaic/Docs/faq-software.html
```

Since you are downloading the source code for the viewer, you'll have to build it and then install it. Each program has its own build process, which should be explained in a *README* or *INSTALL* file, so we can't tell you exactly how to build each program. We can, however, walk you through the basic process. Let's use **xv**

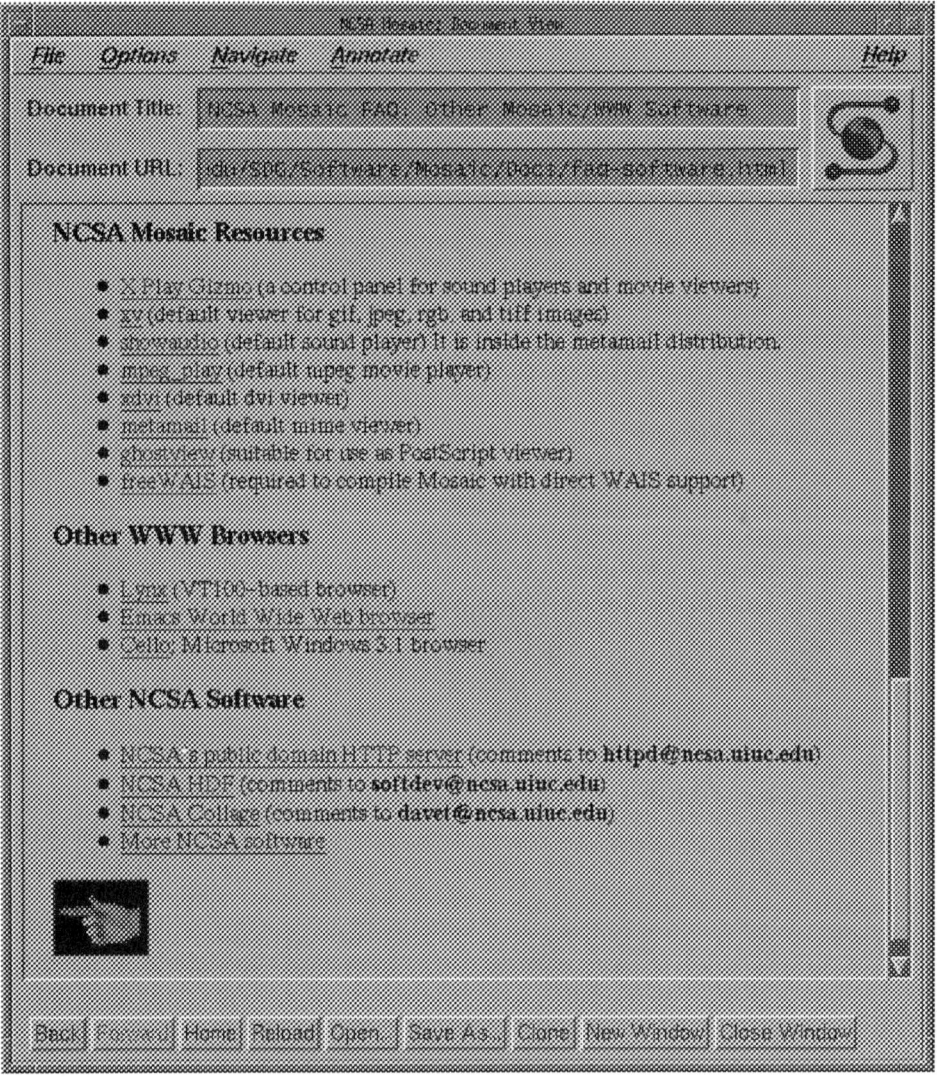

Figure 6-1. NCSA Mosaic viewers

as an example. Follow the **xv** link on the *Other Mosaic/WWW Software* page to go to the FTP server where **xv** is available. The URL is:

```
ftp://ftp.cis.upenn.edu/pub/xv
```

To download, build, and install the program:

1. Create a directory for the source code. Where you put this depends on how your system is configured. On our system, we put it in */usr/local/src/xv.*

2. Click on the link for the latest release of **xv**, which at this time is *xv-3.00a.tar.Z*. Mosaic connects to the FTP server and starts downloading the file. This may take a long time as the file is almost three megabytes.

3. When Mosaic finishes retrieving the file, it decompresses it using **uncompress** because the file has a *.Z* extension. Now Mosaic prompts you for a filename with the **Save As** dialog box. Enter the full path of the directory you've created and pick a filename, such as *xv.tar*.

4. Now you have a UNIX tar archive. Unpack the archive with the following command:

```
% tar xvf xv.tar
```

This creates an *xv-3.00a* subdirectory that contains the source code for **xv**.

5. Change to this directory and follow the instructions in the *INSTALL* file to build **xv**. This program is shareware, so be sure to read the *README* file for shareware information.

6. Once you've built **xv**, install the binary in a standard location, such as */usr/local/bin*. You'll need superuser privileges to do this.

You'll need to follow this basic process for each of the external viewers that you want to install on your system.

Getting the Big Picture

Most of the files on the Web (aside from HTML files, of course) are graphics files. You may be thinking that Mosaic can already display graphics, since *GNN* contains graphics, but as far as the Web is concerned, there are actually two kinds of graphics. Inline graphics are arranged on HTML pages, while linked graphics are standalone graphics files that require an external viewer like **xv**. There are several graphics formats, although GIF and JPEG are the most common on the Internet.

GIF is an 8-bit indexed color file format, while JPEG is a compression standard for 24-bit color. Quality depends on the level of compression, but JPEG images are generally better quality than GIF images.

To view some of the great graphics on the Net, let's go to the *Space Telescope Science Institute*'s page of recent Hubble Space Telescope images. The URL is:

```
http://marvel.stsci.edu/EPA/Recent.html
```

This page, shown in Figure 6-2, contains thumbnail images of photographs taken by the Hubble Space Telescope. Clicking on the image downloads a larger JPEG version of the image. There's also an icon labeled GIF, which you can click on to see the GIF version of the image. The caption icon lets you see a text file about the photograph. Let's go ahead and get the JPEG version of the Orion Nebula.

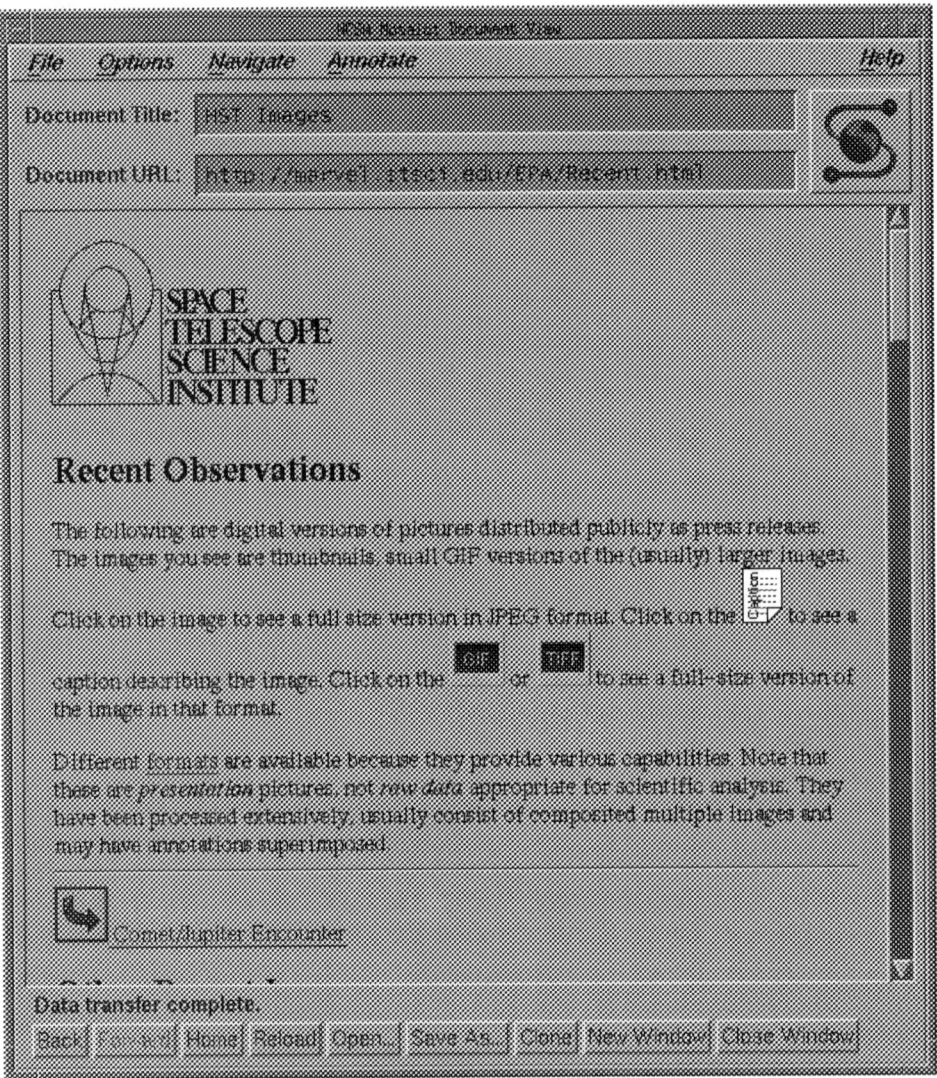

Figure 6-2. Hubble Space Telescope images

Click on the thumbnail photo for the image to get Mosaic to retrieve the image. When the download is complete, Mosaic will launch **xv** (if it's installed) and display the file as shown in Figure 6-3.

When you download an image, Mosaic does not save the file to your system. Fortunately, **xv** provides a way for you to save the image. As you can see in Figure 6-3, **xv** does not provide a menu bar or other visible controls. All functionality of **xv** is accessed through a control panel that appears when you press the third

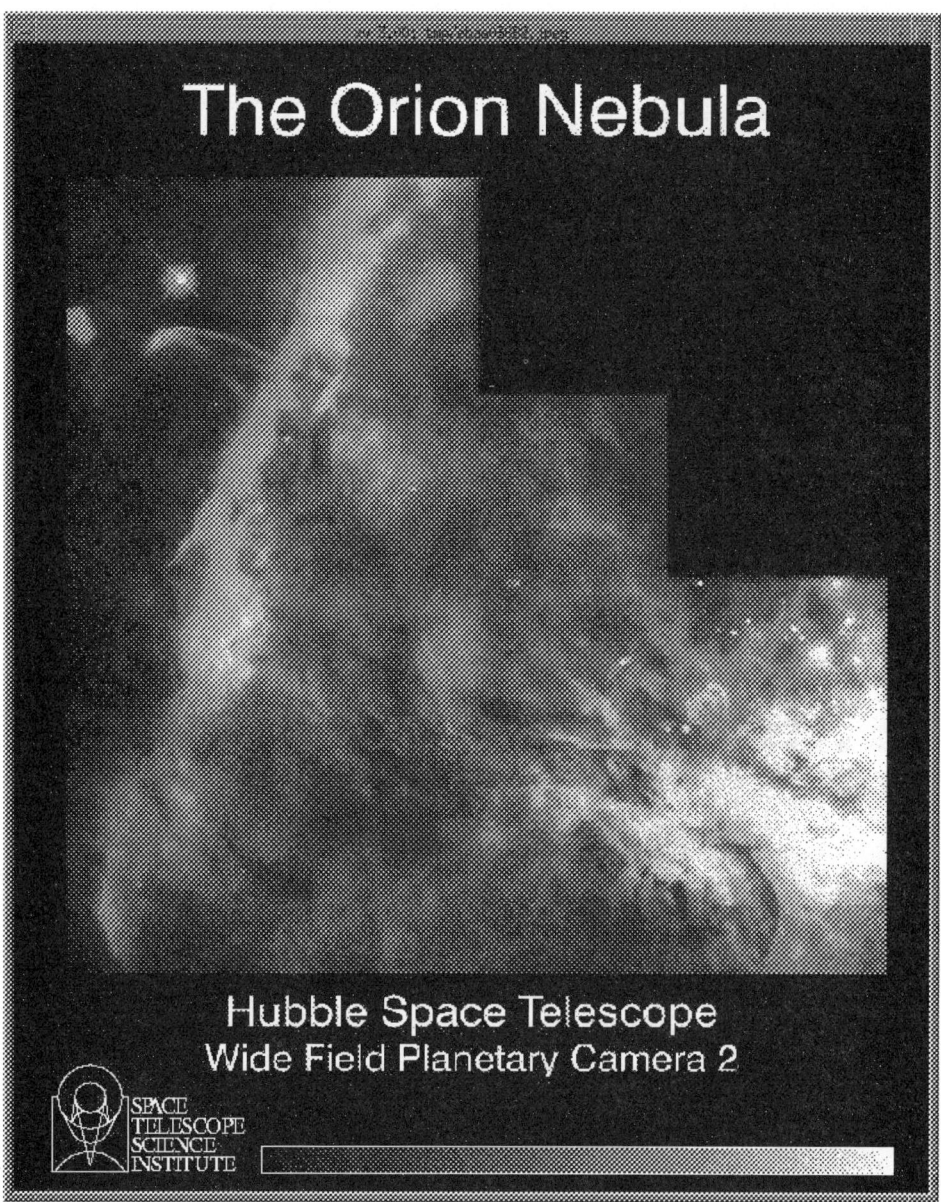

Figure 6–3. The Orion Nebula

mouse button over the image. As shown in Figure 6-4, this control panel provides a **Save** button. It also has a **Quit** button that allows you to exit the viewer. **xv** is a full image editing program, so there's a lot you can do with images, including rotating, scaling, and cropping.

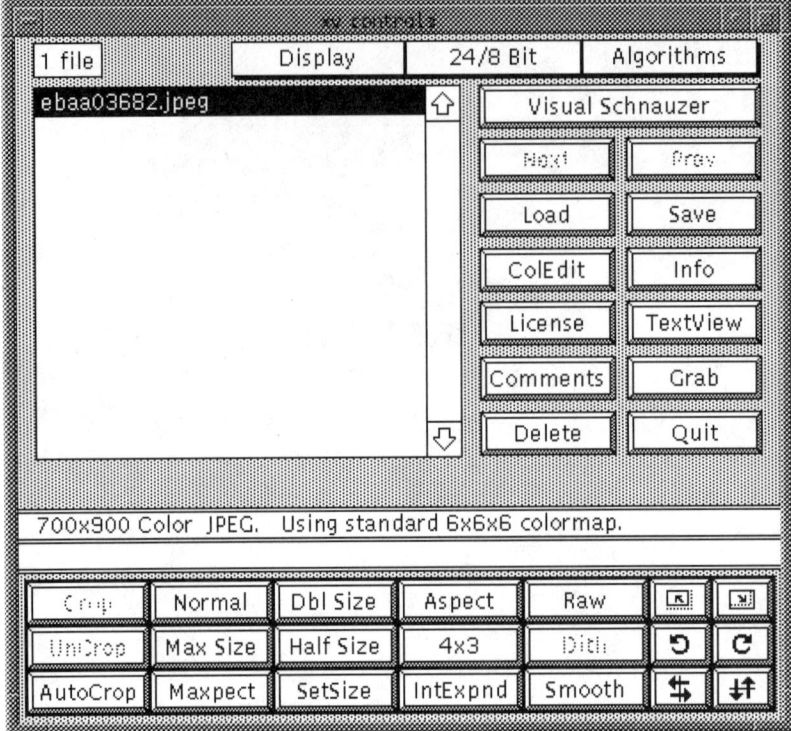

Figure 6-4. The xv control panel

Mosaic uses **xv** as the default viewer for all types of images, except X window dumps. Mosaic handles X window dumps using another viewer, **xwud**, which is the counterpart to **xwd**, a utility that creates an X screen dump. If you follow a link to an X window dump file, which typically has the file extension *.xwd*, Mosaic displays it using **xwud**. This program merely displays the image in a window; there are no controls. To remove the viewer, simply click any mouse button over the image. **xwud** is a supported X client, so it should be present on every system running X.

Digital Drive-In

Playing movies on your computer is one of the cooler ways to waste time at work. Actually, digital video has the potential to be quite useful, as well as fun. Imagine reading an entry from Nixon chief of staff H.R. Haldeman's diaries and being able to view a home movie he took on the day of the journal entry. Or learning a new software program and watching a movie that demonstrates a difficult function. Or reading an author's work and seeing an interview with him.

These are all great uses of video on the Net. There aren't many cases where video and text are integrated very tightly, however. Most video clips on the Internet are random clips of a minute or less.

In Digital Drive-In, a *GNN* special feature, D.C. Denison explains the state of digital video:

> It's the Internet's final frontier: moving pictures. Every cyberspace news story, when they get to that inevitable "future of the net" section, mentions the eventual delivery of digital video. So where is it?
>
> *GNN* decided to find out. This involved short bursts of net surfing followed by long stretches of downloading. (A tip for prospective Internet movie downloaders: develop a time-consuming hobby, like rug weaving.) Fortunately all the searching, and waiting, led to a happy discovery: digital movies are already on the net in growing numbers. True, some of them look like animated postage stamps, but they have the spunky appeal of an embryonic art form.

To visit the Digital Drive-In, click on the **Digital Drive-In** icon on the *GNN Home* page. Among the movies featured in the Digital Drive-In is some footage from the Raleigh, North Carolina *News and Observer*'s Web server. The *News and Observer* runs a series of features called "Carolina Discoveries," which profile different spots around the state. A story on North Carolina's waterfalls includes two MPEG movies of waterfalls. To see these movies, click on the **GO** button.

This takes you to a page with links to the two movies. This page tells you the format, file size, and length of the clips. "Views of the cascading water" is a 640K MPEG movie that runs 28 seconds, while "The falling waters and the green forest create a tranquil scene" is a 480K MPEG movie that runs 24 seconds. Getting movies from the Net involves a lot of waiting, so it's usually better to start with smaller clips since they take less time to download. In this example, we'll get the "tranquil scene" video.

When you click on the link, Mosaic starts downloading the movie. When the file is downloaded, Mosaic launches **mpeg_play** to play the movie. Movies tend to use a large number of colors; keep the pointer in the movie window so that you see the movie in the appropriate colors. The program will quit when the movie finishes. To remove the program before the movie is done, close the window (if that is supported by your window manager), or kill the window.

As with images, when you download a movie, Mosaic does not save it to your system. However, unlike **xv**, the **mpeg_play** program does not provide a way to save the movie. If you want to save a local copy of an MPEG file, set the **Load to Local Disk** option on the **Options** menu and follow the link again. Once Mosaic has retrieved the file, you will be prompted to enter a filename. If you know in advance that you are going to want to save a movie file, you can avoid retrieving the data twice. Use the **Load to Local Disk** option to save the file and then play it yourself using **mpeg_play**.

Digital video is definitely not the big screen. In fact, it's the very small screen. The *News and Observer*'s Eric Harris says: "When it comes to digital video, we're sort of in the black-and-white TV age."

Sound Waves

There are all kinds of sounds available on the Internet, from music servers like the Internet Underground Music Archive, the U2 server and the Elvis server, to sound bytes from Internet Talk Radio and The Late Show with David Letterman. One of the most popular music servers on the Internet is the Internet Underground Music Archive, which was awarded a Best of the Net award from *GNN*. "The Net's first free hi-fi music archive," the IUMA is dedicated to promoting unknown and unavailable artists over the Internet.

To use it, click on the Internet Underground Music Archive on the *Mosaic Handbook Hotlist* or enter the IUMA's URL:

```
http://www.iuma.com/IUMA/index_graphic.html
```

When you get to the IUMA, you'll see one of the hippest home page designs on the Internet, with options to check out bands by artist, label, location, song title, and interactively. You can also select the **Fresh Catches** option to listen to new tracks. Figure 6-5 shows the IUMA home page.

The *Fresh Catches* page describes the music available and provides several links to various versions. There are stereo and mono versions of the whole cut, which typically weigh in at 4 to 5 megabytes, as well as much smaller 15-second samples, which are *.au* files.

Following the smaller-is-better rule of downloading, choose one of the smaller samples. When the file transfer is complete, Mosaic launches **showaudio** to play the sound. This program simply outputs the sound file to the speaker on your system.

As with movies and images, when you download a sound file, Mosaic does not save it to your system. Since **showaudio** does not provide a way to save the sound, you need to use the **Load to Local Disk** option to save a local copy.

Formatted Documents

While online publications are becoming more common as the Web grows, there's no reason to believe that the printed page is going to become obsolete any time soon. In fact, it's quite common to see links to formatted documents, such as PostScript files, in Web documents. When you follow a link to a PostScript file (*.ps*), Mosaic displays the file using the **ghostview** viewer, as shown in Figure 6-6.

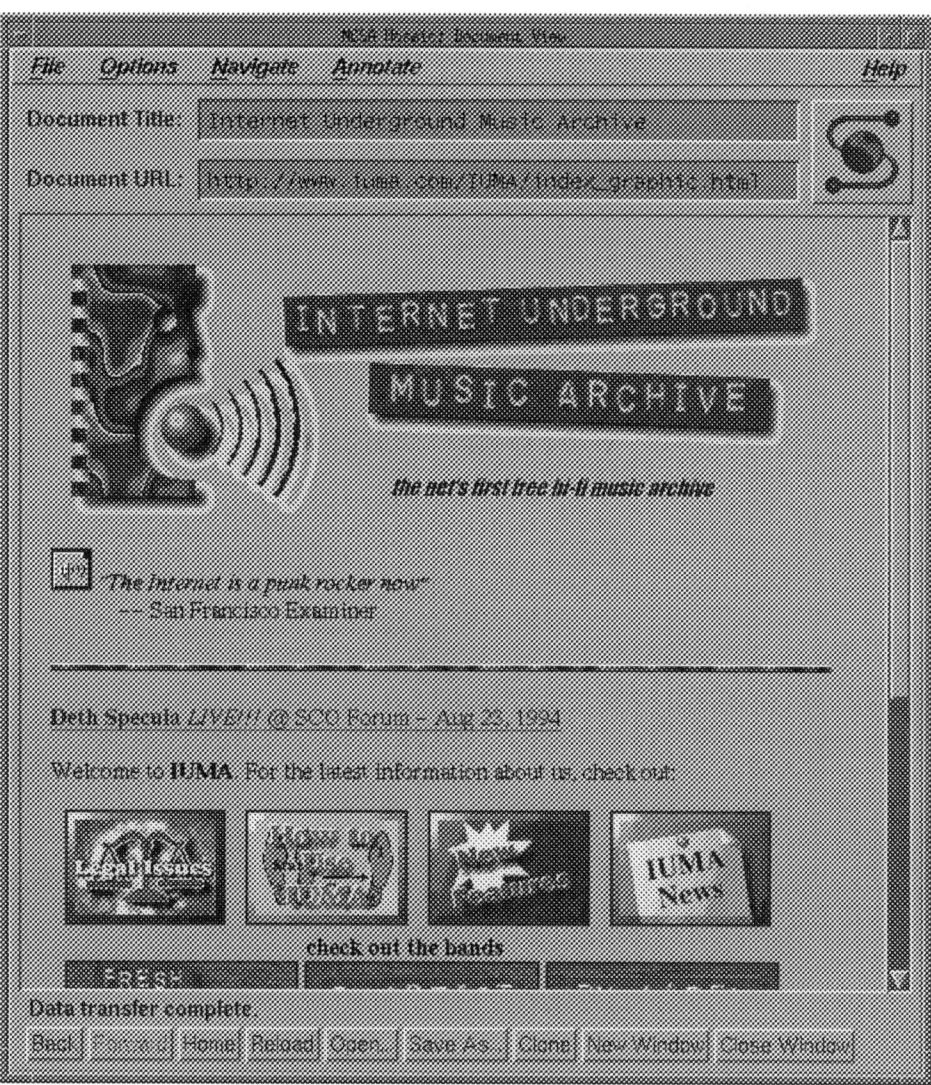

Figure 6–5. Internet Underground Music Archive

As you can see in Figure 6-6, **ghostview** provides a number of controls for manipulating the file. Most PostScript files span multiple pages; use **Next** and **Previous** on the **Page** menu to move forward and backward in the document. The **File** menu contains a **Save** command so you can save a local copy of the file, as well as the **Quit** command that allows you to exit the viewer.

TeX is another common document formatting language. TeX produces device-independent output files known as DVI files. If you follow a link to a DVI file, Mosaic displays the file using **xdvi**.

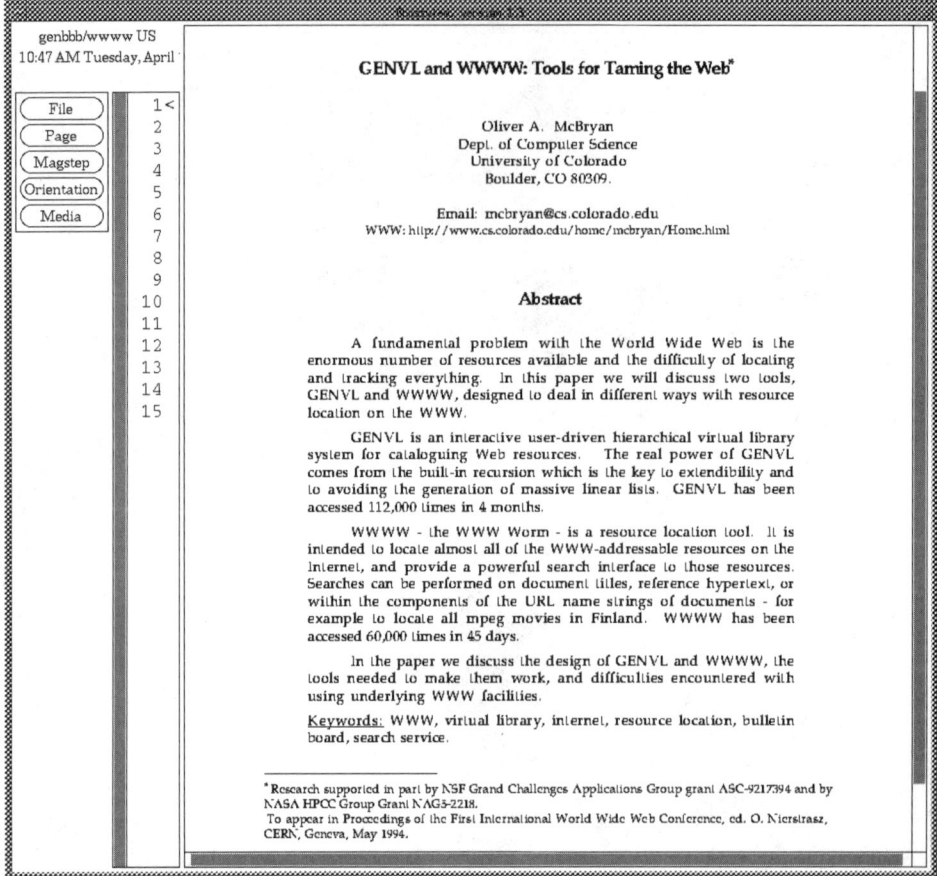

Figure 6-6. A PostScript file displayed with ghostview

Extending Multimedia Support

Multimedia support in Mosaic is based on a mechanism originally developed for email, the Multipurpose Internet Mail Extensions, or MIME. MIME defines a set of multimedia content types and subtypes that specify the type of data in the body of an electronic mail message. For example, *image/x-xwd* indicates that a mail attachment is an X window dump. MIME uses something called a mailcap (for "mail capabilities") file to specify the applications used to display the different types of data.

In MIME, the names of multimedia content types are defined by mail header lines, which are read by a mail program and acted upon rather than being displayed to the user. This mechanism obviously won't work for Mosaic. Instead, Mosaic relies on a system of file extensions to identify multimedia types.

Mosaic's mappings of file extensions to MIME content types, and from MIME content types to external viewer programs, are compiled into the program. However, you can override or extend the definitions by creating an extension map file and/or a mailcap file. The extension map file lists the associations between file extensions and MIME types. For example, the *.ps* file extension maps to the MIME type *application/postscript*. The mailcap file in turn lists the associations between MIME types and external viewers. For instance, the type *application/postscript* is mapped to the **ghostview** program.

There are three common things you might want to do to extend Mosaic's handling of multimedia types:

- Replace a default viewer with another one you prefer. For example, let's say you're using the HP VUE environment; you might want to use VUE's **imageview** program instead of **xv** to display images. To do this, you'd create a mailcap file to associate the various image types with **imageview** instead of **xv**.

- Recognize a new type of multimedia format. For example, let's say you have access to a TGA (Targe Image File) graphics and the **xli** program to display it. You would first have to define an extension mapping to associate the file extension for this type with a MIME content type. Then you'd create a mailcap entry to associate that content type with the program to view it.

- Cause a hyperlink to execute a local shell script.

We explore each of these scenarios in detail, along with the syntax of the mailcap and extension map files.

Using an Alternate Viewer

If you want to replace one of the default viewers, all you have to do is map the appropriate MIME content types to the new viewer in a mailcap file.* You don't need to worry about the extension map file; the file extensions are already associated with the correct MIME types for Mosaic's default behavior.

But before we can look at the syntax of the mailcap file, we need to tell you some more about MIME types. MIME defines the content types shown in Table 6-3.

---

* If you simply want to try out a different viewer quickly, you can use a symbolic link to handle the customization. For example, on an HP machine that has audio capabilities, you could try the **send_sound** program for playing audio files by setting up the following symbolic link:

```
% ln -s /usr/audio/bin/send_sound showaudio
```

This creates a symbolic link in your current directory; in order for the link to work, this directory needs to be in your PATH.

Table 6–3: MIME Content Types

Type	Use
text	Represent textual information
multipart	Combine several types
application	Transmit application or binary data
message	Encapsulate another message
image	Transmit image data
audio	Transmit audio data
video	Transmit video data

Of these types, *image, audio, video, application,* and *message* are relevant to our discussion of external viewers. Each content type has subtypes that are defined to further specify the format of the data. For example, the *mpeg* subtype of *video* specifies the MPEG video format.

As we mentioned earlier, the default mapping of MIME types to viewers is compiled into Mosaic. Table 6-4 lists the default mapping.

Table 6–4: Default Mapping of MIME Types to Viewers

Content Type	Viewer
audio/*	showaudio %s
image/xwd	xwud -in %s
image/x-xwd	xwud -in %s
image/x-xwindowdump	xwud -in %s
image/*	xv %s
video/mpeg	mpeg_play %s
application/postscript	ghostview %s
application/x-dvi	xdvi %s
message/rfc822	xterm -e metamail %s

As you might guess from Table 6-4, an asterisk (*) matches all of the subtypes of a particular MIME type. Thus, the *audio/** specification applies to all of the subtypes of the *audio* type. The entries for *image* demonstrate how you can handle particular subtypes with one viewer and use another viewer for everything else. The *xwd, x-xwd,* and *x-xwindowdump* subtypes all identify data as being an X window dump. The order of the *image* mappings is important; the specific mappings are defined before the wildcard entry so that they take precedence.

Specifying mailcap entries

Since Mosaic defines its default mapping internally, there is no default mailcap file for you to edit. Instead, you have to create a mailcap file with entries that describe your desired use of external viewers. For example, on an HP machine running

VUE, you might want to use the **imageview** program to display all types of images. The following mailcap file performs that customization:

```
# Use 'imageview' for all types of images
image/*; imageview %s
```

A mailcap file consists of a set of entries, in which each entry describes the handling of a particular type of data. A mailcap entry consists of two fields separated by a semi-colon.* The first field, the content-type field, specifies the type of data that the entry handles; the second field, the view-command, describes how the data is to be displayed. Each entry in a mailcap file is terminated by a newline; a long entry can span multiple lines if each non-terminating line ends with a backslash (\). Blank lines and lines that begin with a pound sign (#) are taken to be comments and are ignored.

The content-type field is a MIME type/subtype specification. As you see in our example, you can use an asterisk as a wildcard to specify all of the subtypes of a particular type.

The view-command field requires a full shell command, including the pathname for the external viewer and any command-line arguments. The command is interpreted by the Bourne shell. Mosaic replaces the *%s* substitution string with the name of the file that contains the actual data, so the viewer displays the appropriate data.

For the mailcap entries you specify to take effect, you need to save the mailcap file in a location where Mosaic can read it. Here you need to decide whether you are making a system or site-wide customization, or simply a personal modification. If your change is a personal one, use the filename *.mailcap* and put it in your home directory. For global changes, put the file in */usr/local/lib/mosaic/mailcap*; you'll need superuser privileges to do this. You can use different filenames if you set the `personalTypeMap` and `globalTypeMap` resources respectively, as we discussed in Chapter 5, *Customizing Mosaic.*

Now, when you start Mosaic, it will use the alternate viewers you have specified. If you want to modify Mosaic's behavior while it is running, you can also do that. First, create or modify your mailcap file as necessary. Then select **Reload Config Files** from the **Options** menu, and Mosaic will read and apply the new mailcap entries.

Entries in a personal mailcap file take precedence over entries in the global file, which in turn take precedence over the default configuration. If you are a system administrator who is setting up Mosaic for an entire site, you should use a global mailcap file for site-wide modifications so that users can specify their own changes in a personal mailcap. As a result of the precedence mechanism, you only have to

---

* Actually, a mailcap entry can consist of more than two fields. The first two fields are required, however. They are also the only fields that are relevant to Mosaic's use of the mailcap file, so they are all we discuss here.

specify mailcap entries for those MIME types for which you want to define alternate viewers. There's no need to redefine entries for the default viewers.

If Mosaic encounters a MIME type it does not recognize, it passes the data to a special **mosaic-internal-dump** viewer. This internal routine dumps the file to your system; Mosaic prompts you for a filename when this happens. You can override this behavior by specifying a viewer for the MIME type `*/*`, but I don't think this is terribly useful as I don't know what viewer you would specify. However, the **mosaic-internal-dump** viewer is useful if there are certain types of data that you always want to dump to disk, rather than view externally. For example, to save all MPEG movie files locally, put the following entry in your mailcap file:

```
video/mpeg; mosaic-internal-dump
```

Now when you follow a link to a movie, Mosaic prompts you for a filename and saves the file, instead of displaying the movie with **mpeg-play**.

Handling a New Document Type

When you follow a link to a document, Mosaic determines the document's MIME type in one of two ways: it gets the type from the document's HTTP server, or it deduces the type from the document's file extension. To make this deduction, Mosaic relies on a mapping between file extensions and MIME types. If you want to configure Mosaic to support a new MIME type, you first need to create an extension map that associates the appropriate file extension with the type. Then you specify a mailcap entry that maps the new type to an external viewer that can display the data.

Mosaic's default internal mapping between file extensions and MIME types is shown in Table 6-5.

Table 6-5: Default Mapping of MIME Types to File Extensions

Content Type	File Extensions
application/octet-stream	*.uu, .saveme, .dump, .hqx, .arc, .o, .a, .bin, .exe*
application/oda	*.oda*
application/pdf	*.pdf*
application/postscript	*.eps, .ai, .ps,*
application/rtf	*.rtf*
application/x-dvi	*.dvi*
application/x-hdf	*.hdf*
application/x-latex	*.latex*
application/x-netcdf	*.cdf, .nc*
application/x-tex	*.tex*
application/x-texinfo	*.texinfo, .texi*
application/x-troff	*.t, .tr, .roff,*
application/x-troff-man	*.man*
application/x-troff-me	*.me*

Table 6–5: Default Mapping of MIME Types to File Extensions (continued)

Content Type	File Extensions
application/x-troff-ms	*.ms*
application/x-wais-source	*.src, .wsrc*
application/zip	*.zip*
application/x-bcpio	*.bcpio*
application/x-cpio	*.cpio*
application/x-gtar	*.gtar*
application/x-shar	*.shar, .sh*
application/x-sv4cpio	*.sv4cpio*
application/x-sv4crc	*.sv4crc*
application/x-tar	*.tar*
application/x-ustar	*.ustar*
audio/basic	*.snd, .au*
audio/x-aiff	*.aifc, .aif, .aiff*
audio/x-wav	*.wav*
image/gif	*.gif*
image/ief	*.ief*
image/jpeg	*.jfif, .jfif-tnbl, .jpe, .jpg, .jpeg*
image/x-tiff	*.tif, .tiff*
image/x-cmu-rast	*.ras*
image/x-portable-anymap	*.pnm*
image/x-portable-bitmap	*.pbm*
image/x-portable-graymap	*.pgm*
image/x-portable-pixmap	*.ppm*
image/x-rgb	*.rgb*
image/x-xbitmap	*.xbm*
image/x-xpixmap	*.xpm*
image/x-xwd	*.xwd*
text/html	*.htm, .html*
text/plain	*.text, .c, .cc, .c++, .h, .pl, .txt*
text/richtext	*.rtx*
text/tab-separated-values	*.tsv*
text/setext	*.etx*
video/mpeg	*.mpg, .mpe, .mpeg*
video/quicktime	*.mov, .qt*
video/x-msvideo	*.avi*
video/x-sgi-movie	*.movie, .mv*
message/rfc822	*.mime*

As you can see, there are quite a few more MIME types here than are handled by the default mailcap values. To simplify our discussion, we've been ignoring many of these types. The truth is that Mosaic handles many of them internally by displaying the data in its browsing area, so these types aren't relevant to our discussion of external viewers.

While you could use a mailcap file to configure Mosaic to display these types of data using an external viewer, there really isn't any good reason to do so.* In a few cases, as with *text/html*, *text/plain*, and *application/x-wais-source*, you cannot override the default behavior. The mappings for these types are hard-coded into Mosaic so that you cannot break the core functionality of the program.

Specifying an extension map

To add support for a new MIME type, you need to create an extension map file that contains the appropriate mapping. For example, if you have access to TGA images that you want to view with Mosaic, use the following extension map entry:

```
# The file extension .tga maps to the image/x-tga type
image/x-tga     tga
```

We've made up a new subtype name, beginning with *x-*, since none exists for TGA. We'll use this same subtype when we specify the viewer for TGA images in a mailcap entry.

An extension map file consists of entries in which each entry describes the file extensions for a single MIME type. You can map each MIME type to one or more file extensions. File extensions are separated by whitespace but not punctuation. Leading whitespace is not allowed—every line should begin with the first character of the MIME type. Comment lines start with a "#".† You should also note that extension mapping in Mosaic is case insensitive.

Just as with mailcap files, Mosaic looks for both a global extension map and a personal extension map. Site or system-wide configurations should be put in */usr/local/lib/mosaic/mime.types*. Your own extension map goes in *.mime.types* in your home directory. You can customize both of these locations with the `globalExtensionMap` and `personalExtensionMap` resources, respectively. Entries in a personal extension map take precedence over entries in a global extension map, which in turn take precedence over the hard-coded defaults.

Specifying a new viewer

Now that you have mapped the new MIME type to the appropriate file extensions, you simply have to specify the external viewer used to display the type. We've already described how to specify a mailcap entry; the process is no different for a new MIME type.

---

* Two exceptions, however, are the *application/x-hdf* and *application/x-netcdf* types. If Mosaic is compiled with internal support for HDF and netCDF, you may want to override the default functionality to display these types of data using an external viewer. For more information about HDF, see *http://www.ncsa.uiuc.edu/SDG/Software/HDF/HDFIntro.html*
† Early releases of Version 2.0 of Mosaic did not support comments, but Version 2.4 does.

For our example, we want to use the **xli** viewer for TGA images, so we would add the following entry to a mailcap file:

```
# Use 'xli' for TGA images
image/x-tga; xli %s
```

Now, when you start Mosaic, it will display TGA images using the **xli** viewer. If you want to modify Mosaic's behavior while it is running, use the **Reload Config Files** command so that Mosaic reads the new extension map and mailcap files.

Executing Shell Scripts

Imagine using Mosaic as a front-end to a number of other applications in a local client/server environment. You could have a document that explains the various applications and provides hyperlinks for each of them. When the user clicks on a link, the application starts running on the local machine. All that's required for this scenario to work is a way to have a link execute a local process—a shell script that can call other programs. You can configure Mosaic to provide this functionality, but doing so raises some security issues. Let's set up the functionality first, and then we'll go over the security concerns.

Configuring Mosaic to execute shell scripts involves creating an extension map and a mailcap entry, so we're really just adding support for a new MIME type. First, put the following mapping in an extension map file:

```
application/x-csh     csh
```

This mapping identifies any files that have a *.csh* file extension as shell scripts. Now put the following mailcap entry in a mailcap file:

```
application/x-csh; csh -f %s
```

This specifies that **csh -f** is used as the viewer for shell scripts. Now when you access a document that Mosaic identifies as a shell script, Mosaic executes the script on your local machine.

For example, say you wanted to have a clock icon be a hyperlink to a shell script that runs the **oclock** application. Create the following shell script:

```
#!/bin/csh
/usr/bin/X11/oclock &
```

To see how the process works, save the script in a file called *clock.csh*. Make sure that you have set up the extension map and the mailcap entry shown above and reloaded the configuration files using **Reload Config Files**. Now select **Open Local** from the **File** menu and open the *clock.csh* file. Mosaic will execute the shell script and you should see the **oclock** application appear on your display. Once you learn how to write HTML files in Chapter 7, *Creating HTML Documents*, you can put links to scripts like this in your Web documents.

Security issues

Clearly, configuring Mosaic so that any random shell script can execute on your local machine is a major security hole. Anyone running a Web server could create a dangerous shell script and set up a link to it. If you follow that link, the script is run on your system, causing whatever damage the author intended.

We want to make it clear right now that the default configuration of Mosaic does not support the *application/x-csh* type or anything else like it. This security hole does not exist *unless* you configure Mosaic to make it exist.

If you want to configure Mosaic so that it can execute shell scripts, there are a few techniques you can use to minimize the security risks. We will briefly present a couple of techniques. For more information on the range of possible techniques, consult the *Executing Shell Scripts Inside Mosaic* page using the following URL: Inside Mosaic"

```
http://www.ncsa.uiuc.edu/SDG/Software/Mosaic/Docs/executing-shell-scripts.html
```

The safest way to handle the security hole is to restrict severely the use of the specially-configured Mosaic client. If you only allow this client to access local files that are known to be safe, then there is no danger of a malicious shell script wreaking havoc on your system. You need to make sure that the specially-configured version of Mosaic is not used to browse the Net. You might want to create a shell script called **xdangerousmosaic** that starts Mosaic using the dangerous mailcap file, just to make the distinction very clear.

If you want to browse the Net with a Mosaic client that can run shell scripts, there's no way to be completely secure. You can protect yourself to some degree, however, by setting up Mosaic so that you can decide whether or not to execute a shell script on a per-script basis. Basically, you need to create a viewer for shell scripts that does the following:

- Takes a filename as a command-line argument.

- Reads the file and displays it.

- Asks you whether or not to execute the script.

- Executes the script only if you say to.

The following shell script, *safe.csh*, is one possible implementation of such a viewer. It uses an X utility called **xmessage** to display the shell script and ask you what to do.

```
#!/bin/csh -f
    xmessage -buttons "Execute this file,Cancel" -file $1
    if ($status == 101) then
            csh -f $1
    endif
```

If you want to use this shell script as a viewer, you need to make sure you have **xmessage** on your system. The source code is available from the X Consortium's FTP server; use the following URL:

```
ftp://ftp.x.org/contrib/utilities
```

Make sure that the **safe.csh** script is executable and that it is in your PATH. You also need to put the following entry in a mailcap file:

```
application/x-csh; safe.csh %s
```

Now when you follow a link to a document of type *application/x-csh*, Mosaic displays the shell script, and you can decide whether or not to execute it.

Recording Audio

In Chapter 2, *Getting Started with Mosaic*, we explained how you can add your own personal comments to a document using annotations. On some machines, notably SGIs, Suns, and HPs, you can record an audio annotation. In order for audio annotations to work, your system needs to have a properly installed audio recording program. You also need to set the recordCommandLocation and recordCommand resources appropriately. (See Chapter 5 for general information on setting resources.)

The recordCommandLocation resource specifies the full pathname of a program that records audio files. The default value is */usr/sbin/recordaiff* on SGI machines, */usr/demo/SOUND/record* on Suns, and */usr/audio/bin/srecorder* on HPs. If this program does not exist when Mosaic starts, Mosaic disables audio annotations.

The recordCommand resource specifies the full command for recording; the first word of the command is the program specified by recordCommandLocation. The default value is **recordaiff -n 1 -s 8 -r 8000** on SGI machines, **record** on Sun's, and **srecorder -au** on HP's. The specified command must take one additional argument: the filename of the new audio file. The program also needs to correctly stop recording when Mosaic sends it a SIGINT signal.

One last bit of work involves making sure that your system has a working microphone. Check that audio input is set to the microphone and the recording volume is high enough. On SGI systems, you can use **/usr/sbin/apanel** to adjust the record volume. On Sun machines, use **/usr/demo/SOUND/gaintool**.

## CHAPTER SEVEN

CREATING HTML DOCUMENTS

The Power of Hypertext
The Hypertext Theory of Relativity
Getting Started
Writing HTML
Creating Your Own Home Page
Using HoTMetaL to Create Documents
Resources

S o far in this book we've talked about viewing other people's World Wide Web pages. Now we're going to turn the tables and show you how to create your own Web pages. It's not something that requires programming experience or any special skills. All you need is access to a Web server on the Internet (one that uses the HTTP protocol) and the ability to tag text files according to the HTML specification.

Writing HTML documents is actually pretty easy. You can create them using any editor that can save files in plain ASCII text format. Most word processors can write ASCII files, and nearly every text editor writes ASCII files normally.

Unfortunately, there are relatively few tools that help in the process. One of them is Mosaic itself, which lets you preview HTML pages located on your local system. Another is HoTMetaL, a WYSIWYG (what you see is what you get) editor for writing HTML. We'll discuss using both of these programs in this chapter.

We'll also go through the standard HTML tags in some detail. While we won't cover every aspect of HTML, we will cover the most common and important tags. You may not be an expert by the time you finish with this chapter, but you will be able to write sophisticated documents for the Web.

The Power of Hypertext

The Web adds a new dimension to writing documents—building hypertext links that connect one document or topic to another. Hypertext is a powerful way to help users navigate through information. To understand just how powerful, think about the way we navigate through printed books. There's a table of contents that describes the content of each chapter; an index that tells you where specific references are located; footnotes and annotations that refer to other sections of the book or to other works; and finally there's the body of the book itself, which (with the exception of mystery novels) most people just flip through and scan for information that catches their eye.

Hypertext incorporates all these modes of navigating and adds the instant gratification of seeing a referenced work or section immediately. Within the pages of a hypertext server, an author can point to other pages of general content, point to specific information, let users jump to other works, and let them move through a collection of information in either a linear or nonlinear way.

In many cases, Web documents are multimedia documents with graphics, sound, and video files, as well as text. This presents the author with yet another question—how to combine and present all of these media in a unified document.

Almost all servers have a *home page*, a front door to the server that provides links to other documents. A home page is a place where you can assert your identity, explain the purpose and scope of your server, and set up links to other documents. Later in this chapter, we'll work on creating your own home page.

The Hypertext Theory of Relativity

HTML is the markup language for World Wide Web documents. A subset of *SGML* (*Standard Generalzed Markup Language*), HTML is a standardized language for creating formatted hypertext documents. It lets you perform two main tasks: defining hypertext anchors and links, and describing the format of the document.

Formatting is defined only in rather general, often relative terms. HTML does not tell Mosaic, for example, "Make this line 36 pt. Palatino." It simply identifies the text as a heading, and Mosaic uses that description to format and display the text.

The reason that HTML describes documents in general rather than specific terms is that there is no single World Wide Web browser that everyone uses. There are several different browsers, and more are likely to be developed in the future. What they have in common is that they are all able to display HTML documents. But they all do it differently.

The differences between browsers tend to reflect the limitations of different computing environments. For instance, Mosaic runs in a graphical user interface, so it can display graphics, type styles, and point sizes. Lynx is for character-based environments, so it makes do with more limited formatting capabilities. Some future computer platform might translate all text into spoken words, and a browser for that system might read plain text in a calm voice and headings in hearty yells.

In addition, not all users have the same set of fonts, so a document that specifies Palatino for headlines might use Courier on a system that doesn't include Palatino. That's a common problem when PC users try to share files, and it's one that HTML avoids by leaving the formatting to the browser.

The basic philosophy of HTML is that authors need not be concerned with the way the document will look; that's the job of the browser. If the file is tagged correctly, each browser will display the document to the best of its abilities.

Getting Started

You already have the most important tool for writing HTML—Mosaic itself. You can use Mosaic to preview documents on your local system by using the **Open Local** command. This works just like the **Open** command in any X application: it launches a dialog box that lets you open a file on your system. Since you're working on local files, this is one time you don't have to be on the network to use Mosaic.

You can also access local files with the **Open URL** command or the **Open** button. In this case, you need to specify the full pathname of the file on your system.

As we go through examples in this chapter, you can try writing your own HTML documents and previewing them in Mosaic. Remember to save your work as text files and to use the extension *.html*.

Let's see what this is all about. First, let's take a look at a real-world document. Figure 7-1 is *GNN*'s *What's Up* page as seen in Mosaic. Here is part of the HTML document that describes the page:

```
<HTML><HEAD>
<TITLE>GNN Home Page</TITLE>
</HEAD><BODY>
<A HREF="/gnn/wel/welcome.html">
<IMG ALT="Global Network Navigator -- Charting the Internet"
SRC="/gnn/graphics/HOME.gif"></A>
<P>
<IMG ALT="What's Up?" SRC="/gnn/graphics/WU.xbm">
<UL>
<LI>
Looking to the Net for election information? In a logic-defying move,
the U.S. Senate has declared a July 23-November 8 moratorium on
electronic postings by Senate candidates to the
Senate gopher server. If it knew better, it might also ban Web
servers such as Ted Kennedy's. Get the scoop in
<A HREF="/gnn/meta/internet/feat/senate/senate-freeze.html">
<B>The Internet Election Freeze</B></A>, this week in the
<A HREF="/gnn/meta/internet/index.html"> Internet Center</A>.
<P>
</BODY></HTML>
```

If that looks discouraging, don't worry. It's really not that bad. In fact, once you get the vocabulary down, HTML is quite a simple beast to master. As you can see from the *GNN* example above, you can create quite sophisticated documents using HTML.

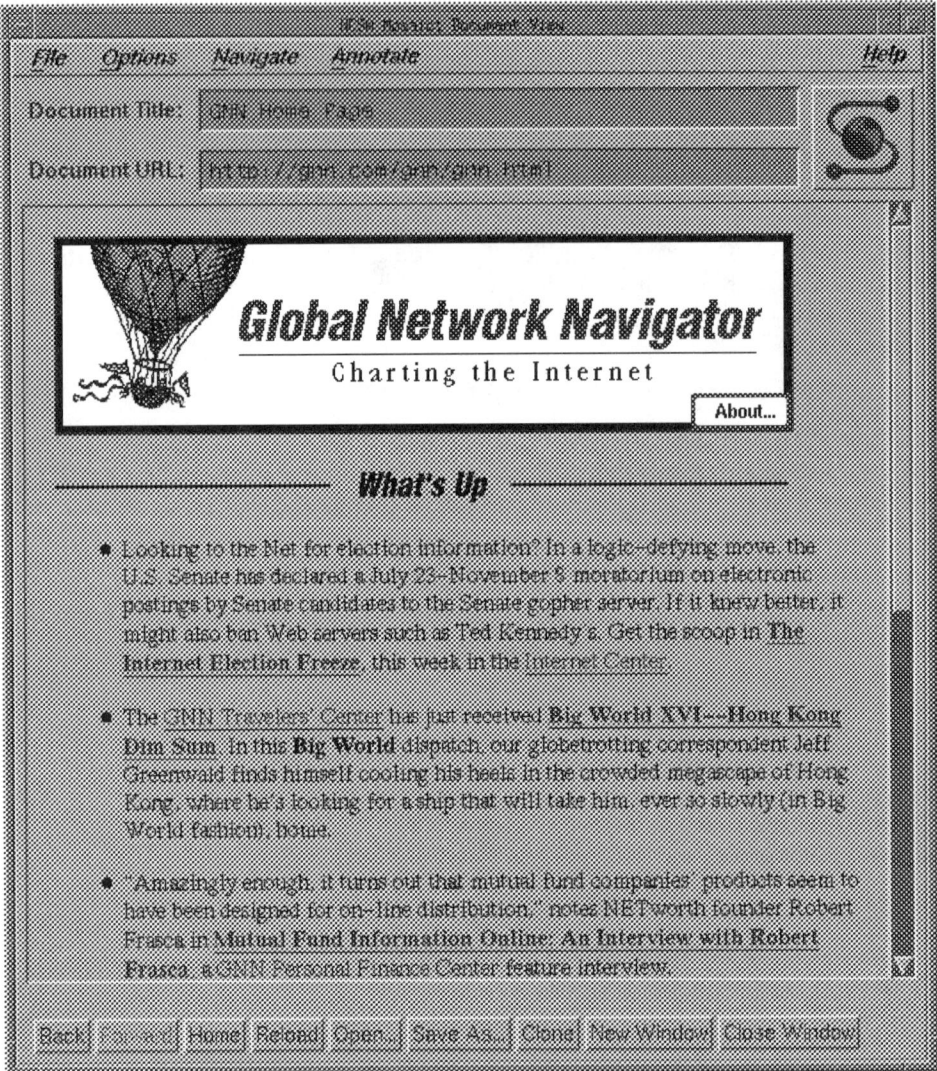

Figure 7-1. Screen shot of GNN's What's Up page

There are three basic conventions of the HTML language, and once you understand them, writing HTML is a breeze. These conventions are tags, attributes, and URLs.

Tags

The most basic element in an HTML document is a tag, which is usually bracketed by the "less than" and "greater than" signs, < and >. Tags often come in pairs and surround text, much like quotation marks, with one tag starting the action and another tag ending it. Ending tags look just like starting tags except for a slash mark preceding the tag name within the brackets. For instance, <H1> is the starting tag for a top-level headline and </H1> is the ending tag. Here's a simple example of how tags are used in HTML:

```
<TITLE>This is the title</TITLE>
<H1>This is a headline</H1>
This is plain text.
```

Some tags work by themselves without ending tags. These tags usually identify special characters or tell the browser to insert something. For instance, the tag &amp represents the ampersand (&). Often tags are nested inside one another. Some tags accept nesting while others do not. Nesting is often used with lists to create an outline format.

Finally, tags are exclusive, not additive. Two tags can't be added together to create a hybrid effect. Each tag has its own formatting, completely independent of nearby tags. For instance, if you have a sentence in italic (using the <I> tag) and want to put a word or two in bold italic, you might think that just placing the bold tags (<B> and </B>) around the words would work:

```
<I>An italic sentence with <B>bold-italic </B>type.</I>
```

It doesn't. Each subsequent tag supersedes the previous tags, so you get regular bold, not bold-italic:

An italic sentence with **bold-italic** *type.*

Combining the tags (<BI>) doesn't work for the same reason. In fact, there really is no way to call out bold-italic type in HTML.

Attributes

With some tags, you need to use attributes to define exactly how the action will work. These attributes vary from tag to tag. They are like multiple-choice questions; there are several possible answers, or values, for each attribute. The syntax for using attributes is:

```
<TAG ATTRIBUTE="VALUE">
```

In this chapter, we'll talk about the most important attributes for each of the tags, but we won't necessarily cover all of them. Refer to Appendix B, *HTML Reference Guide*, for more information about these attributes.

URLs

Attributes are often used to specify files as links. To specify a file, use the document's URL as the value of an attribute. For example, IMG, the tag used to include a graphic or figure, takes the attribute SRC (for "source") to indicate which file to use. In this case, the document's URL is the value of SRC:

```
<IMG SRC="http://gnn.com/graphics/HOME.gif">
```

For a more detailed discussion of URLs, see Chapter 2, *Getting Started with Mosaic.*

Writing HTML

There are two steps in creating a page for the Web—formatting the document and building links to other files. To start, let's go through a simple HTML document. This is the HTML document for the home page of a fictional server about the Marx Brothers comedy team. Figure 7-2 shows how the page appears in Mosaic.

```
<HTML>
<HEAD>
<TITLE>The Marx Brothers Home Page</TITLE></HEAD>
<BODY>
<H1>The Marx Brothers Web Server</H1>
Welcome Marx Brothers Fans!
<HR>
Get Information About The Brothers By Clicking On Their Names:
<P><A HREF="groucho.html">GROUCHO</A>
<P><A HREF="harpo.html">HARPO</A>
<P><A HREF="chico.html">CHICO</A>
<P><A HREF="zeppo.html">ZEPPO</A>
</BODY></HTML>
```

Identification Tags

An HTML document consists of several tags that give information to the browser but don't actually affect the content. These tags give the title of the document and tell the browser when the header starts and ends, when the body starts and ends, and so on.

Document identifier tag

```
<HTML> and </HTML>
```

The Marx Brothers document opens with the <HTML> tag. <HTML> is the opening tag for all Web documents. It tells the Web browser that this is in fact an HTML document and not some other structured document. </HTML> marks the end of the document. Note that everything else in the document is nested inside these two tags. In fact, Mosaic and most other browsers do not insist on the use of these tags, but using them may prove to be more important in the future.

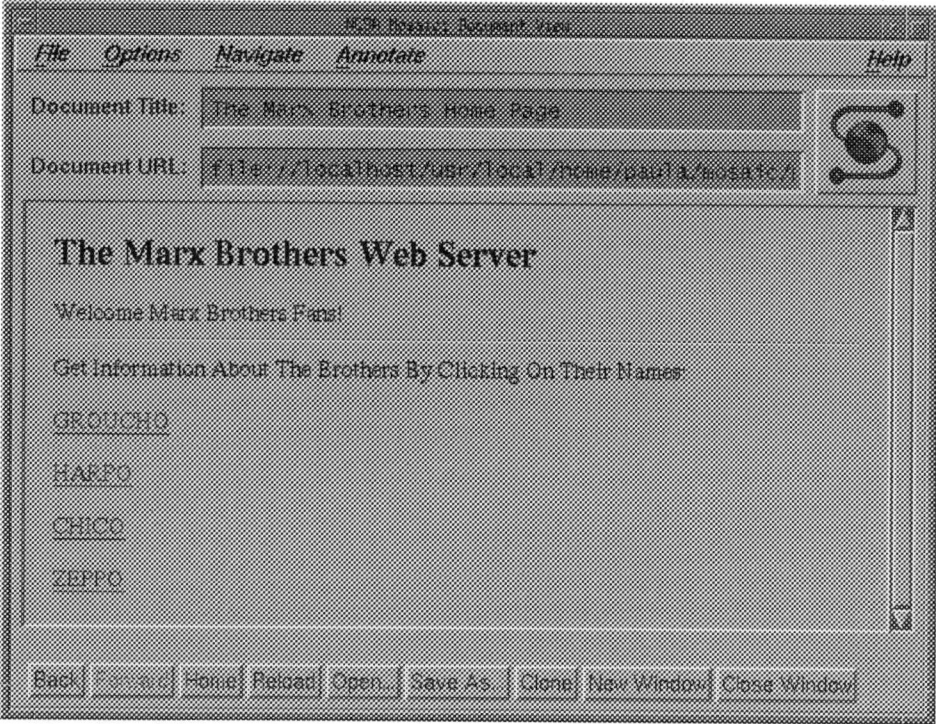

Figure 7–2. Marx Brothers Home Page

Header

<HEAD> and </HEAD>

While there are actually several elements that can be included in the header, the only important one is the title.

Title

<TITLE> and </TITLE>

The title is the name of the document as it appears in the browser's title window, history list, and hotlist. The title tag is part of the header, thus it needs to be within the two header tags.

There are a few technical rules worth mentioning here:

- There may only be one title in any document.

- The title cannot contain anchors (explained later), paragraph marks, or text formatting.

- It is not normally displayed in the text of a document itself, although the opening heading could consist of the same text as the title.

- While there is technically no limit to the length of a title, it's a good idea to keep it less than 64 characters. This is because some browsers may truncate it in window titles, menus, and hotlists.

- Each document within the collection of documents should have a unique title.

- The title should describe the page out of context. That is, it should refer to the whole collection of documents, not just a specific document. You can imagine how confusing it would be if you followed a hypertext link only to arrive at a page labeled merely "Home Page."

In the following example, the title is nested within the header tags, which in turn are nested within the document identifier tags. The ellipsis represents the body of the document, which is itself nested within the HTML tags.

```
<HTML>
     <HEAD>
          <TITLE>The Marx Brothers Home Page
          </TITLE>
     </HEAD>
          . . .
</HTML>
```

Body identifier

```
<BODY> and </BODY>
```

We're almost ready to start writing the document, but there is one more technical item. The body tag indicates that we're ready to start the actual document. Now you might think that since we explicitly ended the header, the Web browser would be able to tell where the body starts, but HTML calls for an explicit tag to start the body. In fact, Mosaic and other browsers don't insist on the use of the body tag, but again, it's a good practice and may be important to future browsers.

Crafting the Page: Formatting Text

HTML provides a number of ways to control the visual presentation of text on the screen. While it doesn't provide precise control over the placement of text and graphics, it does enable you to specify a great deal about the way your page is structured.

Headings

```
<H1> and </H1>  . . .  <H6> and </H6>
```

There are six levels of headings, with <H1> having the most emphasis and <H6> having the least. Exactly how these headings are displayed is up to the different browsers. Mosaic displays <H1> in large bold text, while Lynx puts the header text in all caps and centers it. The other header elements, <H2> through <H6>, are of gradually reduced emphasis.

Don't use header elements below <H3>, because the display of these minor levels is notoriously inconsistent between browsers; a small but readable header in one browser may be indecipherable in another. More importantly, if you feel the need to have more than three levels of information, consider breaking the document up into several smaller documents and linking the documents to each other. Each document could then have its own <H1> element.

In the following example, we've added the body tag, an <H1> header, and some plain text. The text between the <H1> tags is the first thing the user will see. Viewed in Mosaic, it will be the biggest text on the page. <H1> indicates the start of the heading text and </H1> indicates the end of it. The next line of text has no formatting codes, so it is presented as regular text. Figure 7-3 is a screen shot of this page in Mosaic.

```
<HTML>
<HEAD>
<TITLE>The Marx Brothers Home Page
</TITLE>
</HEAD>
<BODY>
<H1>The Marx Brothers Web Server
</H1>
Welcome Marx Brothers fans!
```

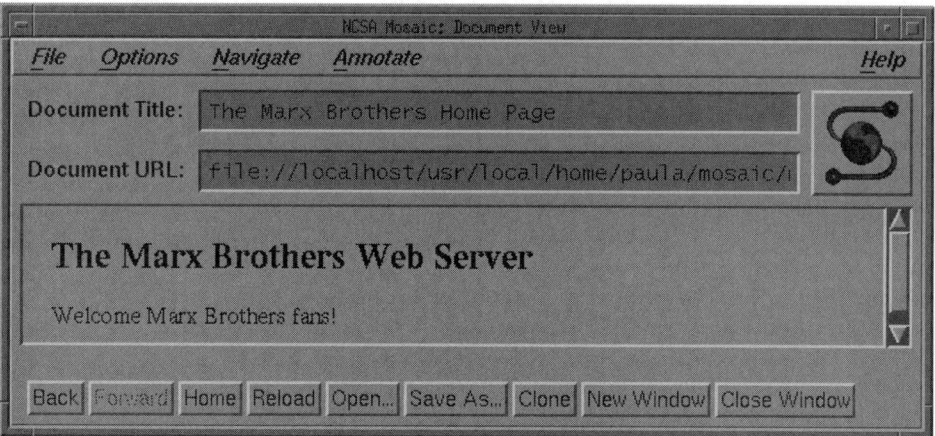

Figure 7–3. Document with an <H1> heading and plain text viewed in Mosaic

Breaking paragraphs and lines

As far as HTML is concerned, the only thing you can do with a keyboard is type text. It does not respond to even rudimentary formatting techniques, such as entering carriage returns or extra spaces. To format text, even to indicate the beginning of a new paragraph, you must use tags. In this section, we'll discuss the tags that let you control the structure of text on the page. Note that these tags do not require ending tags.

Paragraphs <P>

The paragraph tag starts a new paragraph. Since carriage returns are ignored, you could simply place paragraph tags at the appropriate place in a block of text, like this:

```
Paragraph one.<P>Paragraph two.<P>Paragraph three.
```

or you could insert returns to make it easier for you to visualize the page, like this:

```
Paragraph one.
<P>Paragraph two.
<P>Paragraph three.
```

The result would be the same—three separate paragraphs. Exactly how those paragraphs would be displayed would, of course, be up to the individual browsers. Most browsers insert space after a paragraph, so there's no need for more than one paragraph tag. In fact you'll want to keep an eye out for redundant paragraph tags, as some browsers (Lynx, for instance) will insert space for every paragraph tag. Mosaic, on the other hand, ignores extra paragraph tags.

**Line Breaks
**

What do you do if want to break a line but you don't want to start a new paragraph? Simple. Use <BR> for a line break. This tag starts a new line but doesn't format a new paragraph. It is commonly used to format a block of text, such as an address:

```
Name<BR>
Address<BR>
Phone Number
<P>
```

Rules <HR>

To make a horizontal rule, don't make the mistake of just typing a bunch of underline characters. Because various browsers may be set up for different line widths, this may create unattractive effects for some users. Instead, use <HR>. It causes a paragraph break and draws a horizontal rule across the screen.

In the following example, we've added paragraph tags, line break tags, and a horizontal rule to the Marx Brothers Home Page. Figure 7-4 shows the display of this document in Mosaic. There are three separate paragraphs on this page. Note that no paragraph tag is used before the horizontal rule because the <HR> tag automatically starts a new paragraph.

```
<HTML>
<HEAD>
<TITLE>The Marx Brothers Home Page</TITLE>
</HEAD>
<BODY>
<H1>The Marx Brothers Web Server</H1>
Welcome Marx Brothers fans!
<P>This server takes as its philosophy Groucho's opening song from
"Horse Feathers":
<P>"Whatever it is, I'm against it<BR>
No matter whose it is or who commenced it,<BR>
I'm against it!"
<HR>
```

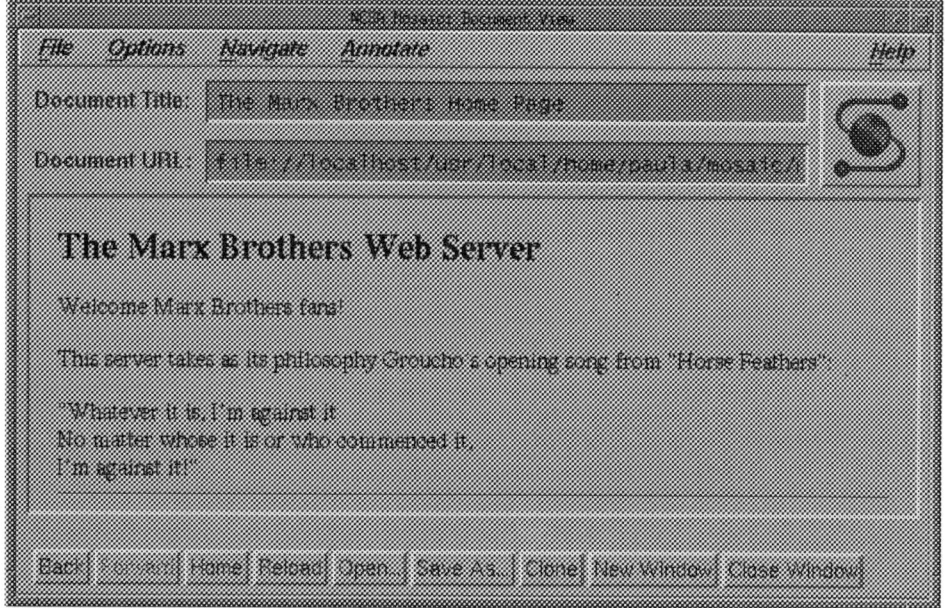

Figure 7–4. Document with paragraphs, line breaks, and horizontal rule viewed in Mosaic

Lists and glossaries

The list and glossary tags can be powerful because they allow for fairly sophisticated formatting through simple tags. Lists are a good illustration of the power of HTML because they let the author generally indicate the nature of the information, while the browsers take care of the exact format.

Lists are simply paragraphs, sentences, phrases or single words presented in an itemized format. There are several kinds of lists. The most commonly used ones are ordered lists and unordered lists. Ordered lists are usually numbered, while most browsers present unordered lists with bullets.

Glossaries have a structure in which each item is a term followed by a definition. The terms are usually short items, while the definitions can be several paragraphs in length. Both glossaries and lists can be nested.

Lists

Entries in unordered lists are preceded by bullets. Entries in ordered lists are preceded by numbers in ascending order. Lists start with an opening tag (<UL> for unordered lists, <OL> for ordered lists) and end with a closing tag. Each item in the list is preceded by the <LI> tag, which does not require a closing tag. The syntax for an unordered list is:

```
<UL>
<LI>Text
<LI>Text
</UL>
```

This example shows an unordered list in HTML, and Figure 7-5 shows the list displayed in Mosaic.

```
Here is a list of the Marx Brothers' Paramount films:
<UL>
<LI>The Cocoanuts (1929)
<LI>Animal Crackers (1930)
<LI>Monkey Business (1931)
<LI>Horse Feathers (1932)
<LI>Duck Soup (1933)
</UL>
```

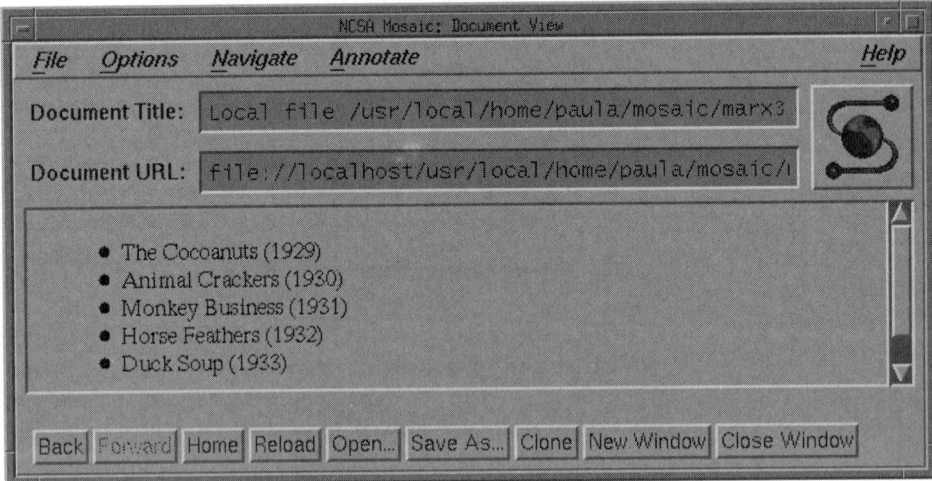

Figure 7-5. An unordered list viewed in Mosaic

The syntax is very similar for ordered lists, with just the opening and closing tags changing:

```
<OL>
<LI>Text
<LI>Text
</OL>
```

Figure 7-6 shows what the previous example looks like in Mosaic if we use an ordered list instead of an unordered one.

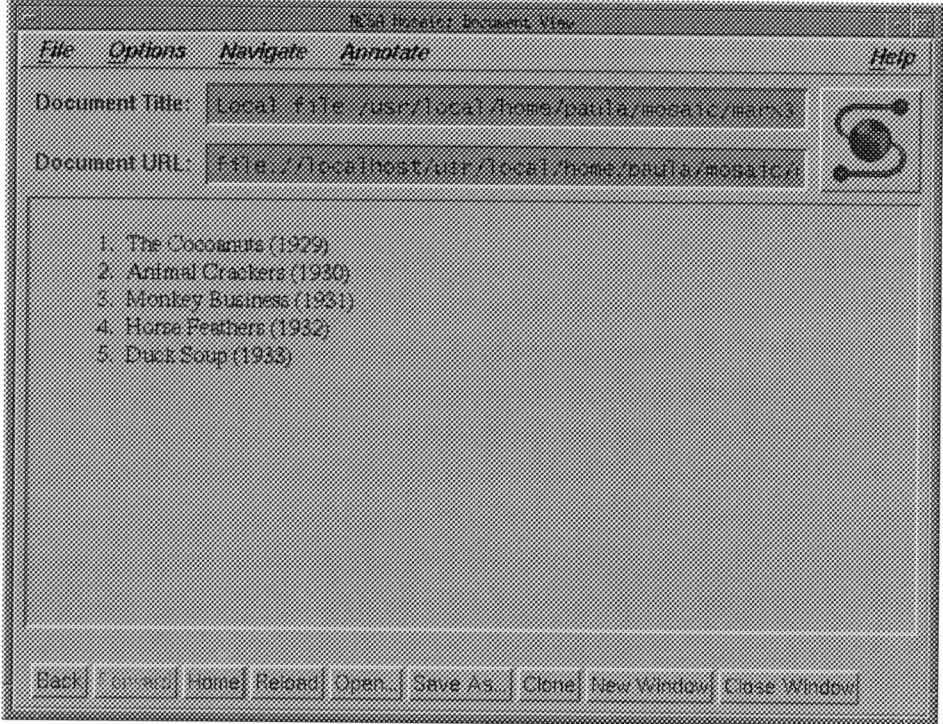

Figure 7–6. An ordered list viewed in Mosaic

Both ordered and unordered lists can be nested to create an outline format, and both kinds of lists can be combined within a larger list. For instance, the following example is a table of contents in which unordered lists are nested within an ordered list. Figure 7-7 shows the list as viewed in Mosaic.

```
<H1>Table of Contents</H1>
<OL>
<LI>Vaudeville Days
        <UL>
        <LI>Fun in Hi Skule
        <LI>Mr. Green's Reception
```

```
                <LI>Home Again
                </UL>
    <LI>On Broadway
            <UL>
            <LI>I'll Say She Is (1924)
            <LI>The Cocoanuts (1925)
            <LI>Animal Crackers (1928)
            </UL>
    <LI>The Paramount Films
            <UL>
            <LI>The Cocoanuts (1929)
            <LI>Animal Crackers (1930)
            <LI>Monkey Business (1931)
            <LI>Horsefeathers (1932)
            <LI>Duck Soup (1933)
            </UL>
    </OL>
```

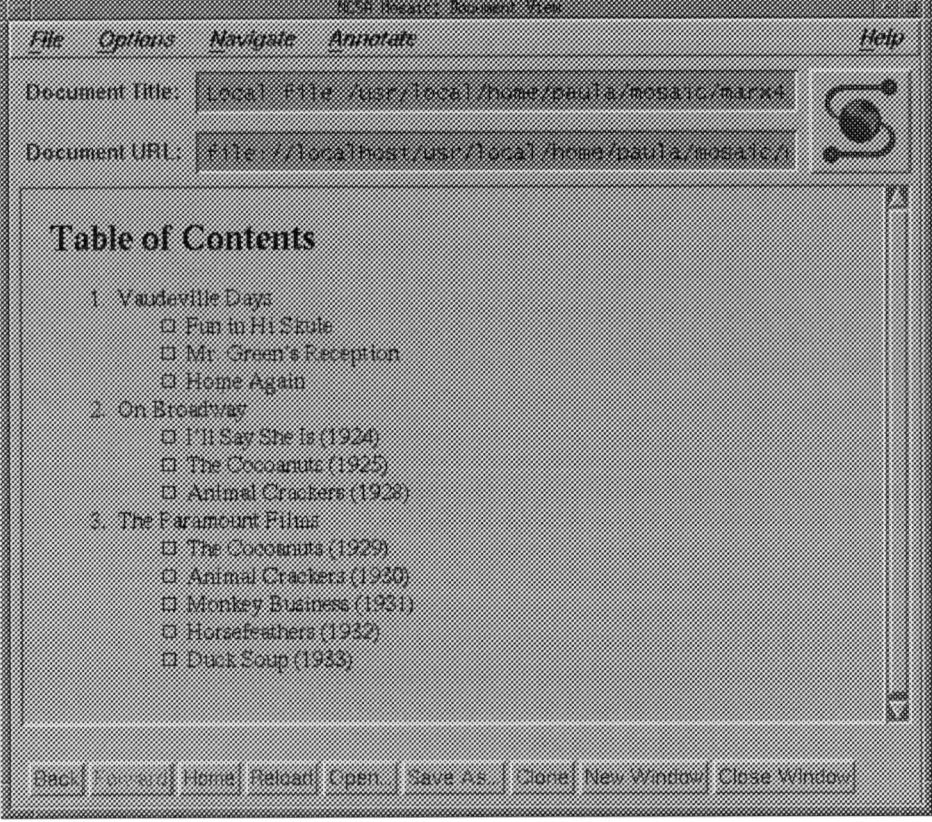

Figure 7-7. Table of Contents with nested lists, viewed in Mosaic

Glossaries

As mentioned earlier, glossaries consist of terms, which are usually short, and longer descriptions, which are indented in Mosaic. Glossaries use four tags:

- `<DL>` to start the glossary
- `<DT>` for the main entry or term
- `<DD>` for the descriptive paragraph, or definition
- `</DL>` to end the glossary

The syntax is:

```
<DL>
<DT>Term One
<DD>Definition of Term One.
<DT>Term Two
<DD>Definition of Term Two.
</DL>
```

The following example gives the HTML for a two-item glossary. Figure 7-8 shows how the glossary is presented in Mosaic.

```
<H2>Marx Brothers Film Summaries</H2>
<DL>
<DT>"The Cocoanuts" (1929)
<DD>Their first film, for Paramount, puts the brothers in Florida during
the land boom of the 1920s. It features the famous "Why a Duck?" routine
with Groucho and Chico.
<DT>"Animal Crackers" (1930)
<DD>Like "The Cocoanuts," based on a Broadway show of the same name,
"Animal Crackers" features Groucho as Captain Spaulding, the African explorer.
<P>It boasts the classic line: "One morning I shot an elephant in my pajamas.
How he got in my pajamas, I don't know."
</DL>
```

Note that `<P>` can be used within definitions to create multiple paragraphs. Other formatting tags, except the heading tags, can also be used. You can also nest ordered and unordered lists within a glossary. For example, you could include an outline (which could include many nested lists) within a glossary definition.

Text attributes

```
<EM> and </EM>
<STRONG> and </STRONG>
<B> and </B>
<I> and </I>
<U> and </U>
```

There are two kinds of tags for text attributes in HTML—physical styles (bold, italic, underline) and logical styles, which let the author format based on his intentions rather than having to specify the exact look of the text. The primary logical

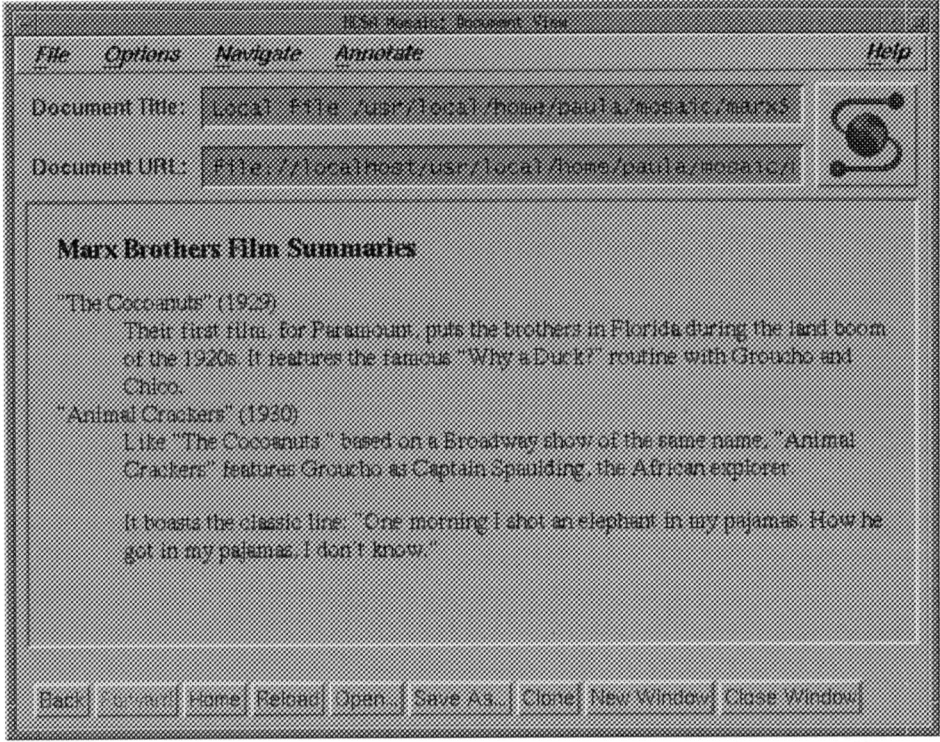

Figure 7-8. HTML glossary as viewed in Mosaic

styles are <EM> (for emphasized text) and <STRONG> (for even more emphasized text). The idea is that emphasized text is visually louder than plain text and stronger text is louder still, as shown below:

```
This is very important: <EM>Always lock the door when you leave.</EM>
<STRONG>Always.</STRONG>
```

Figure 7-9 shows how this is presented in Mosaic. As a rule, you should use <EM> and <STRONG> instead of the physical styles (<B>, <I>, and <U>). This is because every browser understands these tags and interprets them in a relative, rather than absolute way. That is, while different browsers display <EM> and <STRONG> differently, they will all display <EM> text as louder than plain text and <STRONG> text as louder than <EM> text.

In X Mosaic and Windows Mosaic, text tagged with <EM> displays in italic, and text tagged as <STRONG> displays in bold. Mac Mosaic underlines the emphasized text and puts strong text in bold. Lynx underlines emphasized text and does the same for strong text.

As for underlining—don't. Underlined text is too easily confused with hypertext links, which are often underlined.

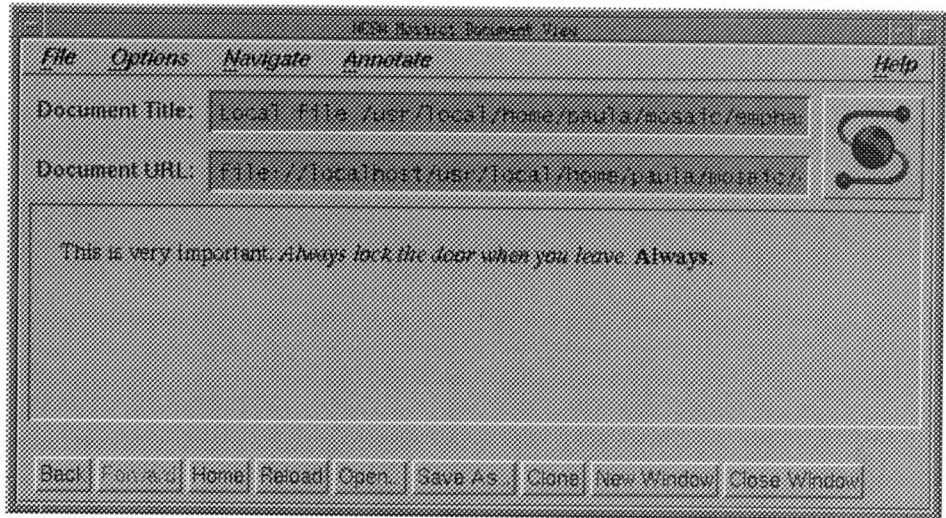

Figure 7-9. EM and STRONG types viewed in Mosaic

Preformatted text

<PRE> and </PRE>

Sometimes you want to control exactly the way text will look. You can do that (within limitations) by using the <PRE> tag. Preformatted text always appears in a monospaced font like Courier, and unlike with other HTML text, carriage returns and extra spaces work. For these reasons, many people use preformatted text for tables, like this:

```
<PRE>
Title               Date
A Night at the Opera   1937
A Day at the Races     1938
At the Circus          1939
Go West                1940
The Big Store          1941
</PRE>
```

You can use most other tags, including hypertext links, within preformatted text.

Address format

<ADDRESS> and </ADDRESS>

This tag was originally intended as a format for contact information at the bottom of a page, but you can use it whenever you want to set a paragraph such as a date apart from the rest of the page. Text appears in italics.

Special characters

What do you do when you want to use characters that have special meanings in HTML? There are four such characters:

<	the left angle bracket
>	the right angle bracket
&	ampersand
"	quote marks

HTML includes character combinations, called escape sequences, to represent these characters in an HTML document. They are:

&lt;	the escape sequence for <
&gt;	the escape sequence for >
&amp;	the escape sequence for &
&quot;	the escape sequence for "

It is important to note that escape sequences are case-sensitive, unlike all other HTML tags. There are many more escape sequences for non-ASCII characters. Some of the more common ones are:

&ouml;	the escape sequence for a lowercase o with an umlaut (ö)
&ntilde;	the escape sequence for a lowercase n with a tilde (ñ)
&Egrave;	the escape sequence for an uppercase E with a grave accent (È)

Weaving Threads: Anchor Links

<A> and </A>

Now for the fun part—creating anchors and hypertext links. As discussed earlier, links are the way that users are guided through a body of hypertext information. In the parlance of HTML, an anchor is the hypertext itself—the element that the user selects in order to go to the linked document. An anchor can be a word, a phrase, a picture, an icon, or anything that can be displayed on an HTML page. The linked item, that is, the place the user goes after clicking on the anchor, can be any file—not just another HTML document, but also a Gopher menu, a WAIS database, an FTP site, etc. For the sake of simplicity, however, we'll talk primarily about linking HTML documents together.

Linking to other documents

By now you're quite familiar with how to recognize and use hypertext links. In this section, you'll learn how to create them. We'll start by discussing how to link to other documents on your system, then we'll move on to linking to other documents on the Internet.

You'll probably start out writing your documents on your local system, but at some point, you'll need to move your files over to an HTTP server to make them available on the Web. For that reason, it's a good idea to use only filenames in your links, not directory names, since your files will have a different path on the server than they do on your local system.

The first step is to create an anchor, which you do with the anchor tag <A>, and the HREF attribute. The anchor tag tells the browser, "Make the following text a hypertext anchor," and HREF tells it, "Link the anchor to this file." Here's the syntax:

```
<A HREF="filename">HYPERTEXT</A>
```

Consider the original Marx Brothers home page shown in Figure 7-10. The mouse is positioned over the word "Groucho," which is displayed as a hypertext anchor. At the bottom of the screen Mosaic displays the name of the file that is linked to this anchor. Here is the HTML that causes Mosaic to display "Groucho" as a hypertext anchor.

```
<A HREF="groucho.html">Groucho</A>
```

This line says: Make the word "Groucho" an anchor that links to the file *groucho.html*. In this case, the file is on the same computer and in the same directory as the active page, so we only gave the filename. But we could link to a file in another directory on the same computer, or to another computer on the Internet.

Let's add to this page a hypertext anchor that links to a document on another server. To do this, we need to give the URL of the linked file. The hypertext will say, "Learn more about the 1930s," and will link to the home page of a collection of documents about the 1930s that exists on a computer called **college.edu**. Here's the HTML:

```
<A HREF="http://college.edu/USHistory/1930s/HomePage.html">Learn
more about the 1930s</A>
```

When users click on the anchor, they are connected to **college.edu** and the linked page is displayed.

When creating links, remember that you can link to any file, not just an HTML page. You can create links to video, audio, graphic, or CAD files. The only proviso is that users need to have external viewers to handle these files, so you'll probably want to stick to the common formats. See Chapter 6, *Using Mosaic for Multimedia*, for more on file formats.

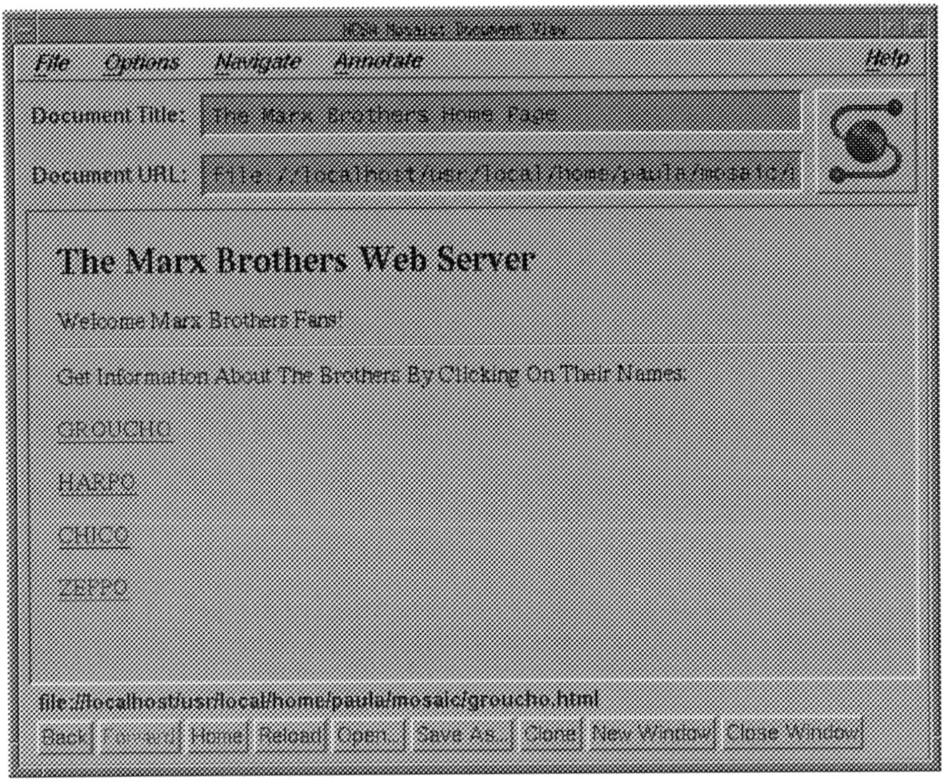

Figure 7–10. Hypertext links displayed in status bar in Mosaic

Naming anchors

Another feature of the anchor tag is the ability to name anchors. This is a helpful navigation technique for large documents. By linking to a named anchor, you can take the user right to a specific part of the page, as illustrated in Figure 7-11. While, in theory, you could link to a named anchor on another server, it's much more common to use names within your own server or within a single page. Let's say you want to set up an anchor to link "Groucho" to an essay later in the same page. The first step is to set up a name for the linked text, using the NAME attribute with the <A> tag. The syntax is:

```
<A NAME="name">TEXT</A>
```

Here's how we would name the essay about Groucho:

```
<A NAME="grouchobio"><B>Groucho Marx: A Life</B></A><P>
Groucho Marx was famous for quick wit, a greasepaint mustache and
eyebrows, and a big cigar. He and his brothers were the preeminent comedians
of film in the 1930s. While Harpo and Chico made a legendary slapstick duo,
often quoting the vocabulary of vaudeville and burlesque in their routines,
```

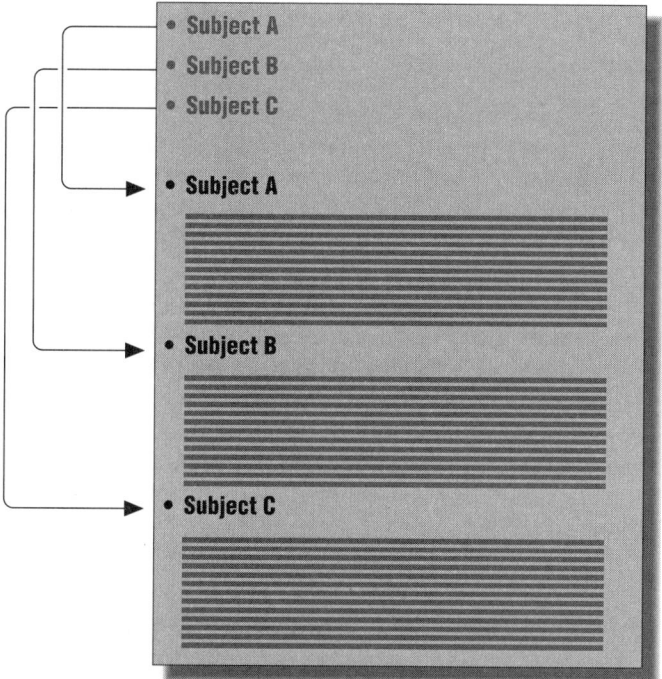

Figure 7–11. Hypertext used to link to text within a document

```
Groucho was without doubt the star of the show. The Marx Brothers started
in burlesque and by the mid-20s were the toast of New York in the Broadway
shows "The Cocoanuts" and "Animal Crackers." Those plays were brought to the
screen as very early talkies in 1929 and 1930. Their film career was
effectively over by the early '40s but Groucho managed a comeback as host of
the game show "You Bet Your Life" in the 1950s.
```

Note that we only named the title of the essay, but we could have named the entire essay, since it is fairly short. Since the hypertext anchor will take us to the beginning of the essay, there's really no point in naming the entire thing.

Now that we've named the paragraph, we can link to it from earlier in the page:

```
Welcome Marx Brothers fans!
<HR>
Get information about the brothers by clicking on their names:
<P><A HREF="#grouchobio"> Groucho</A>
```

The last line of the above code now says: Make "Groucho" an anchor and, when the user clicks on it, link to the text named "grouchobio."

Any text can be named, even another anchor. Remember that NAME is an attribute, just like HREF. Here's the syntax for naming text that is also a hypertext anchor:

```
<A HREF="linked-file" NAME="#name">Hypertext anchor</A>
```

Inserting graphics

```
<IMG>
```

The combination of graphics and text is one of the things that make the World Wide Web so interesting. In our Marx Brothers server, we could include photos of the brothers, stills from their films, illustrations of them, and so on.

There are two ways to present graphics in the World Wide Web—inline graphics (those that appear within the page) and linked graphics (stand-alone files reached by links). HTML only supports the XBM and GIF file formats for inline graphics; however, if you link to a graphics file, it can be in any format—provided that users have the external viewers with which to view them. The most common file formats are JPEG and GIF; it's probably a good idea to convert graphics to one of those formats. (Chapter 6 has more information about file formats and viewers.)

The tag for inserting an inline graphic is <IMG>. Since the tag doesn't refer to text, there's no end tag involved. This tag always requires a source attribute (SRC), which defines the name of the file to insert. The value for the SRC attribute can be any URL. The URL can point to a GIF or XBM file on any computer on the Internet, although it's probably safer to maintain inline graphic files locally, just in case the other computer is inaccessible.

There are two other attributes that can be included in the tag:

- ALIGN specifies how graphics and/or text should align. The values are TOP, MIDDLE, and BOTTOM. They tell the browser to align nearby text with the top, middle, or bottom of the graphic.

- ALT defines some alternate text to be used in case a browser cannot display graphics. This is important for users of non-graphical browsers such as Lynx. If the graphic is an integral part of your content, you'll want to be sure to specify some alternate text.

Let's say we want to insert a photo of Groucho before his name and have the accompanying text line up with the bottom of the image. For Lynx users, we'll display the phrase "[Photo of Groucho Marx]." Here's the tag:

```
<IMG SRC="groucho.gif" ALIGN=BOTTOM ALT="[Photo of Groucho Marx]">
```

Inserting graphics as anchors

We can also insert a graphic and make it an anchor for a hypertext link. Here the photo of Groucho is an anchor to the specified file:

```
<A HREF="marxbros.html"><IMG SRC="groucho.gif" ALIGN=BOTTOM></A>
```

One common use of graphics as anchors is for custom bullets. Instead of using an unordered list, which uses bullets, you can put postage-stamp size graphics in front of text and have them do double duty as custom bullets and hypertext links. It's a good way to give your page some personality. If you wanted to use a picture of Groucho as linked bullet, for instance, you might write:

```
<P><A HREF="file1.html"><IMG SRC="groucho.gif" ALIGN=BOTTOM></A>Information
about Groucho's life
<P><A HREF="file2.html"><IMG SRC="groucho.gif" ALIGN=BOTTOM></A>Information
about Groucho's family
<P><A HREF="file3.html"><IMG SRC="groucho.gif" ALIGN=BOTTOM></A>Information
about Groucho's work
```

Figure 7-12 shows how this list looks in Mosaic.

Creating Your Own Home Page

If first impressions really are the most important, you'll want to pay particular attention to your home page. The home page is the first document users come to when they contact your server. It introduces users to your service, tells them what kind of information they'll find, and provide links to documents on your server or others. Beyond that there really are no rules for home pages. Companies, colleges, publications, scientists, students . . . they all have Web servers on the Internet, with very different home pages. In this section, we'll take a look at some of the different home pages out there and discuss how you can make the right impression.

A personal home page occupies a unique niche on the World Wide Web: it represents the Web at its most basic and at its most eccentric. We can lay the blame for this multiple-personality disorder on evolution. From its simple text-based roots in CERN, the WWW home page has rapidly grown into a flexible self-publishing tool. It can now serve as anything from a conservative, professional-looking front door on the Net, to a medium of personal expression that intersects with autobiography, e-zines, and science fiction.

What should you put in your home page? Here are a few thoughts (with the linked servers shown in brackets), taken from *GNN*'s Netizens feature, written by D.C. Denison:

Be Professional:
> I graduated from Utah State University [USU] with a degree in Music [Internet Underground Music Archives], and now I work with the Global Network Navigator [GNN].

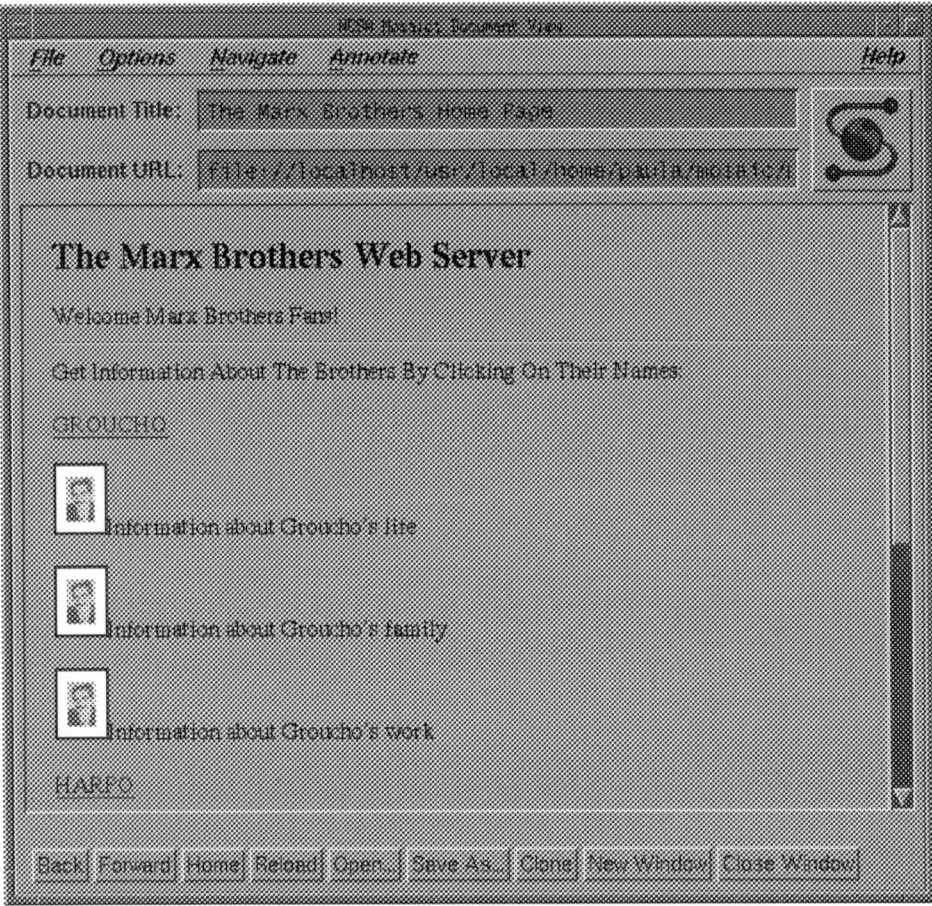

Figure 7–12.   Custom bullets used as hypertext anchors

Wax Literary:

It was a <u>dark and stormy night</u> [weather server]. Nancy Drew leaned back in her trusty <u>'62 T-bird</u> [rec.auto.classic] and turned the radio dial to <u>KKSF</u> [SF radio station Web site].

Get Up Close and Personal:

I live with an amazing standard poodle named <u>Willie</u> [picture of Willie], and love to ponder <u>the meaning of life</u> [philosophy gopher] while watching <u>basketball</u> [GNN Sports Page]. The latest important news I found on the Net is the lineup for <u>Woodstock '94</u> [Adam Curry's Web server].

Be an Information Kiosk:

Here is a list of all the free <u>Mac software</u> on the Net [Internet Computer Index], all the online guides to <u>cyberspace</u> [GNN Gold Mine], and a list of all the Internet <u>bicycle information</u> [cycling gopher].

The attitude you decide on will tell you a lot about the other aspects of designing your page. If you're creating a professional page, you'll want your photograph to be professional and your links to be clearly identified. If you're being more personal, you can embed lots of links within text, make inside jokes, show off your homemade computer art, and so on.

To help you get started with that first home page, here are a couple of templates. All you need to do is fill in the blanks, and you're off and running. This template is the HTML for a generic personal home page. It uses an inline image, unordered lists and some links, as well as the <ADDRESS> tag.

```
<HTML><HEAD>
<TITLE>YourName's Home Page</TITLE></HEAD><BODY>
<H1>YourName's Home Page</H1>
<IMG SRC="YourPicture.gif"> picture title
<H2>Where I work/go to school</H2>
I work at <A HREF="URL here">company/school name</A>.
<H2>Hobbies</H2>
<UL>
<LI>description
<LI>description
<LI>description
</UL>
<H2>Personal Hot List</H2>
<UL>
<LI><A HREF="URL here">description</A>
<LI><A HREF="URL here">description</A>
<LI><A HREF="URL here">description</A>
</UL>
<ADDRESS>YourName (YourEmailAddress@host.domain) </ADDRESS>
</BODY></HTML>
```

You can fill this out and use it as your home page or customize it as you wish. Figure 7-13 shows a filled-out version of this page.

The following template is a somewhat more complex form, featuring custom bullets in glossaries, as well as inline images and plenty of links. Try filling out this template and previewing the results in Mosaic.

```
<HTML><HEAD>
<TITLE>My Favorite Things</TITLE></HEAD>
<BODY>
<H1>These Are a Few of My Favorite Things</H1>
This page is all about the things I like.
<DL>
<DT>
<IMG ALIGN=BOTTOM SRC="picture.gif">
<A HREF="startrek.html">Star Trek: The Next Generation</A>
<DD>
<I>My all time favorite TV show</I>
</DD>
</DT>
```

Figure 7-13. Personal home page

```
<DT>
<IMG ALIGN=BOTTOM SRC="picture.gif">
<A HREF="bogart.html">Casablanca</A>
<DD>
<I>My all time favorite movie</I>
</DD>
</DT>
<DT>
<IMG ALIGN=BOTTOM SRC="pics/whiteball.gif">
```

```
<A HREF="ulysses.html">Ulysses by James Joyce</A>
<DD>
<I>My all time favorite book</I>
</DD>
</DT>
</DL>
</H2>
</LI>
</BODY></HTML>
```

Using HoTMetaL to Create Documents

While HTML is a relatively simple tagging language, it is easy to make mistakes. If you miss an end tag somewhere, your whole document may be displayed in bold or as <H3> text. If the mistake occurs in a large document, it may be rather difficult to find and correct. At the very least, your fingers will get tired from typing out all those tags.

One solution is a new program called HoTMetaL, available in both freeware and commercial versions. There is a link for downloading HoTMetaL on the *Mosaic Handbook Hotlist*, or you can download it yourself using the URL:

```
ftp://ftp.ncsa.uiuc.edu/Web/html/hotmetal/SPARC-Motif
```

Developed by SoftQuad for X and Windows, HoTMetaL solves some of the problems of writing HTML from scratch. For starters, the **Insert Element** command on the **Markup** pull-down menu gives you a list of all the tags, so you don't have to keep them all in your head.

In addition, HoTMetaL is a rules-based program, so it won't let you make any bone-headed mistakes. For instance, whenever you insert a tag, say <H1>, HoTMetaL automatically inserts the appropriate ending tag. All of this saves you from the endless typing of tags. In fact, HoTMetaL's rules are a good bit stricter than they currently need to be, since Mosaic and other browsers are fairly forgiving of documents that don't adhere to the letter of the law. For this reason, HoTMetaL gives you the option of turning off the rules. As the program's manual notes, however, future browsers are likely to be more insistent on proper tagging, so it's a good idea to use HoTMetaL's rules.

HoTMetaL is more than just a fancy macro program; it's also a WYSIWYG editor. Titles, headers, and other tagged text are displayed in different fonts and point sizes to give you an idea of what the document looks like as you're writing it. The display of all tags is configurable by the user.

Another strong point of this freeware program is that it allows you to save templates, which is useful if you have many documents with similar structure. Figure 7-14 is a screen shot of the HoTMetaL interface.

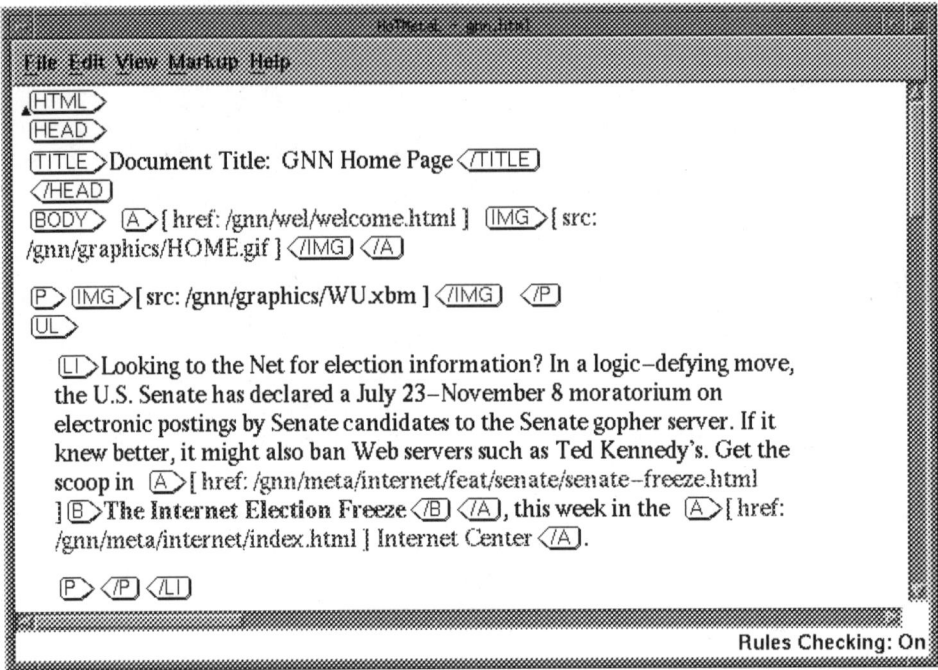

Figure 7–14. The HoTMetaL interface

Marking Up

The primary menu is the **Markup** menu, which lets you insert and edit HTML tags. To get started, you use the **Insert Element** command to bring up a scrolling box of possible tags. By selecting one of the tags, you insert both the opening tag and the closing tag. If you try to insert an element with the cursor positioned where no tags are allowed, HoTMetaL disables the **Insert Element** command. The **Insert Element** dialog also has a checkbox labeled **Include Required Elements**. When this is checked, sub-elements to a tag are automatically inserted along with the tag. For instance, inserting <HTML> automatically inserts <HEAD> as well.

You can edit the attributes and URLs of an element by using the **Edit Links and Attributes** command. Select an element and then choose this command from the **Markup** menu. This brings up a dialog box with the name of each attribute and either a drop-down menu with possible values or a text box for specifying a name of some kind. For instance, if you select an IMG tag, the dialog box will show the ALIGN attribute with the choices TOP, MIDDLE, BOTTOM. Simply select another choice and the element is edited. The dialog box also has text fields for editing the URLs specified with HREF or SRC.

The **Surround** command lets you select text and then surround it with a tag. For instance, you might decide to change a line from plain text to an <H3> heading.

To do this, select the text, choose **Surround**, and then pick **H3** from the menu. HoTMetaL will put an <H3> tag before the text and </H3> after it.

Rules Checking

HoTMetaL prevents markup errors essentially by removing temptation. The program presents a restricted list of tags, so that only correct tags are available from the **Insert Element** dialog box. This list changes according to the element within which the cursor is positioned. In addition, HoTMetaL disables commands that would cause the document to be incorrectly coded. If at any point this all gets too restrictive, you can turn Rules Checking off by selecting the toggle command **Turn Rules Checking On/Off**. You might want to do this while you perform an intermediate step that temporarily makes the tagging incorrect.

Viewing

While HoTMetaL provides a number of commands for controlling the presentation of text, including the ability to set font families, point sizes and spacing, it's not the same as previewing in Mosaic. These settings bear no relationship to the way Mosaic will present the document. To make the previewing more useful, HoTMetaL has a **Preview** command on the **File** menu, which launches Mosaic and loads the document.

There are two windows, launched from the **View** menu, that help in checking the construction of your document. **Show Structure View** (shown in Figure 7-15) brings up a window that shows the hierarchy of the entire document. Each line represents a new element and has a start tag, an end tag, and the text between them. The lines are indented to show the nesting of tags.

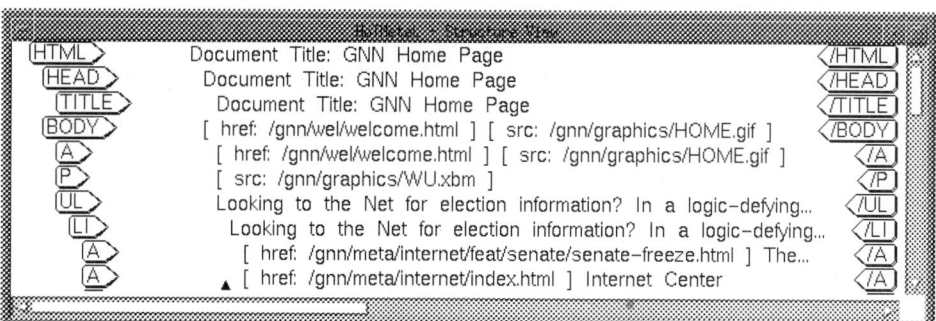

Figure 7-15. HoTMetaL's Structure View

For a close-up look at the structure of the selected element, use **Show Link and Context View**. When the selected element is nested within other elements, this window will show the hierarchical sequence up to the selected element. It doesn't show tags before or after the current hierarchy.

While you're still not an HTML expert, you're well on your way now. While we haven't covered every single thing you can do with HTML, you know enough now to create pages as sophisticated as most of what you see on the Web.

Resources

A Beginners Guide to HTML
http://www.ncsa.uiuc.edu/General/Internet/WWW/HTMLPrimer.html

A Beginners Guide to URLs
http://www.ncsa.uiuc.edu/demoweb/url-primer.html

HTML Quick Reference
http://kuhttp.cc.ukans.edu/lynx_help/HTML_quick.html

Hyper Text Markup Langugage (HTML)
http://info.cern.ch/hypertext/WWW/MarkUp/MarkUp.html

Style Guide
http://info.cern.ch/hypertext/WWW/Provider/Style/Overview.html

WWW Names and Addresses
http://info.cern.ch/hypertext/WWW/Addressing/Addressing.html

World Wide Web Initiative
http://info.cern.ch/hypertext/WWW/TheProject.html

ISO Latin Characters
http//info.cern.ch/hypertext/WWW/MarkUp/ISOlat1.html

## CHAPTER EIGHT

FUTURE DIRECTIONS

W3O
WWW Project Information
VRML: Visualizing Web Space

The Mosaic interface and the World Wide Web information architecture will continue to evolve in new directions. In this chapter, we try to indicate what some of those directions might be and to describe how you can join in the discussions on the Net where the new developments are happening.

We begin with a story from *GNN NetNews* on W3O, the organization created by the Massachusetts Institute of Technology (MIT) and the European Laboratory for Particle Physics (CERN) to shape the future of the WWW. We also include a *GNN* interview by D.C. Denison with Professor Michael Dertouzos of MIT, a key player in creating this international organization. He talks about the goal of creating a Web that includes online entertainment, commerce, and education, and what needs to be done to make this happen.

Also in this chapter, we catalog the newsgroups, mailing lists, and Web servers where you can follow the most recent developments, such as the Virtual Reality Markup Language.

W3O

Almost from the beginning of the World Wide Web initiative at CERN, project leader Tim Berners-Lee recognized the need for a separate organization that could help to develop WWW standards, as well as much of the common code base. In the summer of 1994 that organization finally emerged, and it was named W3O. The organizing sponsors of W3O consortium are MIT and CERN. Berners-Lee will move from CERN to MIT to serve as the director of W3O.

At MIT, the Web initiative will be based at the Laboratory for Computer Science. Professor Michael L. Dertouzos is the director of the Lab. Dertouzos said that W3O aspires to "enhance the Web by developing the 'bulldozers and backhoes' of the information age, that will work for us—not the other way around, as is often the case today.

"We envision an information market where information and information services can be purchased, sold, or exchanged freely so as to improve the economic well-being and the quality of life of people throughout the world, and as a medium for education and the nurturing and integrating of different cultures."

W3O is expected to receive the enthusiastic support of the European Union. "It is of the utmost importance that these computer frameworks be worldwide frameworks," said Dr. Martin Bangemann, the Commissioner of the European Union in charge of industrial policy, information technologies and industries, and telecommunications. "The European Union intends to support this cooperative activity as an important step toward the Global Information Society," he said.

Dr. George Metakides, director of the European Strategic Program for Research and Development in Information Technologies (ESPRIT), which reports to Dr. Bangemann, commented, "Common information navigation tools will be essential for the development of the Global Information Infrastructure. This development of the World Wide Web provides a concrete example that will help us to understand better the transition to the information society."

At the time of the W3O announcement, Tim Berners-Lee commented, "The Web was conceived as a representation of mankind's knowledge, society, and commerce." It is becoming more secure, more interactive, and developing greater richness of meaning. An international base seemed essential to support its very rapid growth and its evolution, while also ensuring its stability.

"Throughout the world, information and communications technologies are generating a new industrial revolution already as significant and far-reaching as those of the past," according to the European Union's Bangemann. "A global information society is emerging which changes the way we work together and the way we live together. The engine driving the transition to the information society is the information infrastructure, which enables us to process, retrieve, and communicate information in whatever form it may take—oral, written, or visual—unconstrained by distance, time or volume."

As you might expect, you can follow the developments at W3O online. As of this writing, there are only a few pages on the Web about W3O, but that should change quickly.

The following URL will get you to the W3O server. (This server may be relocated to MIT.)

```
http://info.cern.ch/hypertext/WWW/Organization/Consortium/W3OSignature.html
```

MIT's Michael L. Dertouzos on W3O

To get a better sense of what W3O might do, as well as what interesting directions the Web might move in, we have an interview with MIT's Professor Dertouzos. This interview was conducted by D.C. Denison and originally appeared in *GNN NetNews* in August of 1994, several weeks after the formation of W3O had been announced.

A secretary gives the visiting reporter a simple way to know when Michael L. Dertouzos has arrived at MIT's Laboratory for Computer Science.

"He's the biggest man who will walk through the door," she says, pointing to the main entrance.

Sure enough, Dertouzos, the director of the Lab and a professor of computer science and electrical engineering at MIT, is easy to spot. Tall and courtly, he sweeps into the office, gathers up a couple of mugs of coffee and some fresh faxes (from Vice President Albert Gore's office, it turns out), and settles down to discuss some big ideas. Like Dertouzos' idea of an "information marketplace," which he has been promoting for 15 years, and the W3O, the brand new international initiative to develop and standardize the World Wide Web.

How did you get interested in the World Wide Web?

I was looking for a mechanism that would allow this Lab to concentrate its future research on the architecture of the global information infrastructure, with the emphasis on global. Second, I wanted something that already had millions of users, so it had the voice of reality, but was bendable. Then reality would bend us back, if we proposed stupid things, and we would bend it back, if we proposed clever or useful things.

I really want this lab to be an architect of tomorrow's information infrastructure. There are going to be so many people out there doing interfaces: Time/Warner will have a movie interface and a news interface; Bill Gates will have his own Microsoft interface, so that if you're in Excel you can hook up with somebody on the other side of the ocean who is also using Excel; the telcos will have an interface, each with its own look and feel; the publishers, the Murdochs, will have their own spin on an interface. Everyone wants to control that, because they see it as a very lucrative market. So there will be no shortage of me-toos, trying to plug you into the infrastructure. But no one's worried about the damn architecture. So I saw this as a fertile ground, for this Laboratory to focus on the architecture. And when I talk about architecture, I'm talking about how machines in one location will understand what the machines in another location want to do. Today, if you look at the Internet, they don't. It's human beings who have to understand. In fact the Web is human browsable.

Is there a better way, in your opinion?

Back in the industrial era, we invented machines, and they replaced our muscles. That was a simple thing to understand. We've also come up with ways to produce food by using only three percent of the population, instead of 50 percent. So what are we replacing in the information revolution? What would you say?

The work of finding and accessing information. The "legwork" it takes to locate sources of information. How's that?

The mundane mind work, if I may generalize from your words. You want to replace some of the mundane mind work. So in this lab, we're trying to work out schemes that will act as bulldozers and backhoes for the mind. That's a nice metaphor. The Web doesn't have bulldozers or backhoes; it has shovels. It welcomes you with lots of shovels that you have to operate. All it is now is a Web that links home pages and other pages all over the world: you click, you cross the ocean or the street, and then your brain has to go to work: you have to figure out, "What do I want to do?" and "What do I have to do?" It's like electronic mail: it does some wonderful things, but it has some terrible disadvantages.

What are its disadvantages?

It's another shovel in your hands. I can click my little finger and create a hundred copies of your message to me, and my response to you, and 100 minds have to at least read the message address to figure out what I'm telling them. Again, it's the human brain being overloaded. It is not evolution, in productivity terms, when you overload an ancient human brain. It's as if the Industrial Revolution came and you started telling people, "Now if you only start working harder with your muscles, we can offer you a lot of utopias." That's bull. It doesn't work. So viewed from that perspective, the current existing networks are nowhere near where we envision them. This is the vision that I have.

So you want to make things simpler.

Correct. But not only simpler. I see it as the human quest to increase productivity, to have others do his work. Technology is there to serve us.

What are the first things we can expect to see on future versions of the World Wide Web?

Recreation. There are 80 million households in the country, and a little over two TV sets in each household. That's more than 150 million TV sets. There are only 30 or 40 million PCs. There is also a well-known, $14 billion market that views videos. So the first application is clearly that one.

Do you think the Web can deliver that kind of entertainment?

Not in its current form. But the Web, suitably modified, could. But we're talking about the infrastructure of the future here, and that infrastructure clearly has to have the architecture to support recreation. So the first things you're going to see will probably be recreation. The Web today goes through slower lines, but there's nothing prohibiting people from running the Web through television's coaxial cable.

And after recreation?

After recreation, I see shopping and mail-order coming right away, because that's natural, once people get used to browsing. Another thrust will come from the business sector, and commerce, by which I mean the whole set of transactions that start with looking for things, move on to negotiations, move on to contracting, and move on to delivery and post delivery. All these steps can be very important, depending on what you're buying or selling. Then there's education, which is the toughest, because although there's plenty of talk about education, there isn't much money. Whereas with entertainment and commerce, there's money and perceived need. So the possibilities for education are beautiful, but will it really happen? The whole area of travel will also be big. But the initial thrust will probably be recreation and commerce. Then I see health care coming in big. There's money there, and the Web can help save both time and money. Financial services and group-work are other areas that show promise.

This seems to be a long way from the current system.

Things always look that way. If you ask people what they want, they generally want 20 percent more than they have—a few more features, smoother operation, etc. But we want to go 150 percent ahead.

How many people will be working on W3O?

I don't differentiate between W3O and the rest of the Lab. We have about 500 people working here, and about half of them will be working on the information infrastructure. But specific W3O people, working on the standard, and issuing new versions—probably around 12.

Is part of W3's appeal its scalability?

W3 is very clean and unmolested by too many fixed ideas, so you can put some things on it. And it can expand. But our own idea, since day one, has been to build this information market. We're interested in a market, not a utility where someone has all the knowledge and sells it. We're not interested in any of these dictatorial models; we want a market where buyers and sellers come together and buy and sell information. It's decentralized.

That's not what many corporations are building now.

No, this is not what's happening today. The scenarios you see today will make it possible for you to watch a movie, but if you want to then sell a service, you won't be able to. So we don't have a market. We don't have an equal place where you and I can transact. We have a broadcast medium, and that's what everybody's after: control, which means broadcast. Never mind if they give you some interaction back, so you can choose what you can buy, it's still broadcast. I've given a name to these models: I call them spiders, because they have a hub, and there's one way out, and they don't let you come back in. There are all sorts of spiders. The European telephone company is a spider: they think that they are going to offer every service you're going to need. That's another spider that prohibits an information market.

If you stop and think about it, it's not in the interest of any single capitalistic agency to promote a universal infrastructure. Any more than it's in the interest of any capitalistic agency to promote a highway system for cars. Who built the highway system in this country? The government. I'm not a socialist, I'm a capitalist, but there are some things that the government has to stimulate. This is one of them. People left to their own devices are going to build spiders, and it will take us 20 years before people will realize, which they will, that there's more money in converting spiders to highways. But by then there may be a lot of things already frozen in place.

How will you head off all these spider-builders?

That's why we're the architects. That's one of our noble duties—to say to people, "Yes, guys, these spiders are great for sending movies to the home, and it's even great to sell L.L. Bean products. But you won't be able to buy, from that home-dweller, his ability to retouch photographs. You won't be able to buy, from that homedweller, his or her ability to work on insurance forms. The way you're going, all you'll be able to get from that homedweller are clicks that are going to say, 'Buy this, sell that, do this, do that.' He cannot put any of his own stuff on. That's fine. We'll offer you an architecture where you can do all that. But our architecture has hooks. So later, when you see the light, and you see that there's some revenue there, we can turn on that hook, and that person can sell." And that person can get on the highway system.

Did you see W3 as a place where a market structure was already working, on a small scale?

W3 already has a great deal of this information market idea in it. It's got two beautiful things. The first is an obvious one, that anyone can produce something. You can create a home page that's as elaborate or as silly as you want. The second part of this is that there are 30 million of you doing this, and it is growing into a beautiful edifice. That's how it will continue to grow: if you do a great Web demo for a health center, then every health center and clinic is going to want to be Webbed. That's how it will work.

It's already working like that.

Yes, but what we have now is a chaotic evolution of servers with no order. The Internet, really, has no order. It's a mud field, and every ten kilometers of mud, you find a little diamond. That's a situation we will be working to improve.

What were the negotiations like, with CERN, when you were trying to put W3O together?

The elements of the deal are really quite obvious. Tim Berners-Lee invented the Web, at CERN, and they have a great understanding of the Web, and a great community of people using the Web. On our part, at MIT, we have the experience with the X Consortium, and our systems work for the last 30 years. And we have architectural research in progress, on the information infrastructure, that is second to none worldwide.

What's going to attract corporations to the W3O Consortium?

Corporations are not stupid. They don't want to miss the next standard. So you offer them a reasonable entry, financially and otherwise, into a consortium, as we did with the X Consortium. You make sure they don't have any spider controls, but you be sure to listen to them, so that they evolve the standard with what they want to see changed, without constraining others from using it. If you get the right balance between openness and response to your users—that is one of the most accepted methods of evolving a standard. It's much faster than an international committee.

Why?

Because you have a standard czar, in this case Tim Berners-Lee, who will be in charge of the consortium. And you have a team of elders, 12 people who will constitute his council. At least half of them will come from the consortium; the other half will be knowledgeable technologists and others whom he will consult. All year long people will be saying, "Gee, Tim, wouldn't it be nice if we had X or Y or Z in there?" Or they're saying, "Tim, that thing that you put in last year—that's a piece of junk." Or they're saying, "That feature you put in, that's fantastic." So he listens to all this, he talks to his elders, then come January 1 he drops the sword and he says, "The next version, number 9, of the W3 standard is this." And the minute he issues that, everybody—and I mean everybody—says "Thank God, we have one place where these decisions are made." That honeymoon lasts precisely one day. The very next day they're back bitching and saying, "Let's make this change, that change . . . " That's how the standard works.

So any company that knows about this process—and they all do—is going to say to themselves, "Hey look, there are some pretty good people at W3O, like the inventor, and CERN, and MIT. Maybe there's just a chance that they're going to do something. Can I afford not to be there?" And we need these people. Because without the manufacturers, who are going to build this stuff, and without the users, and without the technologists, who we represent, we don't have anything. You've got to have all three components: users, makers, and researchers.

How much of a role are you going to play?

This subject happens to be a rather serious interest of mine, the information infrastructure. I'm writing a book on it. So I'll stop in and ask questions, but I'm not going to interfere. This is really better left to other people. But I'll be watching, making sure that we carve a path that is going to open the usage of these things to the world, and create an infrastructure, rather than create a spider.

How will you roll out advances to WWW?

By a system of what I call protocol grafts. You know the way you graft a branch on a tree and it either takes or it doesn't? We are going to be declaring, in a given standard version, that "Here is the standard, and here is the graft region that has the six new things in it. They are not part of the standard; they are for people who want to play. But please send your comments." In the next version, based on the comments, two of these six grafts might make it into the standard, three might drop off, and one might stay for another year of observation. And three new grafts might be added. That's how I plan to resolve these tensions in an orderly way. Otherwise, the Web is going to remain a human-browsable network, which is not very useful. And my people's great ideas will remain unsorted, as to which ones are bull or great.

What would be an example of a graft?

Let's say an automated vocabulary, with 100 nouns and 100 verbs, which every server on the Web that implements that standard can now understand. The verbs could be of the form, "Have you?" or be declarative, of the form, "I sent you," or "I ask you to send me" or "I ask, do you have?" or "Can you show me how?" And there may be one hundred nouns, having to do with "a file named __" or "a picture named ___" or statements of the form "I don't understand." So maybe we announce, "We're putting in this graft extension, a little language that augments the Web, and if you install this software, then you'll be able to not only finger-click, but do some things automatically." So we'll try it as a graft. Nobody is compelled to use it. In fact, if you want simplicity, ask for the version without this. Then, whenever somebody hits you with it, they will get back the message, "Sorry, this node does not understand graft #16." But people being as adventurous as they are, they'll go for the grafts.

The Internet doesn't lack for adventurous people.

That's right. You have 15 million adventurous people. Even if half of them say "screw it," that still leaves enough for me to know if a given graft will take or not. And I'm not just talking about the techies. I want to get the regular human beings. So look for deals with some of the entertainment companies.

When will we see the first new version of WWW coming out of W3O?

I expect nothing before a year and a half. Tim Berners-Lee will start in September (1994). If we assume version 1.0 was what happened in Geneva, the very earliest you can expect to see version 2.0 will be January '96. Maybe.

WWW Project Information

The largest repository of the information about the WWW is online, and organized at CERN. The URL for the WWW Project is:

```
http://info.cern.ch/hypertext/WWW/TheProject.html
```

You will find various lists of resources, as well as pointers to technical information about the Web. We have summarized the key information resources below.

WWW Newsgroups

If you're interested in following, or taking part in, the development of the Web, you can participate in several newsgroups. Here is a list of Web-related newsgroups.

comp.infosystems.www.users

This newsgroup is the best starting place for learning about using the Web. It is a forum for the discussion of Web browsers and their use with various Internet information sources. Among the topics covered in this group: new user questions, client setup questions, client bug reports, questions on how to locate information on the Web, and comparisons between various client packages.

comp.infosystems.www.providers

This newsgroup is a forum for the discussion of Web server software and presenting information to users. Topics covered include: general server design, setup questions, server bug reports, security issues, HTML page design, and other concerns of information providers.

comp.infosystems.www.misc

A forum for general discussion of Web-related topics that are not covered by the other newsgroups in the hierarchy. According to CERN, "This will likely include discussions of the Web's future, politicking regarding changes in the structure and protocols of the Web that affect both clients and servers, etc."

Mailing Lists

To join any of the CERN mailing lists, send email to *listserv@info.cern.ch* with the following message:

```
subscribe list-name your-name
```

in the body of the message. For example:

```
subscribe www-announce "Dale Dougherty"
```

If you need more information about CERN's mailing lists, use the following URL:

```
http://info.cern.ch/hypertext/WWW/Administration/Mailing/Overview.html
```

The CERN mailing lists are described in the sections that follow. Many are available in archive form. If the archive is organized by a program called **Hypermail**, the messages can be viewed sorted by date, subject, or author.

www-announce

A mailing list for anyone interested in WWW, its progress, new data sources, or new software releases. There is also an archive of the list, which is accessible through Mosaic. The URL for the archive is:

```
http://info.cern.ch/hypertext/WWW/Archive/www-announce
```

www-html

Technical discussions of HTML and HTMLPlus. This is a technical mailing list consisting of design discussions only. This is not the place to ask basic questions about writing HTML, but if you're interested in following the nitty-gritty of the HTML language, you may want to subscribe to this list.

There is also a hypertext-based archive for this mailing list at:

```
http://info.cern.ch/hypertext/WWW/Archive/www-html
```

www-proxy

This mailing list is for a technical discussion about WWW proxies, caching, and future directions.

www-talk

Technical discussion for those developing WWW software or with a deep interest in WWW. (Please keep this to WWW technical design only, *not* general questions from non-developers.) See the hypertext archive at:

```
http://gummo.stanford.edu/html/hypermail/archives.html
```

VRML: Visualizing Web Space

The idea behind the Virtual Reality Markup Language (VRML) is to create a non-proprietary, platform-independent language, much like HTML, that would allow authors to create virtual reality "scenes." Users of virtual reality servers would be able to walk around a space and push open doors to other parts of the Web. While, as of this writing, VRML is still very much in the "talking about" phase, there is a working specification for VRML, developed by Mark Pesce and Anthony Parisi of the Labyrinth Group in San Francisco.

VRML Resources

The VRML Web site contains papers, specifications, and links to other VR-related projects. The URL is:

```
http://www.wired.com/vrml/
```

You can subscribe to the www-vrml mailing list by sending email to:

```
majordomo@wired.com
```

with the following in the body of the message:

```
subscribe www-vrml your-email-address
```

MOSAIC REFERENCE GUIDE

The Control Panel
The Menus

While using Mosaic is a farily intuitive experience, the program includes several features that are quite helpul in managing your Mosaic session. This appendix provides a comprehensive guide to Mosaic's control panel and menu commands. The interface is described in Chapter 2, *Getting Started with Mosaic.*

The Control Panel

The control panel contains buttons that help you navigate with Mosaic. These buttons run across the bottom of the Mosaic window.

Back and Forward

On the left end of the control panel is the **Back** button. You use this button to display the page you were last viewing. Next to it is the **Forward** button. It works the same way, only in reverse. Normally the **Forward** button is dimmed; if you use the **Back** button, the Forward button becomes active, allowing you to return to your most recently downloaded page.

It's kind of like adding pages to a book. Every time you download a new page, you are adding that page to the back of your book; that page then becomes the last page of the book. Flipping back brings you to pages that were downloaded earlier; flipping forward takes you to pages added later.

This navigation process works well while moving through documents held in the cache. It gets a bit confusing, however, if you move too far back. When you move to a document that is not in the cache, Mosaic will download that document; that file will then become the most recent document. The solution is to use **Back** and **Forward** only to move in small increments; use **Window History** or **Hotlist** to take larger steps.

Home

To the right of **Back** and **Forward** is the **Home** button. Clicking on this brings you back to your home page. This can be a handy tool if you get confused about where you are and how you got there. Like the Land of Oz, the Web can be a fantastic adventure, but sometimes you'll find, just like Dorothy, "There's no place like home." You don't have to click your heels together three times, though; just click the **Home** button once and you'll be back at your Home Page.

Reload

This button simply downloads the same page over again. It is useful when Mosaic has a problem accessing a server or displaying an image on your screen. Just press **Reload** to try again.

Open

The **Open** button brings up a dialog box that asks you for a URL. Mosaic will then contact the server and get the file for you. Because you have to enter the whole string by hand, it's quite easy to make a mistake. If you get an error message, check to make sure you entered the URL correctly. Some directories and filenames are case-sensitive, so make sure you entered the URL exactly.

Save As

This button lets you save the current document to your system, as plain text, formatted text, PostScript, or an HTML document. You need to specify the directory and filename used for the document. Be sure to use an *.html* file extension for HTML documents.

Clone and New Window

Mosaic lets you open numerous windows, so you can keep many different documents open on your screen at the same time. This can save quite a bit of time in going back and forth to your most frequently used documents. For instance, you could keep *GNN* open in one window and explore other Web offerings in another window. Then, instead of having to find your way back to *GNN*, just switch to the *GNN* window.

When you click on **New Window**, Mosaic opens a new **Document View** window and displays your home page. Clicking on **Clone**, however, causes Mosaic to open a new window and duplicate the contents of the current window.

Close Window

You can close a Mosaic window by pressing the **Close Window** button. If you only have one open Mosaic window, pressing this button causes the program to exit.

The Menus

There are five menus in Mosaic: **File**, **Options**, **Navigate**, **Annotate**, and **Help**. These menus let you manage files, change display characteristics, navigate the Web, annotate documents, and display online help. If you've installed Mosaic from the CD, your version will also have a **Documents** menu that gives you quick access to various *GNN* publications.

Mosaic provides keyboard shortcuts in the form of *hot keys* for many of its menu commands. You can simply press the key to use the command; this is useful if you don't like mousing around. Most hot keys are case-insensitive, so it doesn't matter if the **Shift** key is pressed.

The File Menu

The **File** menu has commands for file management operations like opening, saving, closing, and printing files.

New Window and Clone Window (*hot keys* n *and* c)

These menu items correspond to the **New Window** and **Clone** buttons on the control panel.

Open URL (*hot key* o)

As described in Chapter 2, **Open URL** lets you enter a URL in a dialog box. This item corresponds to the **Open** button on the control panel. After you enter a URL, Mosaic contacts the server and gets the document for you.

Open Local (*hot key* l)

When you're writing HTML documents, it's quite helpful to preview them in Mosaic. To view HTML documents on your system, use the **Open Local** command. It opens a standard file selection dialog box showing directories and files. **Open Local** is handy when writing HTML documents because mistakes are sometimes hard to catch when looking at ASCII text, but they become glaringly obvious when displayed in Mosaic. Remember, you must give your HTML documents a name with the extension *.html*. If you don't, Mosaic will display the file as plain text. You can also use **Open Local** to view non-HTML files on your system.

Reload Current and Reload Images (*hot key lowercase* r)

The **Reload Current** command corresponds to the **Reload** button on the control panel. It retrieves the current document from the Net and redisplays it. This command, however, does not reload cached images. To reload the current document and its images, use **Reload Images**.

Refresh Current (hot key uppercase R)

This command redisplays the current document without reloading it from the network. This is useful to restore image colors and remove disturbances due to console messages.

Find in Current (hot key s)

The **Find in Current** command lets you search the current document for a text string, which is highlighted in the document when found. The dialog box includes two toggle buttons, one for matching case and one for starting from the top of the document.

View Source (hot key d)

This command lets you see the HTML version of a document, as well as its URL. It's useful for people who are previewing their HTML documents in Mosaic or who want to see how somebody else achieved a certain result. You can use cut-and-paste from the **View Source** window if you want to transfer some text.

Save As

This command lets you save the current document to your system, as plain text, formatted text, PostScript, or an HTML document. You need to specify the directory and filename used for the document. This comes in handy if there's a long, particularly useful document that you want to read offline. Just save it as HTML and use the **Open Local** command to view it in Mosaic. Saving as text is better if you plan to put the document in a document of your own, for instance, a memo that you create in a word processing or page layout program.

Print (hot key p)

Selecting the **Print** option prints all pages in the current document. You get to specify the print command used, as well as the format of the printed document.

Mail To (hot key m)

This command lets you mail the current document to another person. The dialog box lets you specify an email address and subject. You also get to choose the format of the mailed document.

Close Window (hot key ESC)

Close Window closes the current Mosaic window. This command corresponds to the **Close Window** button on the control panel.

Exit Program

Exit Program closes all Mosaic windows and quits the program. A confirmation dialog box is posted to allow you to cancel the action.

The Options Menu

The **Options** menu has commands for setting various aspects of Mosaic's appearance and behavior. Many of these commands are described in Chapter 5, *Customizing Mosaic.*

Fancy Selections

When this option is selected, if you use X cut-and-paste to transfer text, the formatting of the text is preserved.

Load To Local Disk

Set the **Load to Local Disk** option if you want to save a document rather than view it. When this option is set and you click on the link, Mosaic prompts you for a filename for the document. This option is most useful for storing large files like sounds and movies.

Delay Image Loading

Setting this option causes Mosaic to delay loading inline images when it retrieves an HTML document. This is useful if you have a slow network connection. Mosaic displays generic image icons instead of inline images. You can retrieve an individual image by clicking on the image icon; use **Load Images in Current** to load all of the images.

Load Images In Current

When delayed image loading is turned on, the **Load Images in Current** command causes Mosaic to retrieve all of the inline images in the current document and redisplay the document.

Reload Config Files

This command reloads the mailcap and extension map files that Mosaic uses to configure its multimedia capabilities. See Chapter 6, *Using Mosaic for Multimedia,* for more information.

Flush Image Cache

Use this command to flush Mosaic's image cache. This is useful if you are working on an HTML document that contains inline images and using Mosaic to view the document. If you don't flush the cache, Mosaic uses the cached images each time you display the document, so you won't see any changes you may have made to the inline images.

Clear Global History

Using the **Clear Global History** command causes Mosaic to erase the history record it stores in order to keep track of visited links. When your history gets large, Mosaic's performance may suffer, so you may want to clear your history periodically.

Fonts

The **Fonts** command posts a submenu that lets you change the fonts Mosaic uses to display HTML documents. The change only remains in effect for the current session of Mosaic.

Anchor Underlines

This command posts a submenu that lets you change the underlining style Mosaic uses for anchor text, or hyperlinks. Any change you make only remains in effect during the current session with Mosaic.

The Navigate Menu

The Navigate menu contains the options that you will use most often as you traverse the Web.

Back and Forward (hot keys b and f)

These menu items correspond to the **Back** and **Forward** buttons on the control panel.

Home Document

This command corresponds to the **Home** button on the control panel.

Window History (hot key lowercase h)

The **Window History** command posts a dialog that contains a list of all the documents you have visited since you first ran Mosaic; it doesn't clear when you quit the program. To go to a document on your history list, double-click on the document name. The **Window History** dialog also contains buttons that let you dismiss the window, mail your history to another person, or get help.

Hotlist (hot key uppercase H)

When you find servers you want to be able to get to quickly, you can add them to your hotlist. The **Hotlist** window has several commands for managing your hotlist.

Add Current

Clicking on this button adds the current document to your hotlist. When you add Web documents, their titles are displayed in the list. When you add non-Web documents, their URLs are displayed.

Go To

Selecting a title and clicking on **Go To** downloads the selected document. You can also go to a document by double-clicking on its title.

Remove

To delete a document from your hotlist, select the document title and click on the **Remove** button.

Edit Title

To change the document title displayed in the hotlist, select the title and click on **Edit Title**. This brings up a window that lets you change the title of the selected document. This is especially handy for non-Web documents, for which Mosaic displays URLs as titles.

Dismiss

Dismiss closes the **Hotlist** window.

Mail To

Mail To allows you to mail your hotlist to another person. The hotlist is mailed as an HTML document consisting of all document titles and URLs in your hotlist. Each title in the document is an active link. You can send your hotlist to a friend, and then that person can save the message, view it with Mosaic, and access the documents on your list.

Help

Help provides help on using hotlists.

Add Current To Hotlist

This option adds the current document to your hotlist, the same as the **Add Current** button in the **Hotlist** window.

Internet Starting Points

This command retrieves a document from the NCSA WWW server that contains links to a variety of Internet services.

Internet Resources Meta-Index

This command retrieves a document from the NCSA WWW server that is intended to be a meta-index of resource directories and indices that are available on the Net.

The Annotate Menu

The **Annotate** menu has commands for making comments on documents that you discover as you explore the Web.

Annotate (*hot key* a)

The **Annotate** command posts a dialog box that lets you add a private comment to the current document. When you view an annotated document, Mosaic adds your comments to the end of the document as a hypertext link.

Audio Annotate

This command allows you to record your voice as an annotation, but it requires special hardware and software that need to be configured properly. This feature is currently available only on SGI, Sun, and HP machines.

Edit This Annotation

When you are viewing an annotation, you can use **Edit This Annotation** to edit your comments. This command is only available when you are viewing an annotation.

Delete This Annotation

Use this command to delete an annotation when you are viewing it.

The Documents Menu

If you are using Mosaic from the CD provided with this book, the **Documents** menu contains commands that take you directly to a number of *GNN* publications. From this menu, you can get to the following documents:

- *GNN Home* page

- *Whole Internet Catalog*

- *GNN Business Pages*

- NCSA's *What's New with NCSA Mosaic* page

- *GNN NetNews*

- *GNN* special publications
- *GNN* registration page

The Help Menu

The Mosaic **Help** menu provides commands that take you directly to a number of documents about Mosaic on the NCSA WWW server. When you use one of these commands, Mosaic opens a new window and then retrieves the document, so you don't have to worry about losing your place when you look for help.

About

This command takes you to NCSA's *About NCSA Mosaic for the X Window System* page.

Manual

Manual retrieves NCSA's online documentation on Mosaic for X.

What's New

This command retrieves NCSA's *What's New with NCSA Mosaic* page.

Demo

The **Demo** command takes you to an NCSA document that demonstrates many of the features of Mosaic.

On Version 2.4

This command takes you to a document with specific help on Version 2.4 of NCSA Mosaic for the X Window System, the latest public domain release.

On Window

On Window provides some basic help on using the **Document View** window.

On FAQ

This command retrieves the *NCSA Mosaic Frequently Asked Questions* document, which contains frequently asked questions and their answers.

On HTML

On HTML takes you to NCSA's online guide to writing HTML documents.

On URLs

The **On URLs** command retrieves NCSA's online primer on Uniform Resource Locators.

HTML REFERENCE GUIDE

Table B-1: Tags

Tag	End Tag	Description
<HTML>	</HTML>	Starts/ends document
<HEAD>	</HEAD>	Starts/ends header
<TITLE>	</TITLE>	Starts/ends title
<BODY>	</BODY>	Starts/ends body
<H1>,<H2>, etc.	</H1>,</H2>, etc.	Starts/ends heading text
<P>	N/A	Starts new paragraph
 	N/A	Inserts line break
<HR>	N/A	Inserts horizontal rule
<EM>	</EM>	Surrounds emphasized text
<STRONG>	</STRONG>	Surrounds stronger text
<B>	</B>	Surrounds bold text
<I>	</I>	Surrounds italic text
<U>	</U>	Surrounds underlined text
<ADDRESS>	</ADDRESS>	Surrounds text in address format
<BLOCKQUOTE>	</BLOCKQUOTE>	Surrounds text in blockquote format
<PRE>	</PRE>	Surrounds preformatted text
<DL>	</DL>	Starts/ends glossary
<DT>	N/A	Precedes term entry in glossary
<DD>	N/A	Precedes term definition in glossary
<UL>	</UL>	Starts/ends unordered list
<OL>	</OL>	Starts/ends ordered list
<LI>	N/A	Precedes entries in list
<A>	</A>	Surrounds anchor; start tag requires attributes
<IMG>	N/A	Inserts inline graphic

Table B–2: Tag Attributes

Tag	End Tag	Attribute	Description	Values
`<A>`	`</A>`	HREF	Defines link destination	File name or anchor name
		NAME	Gives symbolic name to anchor	Any one-word name
`<IMG>`	N/A	SOURCE	Defines image source file	File name
		ALIGN	Specifies alignment	TOP, MIDDLE, or BOTTOM
		ALT	Specifies alternate text	Any text

LIST OF X RESOURCES

This appendix lists all of the X resources you can use to customize Mosaic's appearance and behavior. The table lists the name of each resource, the appropriate data type for specifying the resource, the default value, and a brief description of the resource. Most of these resources are described in more detail in Chapter 5, *Customizing Mosaic.*

activeAnchorBG
>**Data Type**: color
>**Default Value**: grey80
>Color for anchor background when anchor is being activated

activeAnchorFG
>**Data Type**: color
>**Default Value**: red
>Color for anchor foreground when anchor is being activated

addressFont
>**Data Type**: font
>**Default Value**: -adobe-times-medium-i-normal-*-17-*-*-*-*-*-iso8859-1
>Font for addresses

anchorColor
>**Data Type**: color
>**Default Value**: blue
>Color for unvisited anchors

anchorUnderlines
>**Data Type**: integer
>**Default Value**: 1
>**Number of lines under unvisited anchors**

annotationsOnTop
>**Data Type**: Boolean
>**Default Value**: False
>Location of annotations

autoPlaceWindows
>**Data Type**: Boolean
>**Default Value**: True
>Automatic placement of Mosaic window

boldFont
>   **Data Type**: font
>   **Default Value**: -adobe-times-bold-r-normal-*-17-*-*-*-*-*-iso8859-1
>   Font for bold, formatted text

catchPriorAndNext
>   **Data Type**: Boolean
>   **Default Value**: False
>   Function of Page Up and Page Down keys

colorsPerInlinedImage
>   **Data Type**: integer
>   **Default Value**: 50
>   Number of unique colors for inline images

confirmDeleteAnnotation
>   **Data Type**: Boolean
>   **Default Value**: True
>   Deleting annotations confirmation dialog

confirmExit
>   **Data Type**: Boolean
>   **Default Value**: True
>   Exiting confirmation dialog

dashedAnchorUnderlines
>   **Data Type**: Boolean
>   **Default Value**: False
>   Dashed lines under unvisited anchors

dashedVisitedAnchorUnderlines
>   **Data Type**: Boolean
>   **Default Value**: True
>   Dashed lines under visited anchors

defaultAuthorName
>   **Data Type**: string
>   **Default Value**: NULL
>   Full name of user

defaultHeight
>   **Data Type**: integer
>   **Default Value**: 700
>   Default Mosaic window height in pixels

defaultHotlistFile
>   **Data Type**: string
>   **Default Value**: .mosaic-hotlist-default
>   Filename for hotlist file

defaultWidth
> **Data Type**: integer
> **Default Value**: 640
> Default Mosaic window width in pixels

delayImageLoads
> **Data Type**: Boolean
> **Default Value**: False
> Delayed inline image loading

displayURLsNotTitles
> **Data Type**: Boolean
> **Default Value**: False
> Display URLs instead of document titles

docsDirectory
> **Data Type**: string
> **Default Value**: NULL
> Location of help documents

documentsMenuSpecfile
> **Data Type**: string
> **Default Value**: /usr/local/lib/mosaic/documents.menu
> Filename for Documents Menu specification

fancySelections
> **Data Type**: Boolean
> **Default Value**: False
> Use fancy HTML selections

font
> **Data Type**: font
> **Default Value**: -adobe-times-medium-r-normal-*-17-*-*-*-*-*-iso8859-1
> Font for normal, formatted text

fixedboldFont
> **Data Type**: font
> **Default Value**: -adobe-courier-bold-r-normal-*-17-*-*-*-*-*-iso8859-1
> Font for bold, fixed-width, formatted text

fixedFont
> **Data Type**: font
> **Default Value**: -adobe-courier-medium-r-normal-*-17-*-*-*-*-*-iso8859-1
> Font for fixed-width, formatted text

fixeditalicFont
> **Data Type**: font
> **Default Value**: -adobe-courier-medium-o-normal-*-17-*-*-*-*-*-iso8859-1
> Font for italic, fixed-width, formatted text

`fullHostname`
> **Data Type**: string
> **Default Value**: NULL
> Fully qualified hostname

`gethostbynameIsEvil`
> **Data Type**: Boolean
> **Default Value**: False
> Broken gethostbyname() on Sun's

`globalExtensionMap`
> **Data Type**: string
> **Default Value**: /usr/local/lib/mosaic/mime.types
> System-wide extension map file

`globalHistoryFile`
> **Data Type**: string
> **Default Value**: .mosaic-global-history
> Filename for global history file

`globalTypeMap`
> **Data Type**: string
> **Default Value**: /usr/local/lib/mosaic/mailcap
> System-wide mailcap file

`gunzipCommand`
> **Data Type**: string
> **Default Value**: gunzip -n -f
> Command for uncompressing gziped files

`hdfMaxImageDimension`
> **Data Type**: integer" .25i
> **Default Value**: 400
> **Maximum height and/or width of HDF images in pixels**

`hdfMaxDisplayedDatasets`
> **Data Type**: integer
> **Default Value**: 15
> Maximum number of HDF displayed datasets

`hdfMaxDisplayedAttributes`
> **Data Type**: integer
> **Default Value**: 10
> Maximum number of HDF displayed attributes

`hdfPowerUser`
> **Data Type**: Boolean
> **Default Value**: False
> Show supporting text in HDF file

header1Font
>   **Data Type**: font
>   **Default Value**: -adobe-times-bold-r-normal-*-24-*-*-*-*-*-iso8859-1
>   Font for first level headers

header2Font
>   **Data Type**: font
>   **Default Value**: -adobe-times-bold-r-normal-*-18-*-*-*-*-*-iso8859-1
>   Font for second level headers

header3Font
>   **Data Type**: font
>   **Default Value**: -adobe-times-bold-r-normal-*-17-*-*-*-*-*-iso8859-1
>   Font for third level headers

header4Font
>   **Data Type**: font
>   **Default Value**: -adobe-times-bold-r-normal-*-14-*-*-*-*-*-iso8859-1
>   Font for fourth level headers

header5Font
>   **Data Type**: font
>   **Default Value**: -adobe-times-bold-r-normal-*-12-*-*-*-*-*-iso8859-1
>   Font for fifth level headers

header6Font
>   **Data Type**: font
>   **Default Value**: -adobe-times-bold-r-normal-*-10-*-*-*-*-*-iso8859-1
>   Font for sixth level headers

homeDocument
>   **Data Type**: string
>   **Default Value**: ✱✱✱
>   Home page document

imageCacheSize
>   **Data Type**: integer
>   **Default Value**: 2048
>   Size of inline image cache in kilobytes

initialWindowIconic
>   **Data Type**: Boolean
>   **Default Value**: False
>   Initial window iconified

italicFont
>   **Data Type**: font
>   **Default Value**: -adobe-times-medium-i-normal-*-17-*-*-*-*-*-iso8859-1
>   Font for italic, formatted text

listingFont
>   **Data Type:** font
>   **Default Value:** -adobe-courier-medium-r-normal-*-12-*-*-*-*-*-iso8859-1
>   Font for computer file listings

maxWaisResponses
>   **Data Type:** integer
>   **Default Value:** 200
>   Maximum number of WAIS matches

percentVerticalSpace
>   **Data Type:** integer
>   **Default Value:** 90
>   Vertical space between paragraphs as percent of normal line height

personalAnnotationDirectory
>   **Data Type:** string
>   **Default Value:** .mosaic-personal-annotations
>   Directory name for annotations

personalExtensionMap
>   **Data Type:** string
>   **Default Value:** .mime.types
>   Personal extension map file

personalTypeMap
>   **Data Type:** string
>   **Default Value:** .mailcap
>   Personal mailcap file

plainboldFont
>   **Data Type:** font
>   **Default Value:** -adobe-courier-bold-r-normal-*-14-*-*-*-*-*-iso8859-1
>   Font for bold, preformatted text

plainFont
>   **Data Type:** font
>   **Default Value:** -adobe-courier-medium-r-normal-*-14-*-*-*-*-*-iso8859-1
>   Font for normal, preformatted text

plainitalicFont
>   **Data Type:** font
>   **Default Value:** -adobe-courier-medium-o-normal-*-14-*-*-*-*-*-iso8859-1
>   Font for italic, preformatted text

printCommand
>   **Data Type:** string
>   **Default Value:** lpr
>   Default print command

recordCommandLocation
> **Data Type**: string
> **Default Value**: system-dependent
> Location of record command for audio annotations

recordCommand
> **Data Type**: string
> **Default Value**: system-dependent
> Record command for audio annotations

reloadReloadsImages
> **Data Type**: Boolean
> **Default Value**: False
> Clear image cache when reloading document

reverseInlinedBitmapColors
> **Data Type**: Boolean
> **Default Value**: False
> Reverse foreground and background for XBM images

sendmailCommand
> **Data Type**: string
> **Default Value**: /usr/lib/sendmail
> Default sendmail command

simpleInterface
> **Data Type**: Boolean
> **Default Value**: False
> Pared down menus and buttons

tmpDirectory
> **Data Type**: string
> **Default Value**: NULL
> Directory name for temporary files

trackFullURLs
> **Data Type**: Boolean
> **Default Value**: True
> Display of format information for links

trackPointerMotion
> **Data Type**: Boolean
> **Default Value**: True
> Display URLs as pointer moves through links

trackVisitedAnchors
> **Data Type**: Boolean
> **Default Value**: True
> Visited anchors displayed in different style

tweakGopherTypes
    Data Type: Boolean
    Default Value: True
    Use Mosaic's Gopher typing mechanism

twirlIncrement
    Data Type: integer
    Default Value: 4096
    Bytes transferred between updates of twirling logo

twirlingTransferIcon
    Data Type: Boolean
    Default Value: True
    Display twirling icon

uncompressCommand
    Data Type: string
    Default Value: uncompress
    Command for uncompressing compressed files

useDefaultExtensionMap
    Data Type: Boolean
    Default Value: True
    Use default file extension to MIME type mappings

useDefaultTypeMap
    Data Type: Boolean
    Default Value: True
    Use default MIME type to external viewer mappings

useGlobalHistory
    Data Type: Boolean
    Default Value: True
    Store global history information

verticalScrollOnRight
    Data Type: Boolean
    Default Value: True
    Scroll bar on right side of Mosaic window

visitedAnchorColor
    Data Type: color
    Default Value: violetred4
    Color for visited anchors

visitedAnchorUnderlines
    Data Type: integer
    Default Value: 1
    Number of lines under visited anchors

xtermCommand
> **Data Type**: string
> **Default Value**: xterm
> Default command for starting terminal window

INSTALLING MOSAIC

Using the CD-ROM
Contents of the CD-ROM
Installing Binaries from the CD-ROM
Getting Mosaic from the Net
Building Mosaic from Source Code

T his book includes a CD-ROM containing Mosaic binaries for a number of different UNIX platforms. The CD-ROM provides Version 2.4 of NCSA Mosaic, the latest public domain version. This version of NCSA Mosaic has been customized for use with this book. It includes the Mosaic Handbook Home Page and *GNN* publications on the **Documents** menu. The CD-ROM includes binaries for the following platforms:

- DEC Alpha OSF/1 1.3

- DEC MIPS Ultrix 4.0

- HP 9000/730 HP-UX 9.01

- IBM RS/6000 AIX 3.2.4

- Intergraph CLIX 7.5

- Silicon Graphics IRIX 5.1 and 4.0

- Sun Solaris 2.3

- Sun SunOS 4.1.3

If you are using one of those platforms and you don't have Mosaic installed on your system, you can install one of the binaries included on the CD-ROM. Otherwise you can get the source code for Mosaic from the Internet and build it for your platform, as we'll describe later in this appendix.

Using the CD-ROM

If you are new to CD-ROMs, you will need to learn about some specific CD-ROM issues before you can access the software on the CD-ROM that accompanies this book.

The CD-ROM can be used in two different ways:

- It can be mounted just long enough for software to be copied onto a local hard disk. In this respect, it is a distribution medium similar to magnetic tapes or floppy disks.

- It can be mounted so that it is always present and available as a local read-only hard disk. It will appear as a filesystem, and you can use familiar UNIX commands to peruse it.

There are several issues that you need to be aware of when using the CD-ROM. The commands and procedures vary depending on what platform you are using, but you should be able to figure out what to do based on the following description.

The CD-ROM Format

The Mosaic CD conforms to the ISO standard 9660. This is sometimes called "High Sierra," but there are differences between the two formats. The ISO 9660 standard is what most CD-ROM drivers will support from now on, even though they will read High Sierra disks.

For UNIX users, ISO 9660 may come as a shock. For example, a directory listing of an ISO 9660 disk might look like this:

```
% ls /cdrom
ALPHA        IBM          SGI5         WELCOME.TXT;1
DEC          INTRGRPH     SOLARIS
HP700        SGI4         SUN
```

ISO 9660 specifies that the filenames are mono-case, and are limited to eight characters with three-character extensions. If the filename doesn't contain a period, one is added at the end of the filename. A "version number" is also appended, following a semicolon. (Version numbers are used in some non-UNIX filesystems such as VMS.) Some systems do not use all these features, so there are several variations that you will encounter.

For example, a file called *readme.txt* may appear as any of the following, depending on what system you mount the CD-ROM on:

```
README.TXT    README.TXT;1    readme.txt    readme.txt;1
```

Directory names are simply eight characters or less and mono-case. A directory called "IBM" can appear as *IBM* or *ibm*.

ISO 9660 also limits directory depth to eight levels.

If your CD-ROM driver program appends version numbers to filenames, you will need to be careful when specifying filenames in commands to the UNIX shell. You will need to escape the semicolon character (;) or single-quote the entire file-name, as shown below:

```
% cp /cdrom/dec/readme.txt\;1 readme.txt
```

```
% cp '/cdrom/dec/readme.txt;1' readme.txt
```

If you don't quote or escape the semicolon, you'll get a message like this:

```
% cp /cdrom/dec/readme.txt;1 readme.txt
Usage: cp [-ip] f1 f2; or: cp [-ipr] f1 ... fn d2
1: Command not found
```

Don't Have a CD-ROM Drive?

If you don't have a CD-ROM drive, don't despair. You can get the Mosaic binaries from the Internet. We'll describe how to do this later in the appendix. But if you don't have a CD-ROM drive, we strongly suggest that you get one. And not just for this disc—CD-ROM is quickly becoming the distribution method of choice, and not just for software.

Mounting the CD-ROM

Under UNIX, the CD-ROM is simply another filesystem (a read-only one). In most cases, the standard *mount* command can be used to mount a CD-ROM. This usually has the form:

```
# mount CD-ROM_device mount_point
```

The CD-ROM device name varies depending on the type of system. If you do not know the device name, consult the documentation that comes with your system. On some systems, the SCSI ID of the CD-ROM device can vary. The SCSI ID will be part of the device name—for example, */dev/rz3c* is the CD-ROM at SCSI ID 3 on a DECstation.

The mount point is simply a directory that will become the parent directory of the CD-ROM when it is mounted.

Most systems do not provide a way for unprivileged users to mount the CD, so you probably need to become the superuser to mount and use the CD-ROM. For this reason, the bulk of this section assumes some knowledge of system administration and superuser commands. If you do not have permission to *su root*, you will need to have your system administrator install the CD-ROM software for you. As the CD is read-only, you may have to specify this fact to the *mount* program or it will generate an error if it tries to open the CD-ROM device for writing. Some systems also need to be told the type of filesystem being mounted (hsfs or iso9660) if it is not the default (usually ufs or nfs). There may be options to the *mount* program that control whether all the ISO 9660 features (such as version numbers) are turned on.

For example, the CD can be mounted on a SunOS 4.1.3 system with the command:

```
# /etc/mount -r -t hsfs /dev/sr0 /cdrom
```

This command mounts the CD (*/dev/sr0*) on the mount point (*/cdrom*) in a read-only fashion (*–r*). If you omit the *–r* option, *mount* will give the following error:

```
mount_hsfs: must be mounted readonly
mount: giving up on:
    /cdrom
```

If you omit the filesystem type of hsfs (High Sierra File System, which preceded the ISO 9660 format), you will get:

```
mount: /dev/sr0 on /cdrom: Invalid argument
mount: giving up on:
    /cdrom
```

The procedure for mounting a CD-ROM varies with each type of operating system. You should consult the manual pages for the *mount* command and look for a mention of CD-ROM, ISO 9660, or High Sierra:

```
% man mount
```

Some examples of *mount* commands for the supported systems are:

- Sun SunOS 4.1.3

  ```
  # /etc/mount -r -t hsfs /dev/sr0 /cdrom
  ```

- Solaris 2.3

  ```
  # /etc/mount -r -F hsfs /dev/dsk/c0t6d0s0 /cdrom
  ```

- IBM RS/6000 AIX 3.2

  ```
  # /etc/mount -r -v cdrfs /dev/cd0 /cdrom
  ```

- DECstation Ultrix 4.x

  ```
  # /etc/mount -t cdfs -o noversion /dev/rz3c /cdrom
  ```

  The **noversion** option will disable the version information on the filenames.

- HP 700 HP-UX

  ```
  # /etc/mount -r -s cdfs /dev/dsk/c201d2s0 /cdrom
  ```

- SGI IRIX 4.x

  ```
  # /etc/mount -o ro,notranslate -t iso9660 /dev/scsi/sc0d5l0 /cdrom
  ```

You can also start up the *cdromd* process:

```
# cdromd -o ro,notranslate -d /dev/scsi/sc0d510 /cdrom
```

To mount the disk, just insert it in the drive. To unmount it, use the *eject* command.

- OSF/1 for DEC Alpha

```
# /usr/sbin/mount -t cdfs -o noversion /dev/rz3c /cdrom
```

Contents of the CD-ROM

The CD-ROM contains a top-level directory for each of the supported platforms. The Mosaic binaries and supporting files for each platform are distributed in the form of uncompressed **tar** files. You will find a **tar** file and a *readme.txt* file in each top-level directory.

We have chosen to distribute **tar** files rather than individual files partly because of ISO 9660 CD-ROM format restrictions. We wanted to be able to use standard UNIX filenames, rather than the more restrictive ISO 9660 filenames. The **tar** format is also most efficient for you, because you will have to copy only one file.

If you are familiar with the way UNIX packages are distributed on the Internet, you will note that on the Net the files are compressed (e.g., *filename.tar.Z* or *filename.tar.gz*). Because ISO 9660 does not allow two extensions and because we had plenty of room on the CD, we chose to include the binaries in uncompressed format.

Installing Binaries from the CD-ROM

If you are using one of the supported platforms, then once you have the CD-ROM mounted, you can proceed to install the Mosaic binary onto your system. If your platform is not one of the supported platforms, you should be able to build Mosaic from the source code, as we'll describe shortly.

Again, the CD-ROM includes binaries for the following platforms:

- DEC Alpha OSF/1 1.3
- DEC MIPS Ultrix 4.0
- HP 9000/730 HP-UX 9.01
- IBM RS/6000 AIX 3.2.4
- Intergraph CLIX 7.5
- Silicon Graphics IRIX 5.1 and 4.0

- Sun Solaris 2.3

- Sun SunOS 4.1.3

The pre-compiled binaries may work on operating system versions slightly older or newer than the ones listed here. If you are uncertain of your operating system version, the *uname* command may help:

```
% uname -a
SunOS ruby 4.1.3_U1 24 sun4m
```

The installation process for Mosaic is quite simple, so we have not provided an installation program. Instead we will walk you through the process step-by-step. Our example installs files in the "standard" locations; consult the documentation for your system to determine the actual directories you should use.

1. To begin the installation, become the superuser and mount the CD-ROM. Then change directories to the mount point you specified for the CD-ROM and see what is there. In our case, we specified */cdrom* as our mount point:

    ```
    # cd /cdrom
    # ls
    alpha        ibm          sgi5          welcome.txt
    dec          intrgrph     sun
    hp700        sgi4         solaris
    ```

    The output could look slightly different depending on the type of the system:

    ```
    ALPHA        IBM          SGI5          WELCOME.TXT;1
    DEC          INTRGRPH     SUN
    HP700        SGI4         SOLARIS
    ```

2. Change directories to the appropriate directory for your platform and check the contents. For example, on a SunOS 4.1.3 system:

    ```
    # cd sun
    # ls
    readme.txt     sun.tar
    ```

3. Now you need to decide where you want to put the *.tar* file, so that you can extract its contents. This directory can be a temporary one, as you'll only need it during the installation process. On our system, we used the directory */usr/local/mosaic*. Create the directory if it doesn't exist, change to it, and copy the appropriate file from the CD-ROM:

    ```
    # mkdir /usr/local/mosaic
    # cd /usr/local/mosaic
    # cp /cdrom/sun/sun.tar sun.tar
    ```

Remember, if your CD-ROM driver uses version numbers, you will need to escape the semicolon:

```
# cp /cdrom/sun/sun.tar\;1 sun.tar
```

4. Now you can unpack the **tar** archive with the following command (or an appropriate command for your own system):

```
# tar xvf sun.tar
```

This extracts the individual files from the **tar** file, displays a list of them as they are extracted, and places them in the current directory:

```
x Mosaic-sun
x Mosaic-sun-lresolv
x app-defaults.color
x app-defaults.mono
x documents.menu
x xbook.html
x gnnicon.gif
x x-hlicon.gif
x x-home.gif
x x-spticn.gif
```

The files you see here are the Mosaic binary, application defaults files, a **Documents** menu specification file, and *.html* and *.gif* files for the Mosaic Handbook Home Page.

5. Once you've unpacked the archive, all that's left is to copy the files to appropriate directories on your system. First, copy the Mosaic binary to an appropriate location, typically */usr/local/bin*. You should also change the name of the binary to just *Mosaic:**

```
# cp Mosaic-sun /usr/local/bin/Mosaic
```

6. Now you need to install the application defaults file for Mosaic. If you are using a color system, copy the color application defaults file to the appropriate location, typically *usr/lib/X11/app-defaults*. Change the filename from *app-defaults.color* to *Mosaic*:

```
# cp app-defaults.color /usr/lib/X11/app-defaults/Mosaic
```

If you have a monochrome system, you should instead copy the file *app-defaults.mono*:

```
# cp app-defaults.mono /usr/lib/X11/app-defaults/Mosaic
```

---

* While the official name of the program is **Mosaic** with a capital "M," you may also want to create symbolic links for the names **xmosaic** and/or **mosaic**, as users may be accustomed to using those names:

```
# ln -s Mosaic xmosaic
```

The application defaults file sets up Mosaic so that the program uses the Mosaic Handbook Home Page we have provided. If you don't install the application defaults file correctly, Mosaic will retrieve the NCSA Mosaic Home Page from the NCSA WWW server instead.

7. To set up the **Documents** menu and the Home Page for Mosaic, first create the directory */usr/local/lib/mosaic*:

```
# mkdir /usr/local/lib/mosaic
```

Now copy the rest of the files to that directory:

```
# cp documents.menu /usr/local/lib/mosaic/
# cp xbook.html /usr/local/lib/mosaic/
# cp *.gif /usr/local/lib/mosaic/
```

The *documents.menu* file sets up the **Documents** menu to provide easy access to *GNN* publications. The *xbook.html* file is the Mosaic Handbook Home Page; the *.gif* files are images used by the Home Page.

You can also put these files into a different directory (i.e., other than */usr/local/lib/mosaic*) if that's more appropriate for your system, but if you do you'll need to make some changes to the application defaults file you just installed. Specifically, you'll need to change the value of the homeDocument resource to point to the correct location of *xbook.html*. The *.gif* files need to be in the same directory as *xbook.html* for the Home Page to display correctly. You'll also need to set documentsMenuSpecfile to the correct location of *documents.menu*. See Chapter 5, *Customizing Mosaic*, for more information about setting these resources.

8. That's it! Now you can test things out. You should probably do that as a normal user, rather than superuser. To run Mosaic:

```
% Mosaic &
```

You should see Mosaic displaying the Mosaic Handbook Home Page, as described in Chapter 2, *Getting Started with Mosaic*.

9. Once you are satisfied that everything is working properly, you can remove the directory where you put the *.tar* file:

```
# rm -r /usr/local/mosaic
```

The final step is to unmount the CD-ROM with the *umount* command, using just the mount point as the argument:

```
# /etc/umount /cdrom
```

Getting Mosaic from the Net

The Mosaic binaries provided on the CD-ROM are also available via anonymous FTP from **ftp.ncsa.uiuc.edu** in */Web/Mosaic/Unix/binaries/2.4*. If you don't have a CD-ROM drive, you can use **ftp** to download the appropriate binary to your system. All of the binaries on NCSA's FTP server are compressed with **gzip**, so you'll need to have this program to uncompress Mosaic. The source code for **gzip** is available via anonymous FTP from **prep.ai.mit.edu** in */pub/gnu*.

If your system is not one of the supported platforms for Mosaic, you may still be able to find a suitable version of Mosaic on the Net. There are a number of unsupported binaries available on NCSA's FTP server in */Web/Mosaic/Unix/contrib*. If you have access to Mosaic on another system, you can also check out the *NCSA Mosaic FAQ: Machines and Systems* document using the following URL:

```
http://www.ncsa.uiuc.edu/SDG/Software/Mosaic/Docs/faq-machines.html
```

This document has information about a number of systems to which Mosaic has been ported, as well as links to sites where the ported versions are available.

We've also made the Mosaic Handbook Home Page available on the Net, so that you can retrieve it if you don't have a CD-ROM drive. The files for the Home Page are available via anonymous FTP from **ftp.ora.com** in the file */pub/nutshell/mosaic/x/xhomepage.tar.Z*.

If you are retrieving a Mosaic binary from the Net, follow these steps to install the program and customize it to use the Home Page:

1. Create a directory where you can store the Mosaic binary and the Home Page *.tar* file, such as */usr/local/mosaic*.

2. Change to this directory and download the Mosaic binary using **ftp**. Uncompress the file using **gunzip** if it has a *.gz* file extension or **uncompress** if it has a *.Z* extension.

3. Install the binary in a standard location, such as */usr/local/bin*. Make sure the program is executable by changing its permissions as follows (you'll need superuser privileges to do this):

    ```
    # cp Mosaic /usr/local/bin/Mosaic
    # chmod 755 Mosaic
    ```

4. Download the Home Page file (*/pub/nutshell/mosaic/x/xhomepage.tar.Z*) from the O'Reilly FTP server (**ftp.ora.com**). Uncompress and unpack the **tar** archive with the following commands:

    ```
    # uncompress xhomepage.tar.Z
    # tar xvf xhomepage.tar
    ```

This extracts the individual files, lists them, and places them in the current directory:

```
x app-defaults.color
x app-defaults.mono
x documents.menu
x xbook.html
x gnnicon.gif
x x-hlicon.gif
x x-home.gif
x x-spticn.gif
```

We've included application defaults files, a **Documents** menu specification file, and *.html* and *.gif* files for the Mosaic Handbook Home Page in this **tar** archive.

5. Install the application defaults file by copying *app-defaults.color* (for a color system) or *app-defaults.mono* (for a black-and-white system) to the appropriate location, usually */usr/lib/X11/app-defaults*. In either case, change the filename to *Mosaic*. For example:

```
# cp app-defaults.color /usr/lib/X11/app-defaults/Mosaic
```

The application defaults file customizes Mosaic to use the Mosaic Handbook Home Page.

6. To set up the **Documents** menu and the Home Page, first create the directory */usr/local/lib/mosaic*:

```
# mkdir /usr/local/lib/mosaic
```

Now copy the rest of the files to that directory:

```
# cp documents.menu /usr/local/lib/mosaic/
# cp xbook.html /usr/local/lib/mosaic/
# cp *.gif /usr/local/lib/mosaic/
```

The *documents.menu* file sets up the **Documents** menu, while the *xbook.html* describes the Mosaic Handbook Home Page. The *.gif* files are images used by the Home Page; they must be present for the Home Page to display correctly.

7. Now you are ready to run Mosaic:

```
% Mosaic &
```

Building Mosaic from Source Code

If you can't find a version of Mosaic for your system, or if you just really want to build it yourself, you can get the source code and build Mosaic. The source for Version 2.4 of NCSA Mosaic for the X Window System is available from NCSA's FTP server (**ftp.ncsa.uiuc.edu**) in */Web/Mosaic/Unix/source/Mosaic-2.4.tar.gz*.

Here are the steps you need to follow to build Mosaic:

1. Create a directory for the source code. Where you put this depends on how your system is configured. On our system, we put it in */usr/local/src/mosaic*.

2. Use **ftp** to download the Mosaic source code from the NCSA FTP server.

3. Uncompress and unpack the file using **zcat**:

   ```
   % zcat Mosaic-2.4.tar.gz | tar xf -
   ```

   If **zcat** is not available on your system, use separate **gunzip** and **tar** commands:

   ```
   % gunzip Mosaic-2.4.tar.gz
   % tar xvf Mosaic-2.4.tar
   ```

   This step creates an *Mosaic-2.4* subdirectory that contains the source code for Mosaic.

4. Change to this directory and follow the instructions in the *README* file to build Mosaic.

5. Once you've built Mosaic, install the binary in a standard location, such as */usr/local/bin*.

6. If you want to customize Mosaic to use the Mosaic Handbook Home Page, follow the instructions given in the previous section for retrieving the Home Page and configuring Mosaic to use it.

GLOSSARY

access provider

See "Internet Service Provider."

anchor

The location of a hypertext link in a document; it can be used to describe the link as it appears in text or graphics as well as the place that the link references.

Archie

A program used to locate files that are publicly available by anonymous FTP.

ARPAnet

An experimental network established in the 1970's that served as a test environment for the software on which the Internet is based. No longer in existence.

attributes

(a) SGML (and HTML) tags may accept attributes that further define their usage, much as parameters are used with command-line options. A tag may be followed by an attribute, which in turn is assigned a particular value.

(b) Configurable characteristics of Mosaic that determine how the program functions and how it displays elements on your screen.

baud

When transmitting data, the number of times the medium's "state" changes per second. For example: a 14.4 baud modem changes the signal it sends on the phone line 14,400 times per second. Since each change in state can correspond to multiple bits of data, the actual bit rate of data transfer may exceed the baud rate. See also "bits per second".

bits per second (bps)

The speed at which bits are transmitted over a communication medium.

browser

A program that interprets and displays HTML documents.

cache

Generically speaking, a location in memory where data is stored for easy retrieval, or the process of storing them. Some versions of Mosaic cache the document previously viewed so you can return to it easily. You can configure Mosaic to hold an additional number of documents and images in the cache. If a document or image is not available in the cache, Mosaic has to return to the Internet to retrieve it.

CERN

The European Particle Physics Laboratory (CERN) in Geneva, Swizterland; Hypertext technologies developed at CERN to allow physicists to share information provided the basis for the World Wide Web.

client

A software application that works on your behalf to extract some service from a server somewhere on the network. Think of your telephone as a client and the telephone company as a server.

dialup

(a) To connect to a computer by calling it up on the telephone. Often, "dialup" only refers to the kind of connection you make when using a terminal emulator and a regular modem. For the technoids: switched character-oriented asynchronous communication.

(b) A port that accepts dialup connections. ("How many dialup ports on your computer?")

dialup account

A type of Internet connection that operates over standard phone lines. Dialup accounts are of two types: shell accounts and PPP/SLIP accounts.

To use a shell account, you typically use a telecommunications program to dial the Internet host and log in. This is a cheap and easy method, but has many limitations; for example, you can't use Mosaic.

A PPP/SLIP account, which requires a high-speed modem, actually puts your computer on the network and allows you to use Mosaic.

See also "Mosaic," "shell," "PPP," "SLIP," and "dedicated line."

download

To transfer data from a remote server to your local system. The FTP program is often used to download files.

DNS

The Domain Name System; a distributed database system for translating computer names (like **ruby.ora.com**) into numeric Internet addresses (like **194.56.78.2**), and vice-versa. DNS allows you to use the Internet without remembering long lists of numbers.

dedicated line

A permanently connected private telephone line between two locations. Dedicated lines are typically used to connect a moderate-sized local network to an Internet service provider. If your Internet connection is provided by a dedicated line, you should be able to use Mosaic. See also "Mosaic" and "dialup account."

Ethernet

A kind of "local area network" (or LAN). It's difficult to define an ethernet because there are several different kinds of wiring, which support different communication speeds, ranging from 2 to 10 million bits per second. What makes an Ethernet an Ethernet is the way the computers on the network decide whose turn it is to talk. Computers using TCP/IP are frequently connected to the Internet over an Ethernet. (Say that three times fast.)

FAQ

An acronym that generally refers to a list of frequently asked questions and their answers, or a question from the list. Many USENET newsgroups and some non-USENET mailing lists maintain FAQ lists (FAQs) so that participants don't spend a lot of time answering the same set of questions.

firewall

See "security firewall."

FTP

(a) The File Transfer Protocol; a protocol that defines how to transfer files from one computer to another.

(b) An application program that moves files using the File Transfer Protocol.

gateway

A computer system that transfers data between normally incompatible applications or networks. It reformats the data so that it is acceptable for the new network (or application) before passing it on. A gateway may connect two dissimilar networks, like DECnet and the Internet; or it might allow two incompatible applications to communicate over the same network (like mail systems with different message formats).

GIF

GIF refers to the Graphics Interchange Format, a graphics file format developed by CompuServe, Inc., which is used on a variety of platforms and systems. GIF is one of the most widely used formats for storing complex graphics, and one of only two formats in which inline images can appear in an HTML document. See also "XBM."

Gopher

A menu-based system for exploring Internet resources; the items are arranged in a hierarchy and each item represents either a file or a directory.

History

A function of the Mosaic browser that keeps track of all the documents you visit and allows you to call them up again.

home page

A home page is the graphical door to the information a server provides. The home page is generally a screen or windowful of information in which all links to related information are included.

host

(a) Generically, a computer.

(b) Sometimes, a computer that provides resources to the Internet; also called an Internet host computer.

Hotlist

A function of the Mosaic browser that allows you to keep a list of the documents you're most interested in and to call them up again.

HoTMetaL

A program from SoftQuad that assists you in formatting documents using HTML codes; available both as freeware and as a commercial product.

HTML

The HyperText Markup Language, a subset of SGML, provides codes used to format hypertext documents. Individual codes are used to define the hierarchy and nature of the various components of the document, as well as to specify hypertext links.

HTTP

The HyperText Transfer Protocol, a fixed set of messages and replies whereby a client and server communicate during a hypertext link.

hyperlink

See "link."

hypermedia

See "hypertext."

hypertext

Any document that contains links to other documents; selecting a link automatically displays the second document.

IAB

See the "Internet Architecture Board."

IETF

See the "Internet Engineering Task Force."

ISP

See "Internet Service Provider."

inline image

An inline image is a graphic image that appears within the current hypertext page. See also "linked image."

Internet

(a) Generally (not capitalized), any collection of distinct networks working together as one.

(b) Specifically (capitalized), the world-wide "network of networks," which are connected to each other using the Internet protocol and other similar protocols. The Internet provides file transfer, remote login, electronic mail, news, and other services.

Internet Architecture Board (IAB)

The group that makes decisions about standards and other important issues.

Internet Engineering Task Force (IETF)

A volunteer group that investigates and solves technical problems and makes recommendations to the Internet Architecture Board (IAB).

Internet resources

Public information available via the Internet.

Internet Service Provider (ISP)

An organization that provides connections to a part of the Internet. If you want to connect your company's network, or even your personal computer, to the Internet, you have to talk to a "service provider."

ISO

The International Standards Organization (or International Organization for Standardization); an organization that has defined a different set of network protocols, called the ISO/OSI protocols. In theory, the ISO/OSI protocols will eventually replace the Internet protocols. When and if this will actually happen is a hotly debated topic.

JPEG

JPEG (pronounced "jay-peg"), which is an acronym for the Joint Photographic Experts Group, refers to a standards committee, a method of file compression, and a graphics file format. The committee originated from within the International Standards Organization (ISO) to research and develop standards for the transmission of image data over networks. The results were a highly successful method of data compression and several closely associated file formats to store the data. JPEG files typically contain photographs, video stills, or other complex images. Since Mosaic cannot display JPEG format files as "inline images," it launches a special viewer window in which the images are displayed.

LAN

See "Local Area Network."

leased line

See "dedicated line."

link

In hypertext documents, the connection from one document to another. See also "anchor."

linked image

A linked image is a graphic image that appears in a file separate from the current hypertext page; it is displayed by selecting a link. See also "inline image."

Local Area Network (LAN)

A grouping of computers that are physically connected within a fairly limited location.

Lynx

A character-based browsing program developed at the University of Kansas.

MIME

The Multipurpose Internet Mail Extensions protocol (MIME), which defines a number of content types and subtypes that allow programs like Mosaic to recognize different kinds of files and deal with them appropriately. The MIME type specifies what kind of file it is, such as image, audio, or video, and the subtype gives the precise file format.

modem

A piece of equipment that connects a computer to a data transmission line (typically a telephone line). Most people use modems that transfer data at speeds ranging from 1200 bits per second (bps) to 19.2 Kbps. There are also modems providing higher speeds and supporting other media. These are used for special purposes—for example, to connect a large local network to its network provider over a leased line.

Mosaic

A graphical browser for the World Wide Web that supports hypermedia. Mosaic is often used incorrectly as a synonym for the World Wide Web.

MPEG

An acronym (pronounced "em-peg") for the Motion Picture Experts Group. MPEG denotes a standards committee, a method of file compression, and a graphics file format. The main application for MPEG is the storage of audio and video data on CD-ROMs for use in multimedia systems. Since Mosaic cannot display MPEG format files as inline images, it launches a special viewer window in which the images are displayed.

MUD/MOO

MUD refers to Multi-User Dungeon, a group of role-playing games modelled on the original "Dungeons and Dragons" games. MUDs have also been used as conferencing tools and educational aids. A MOO is an object-oriented MUD. Some experimental Web servers are set up with interactive MUD/MOO interfaces.

multimedia

Documents that include different kinds of data; for example, text, audio, and video.

NCSA

The National Center for Supercomputing Applications; NCSA produces a public domain version of the Mosaic browsing program and licenses the technology to developers.

NFS

The Network File System; a set of protocols that allows you to use files on other network machines as if they were local. So, rather than using FTP to transfer a file to your local computer, you can read it, write it, or edit it on the remote computer—using the same commands that you would use locally. NFS was originally developed by Sun Microsystems, Inc., and is widely used.

NSFNET

The National Science Foundation Network; the NSFNET is *not* the Internet. It's just one of the networks that make up the Internet.

OSI

Open Systems Interconnect; another set of network protocols. See "ISO."

packet

A bundle of data. On the Internet, data is broken up into small chunks, called "packets"; each packet traverses the network independently. Packet sizes can vary from roughly 40 to 32,000 bytes, depending on network hardware and media, but packets are normally less than 1500 bytes long.

port

(a) A number that identifies a particular Internet application. When your computer sends a packet to another computer, that packet contains information about what protocol it's using (e.g., TCP), and what application it's trying to communicate with. The "port number" identifies the application.

(b) One of a computer's physical input/output channels (i.e., a plug on the back).

Unfortunately, these two meanings are completely unrelated. The first is more common when you're talking about the Internet (as in "**telnet** to port 1000"); the second is more common when you're talking about hardware ("connect your modem to the serial port on the back of your computer").

PPP

Point-to-Point Protocol; a protocol that allows a computer to use the TCP/IP (Internet) protocols (and become a full-fledged Internet member) with a standard telephone line and a high-speed modem. Although PPP is less common than SLIP, it's quickly increasing in popularity.

PPP/SLIP account

See "dialup account."

protocol

Simply, a definition of how computers will act when talking to each other. Protocol definitions range from how bits are placed on a wire to the format of an electronic mail message. Standard protocols allow computers from different manufacturers to communicate; the computers can use completely different software, providing that the programs running on both ends agree on what the data means.

proxy server

A server on the Internet that provides indirect Internet access to systems excluded from a direct connection by a security firewall.

RFC

A Request For Comments; a set of papers in which the Internet's standards, proposed standards, and generally agreed-upon ideas are documented and published.

router

A system that transfers data between two networks that use the same protocols. The networks may differ in physical characteristics (e.g., a router may transfer data between an Ethernet and a leased telephone line).

security firewall

A system that isolates an organization's computers from external access, as through the Internet. The organization sometimes provides some Internet access through use of a proxy system. The firewall is intended to protect other machines at the site from potential tampering from the Net.

server

(a) Software that allows a computer to offer a service to another computer. Other computers contact the server program by means of matching client software.

(b) The computer on which the server software runs.

service provider

See "Internet Service Provider."

SGML

Standard Generalized Markup Language; a set of codes used to format documents. Individual codes are used to define the hierarchy and nature of the various components of a document; for example, as headers, options, variables, etc.

shell

On a UNIX system, software that accepts and processes command lines from your terminal. UNIX has multiple shells available (e.g., C shell, Bourne shell, Korn shell), each with slightly different command formats and facilities.

shell account

See "dialup account."

SLIP

Serial Line IP (Internet Protocol); a protocol that allows a computer to use the Internet protocols (and become a full-fledged Internet member) with a standard telephone line and a high-speed modem. SLIP is being superseded by PPP, but still in common use.

tags

In HTML, tags are the codes that determine both the structure of information within a document and its presentation.

TCP/IP

Transmission Control Protocol/Internet Protocol; the most important of the protocols on which the Internet is based. TCP is a reliable connection-oriented protocol; IP allows a packet to traverse multiple networks on the way to its final destination.

TELNET

(a) A "terminal emulation" protocol that allows you to log in to other computer systems on the Internet.

(b) An application program that allows you to log in to another computer system using the TELNET protocol.

TIFF

The Tag Image File Format, a graphics file format developed by Aldus Corporation, which has become a standard format found in most paint, imaging, and desktop publishing programs. TIFF is both powerful and flexible, and allows for storage of grayscale and color images.

URL

Uniform Resource Locator; the address of a document on the World Wide Web. The address is contained in a link, which a client interprets in order to connect with the proper server.

USENET

An informal, rather anarchic, group of systems that exchange "news." News is essentially similar to "bulletin boards" on other networks. USENET actually predates the Internet, but these days, the Internet is used to transfer much of the USENET's traffic.

Veronica

A service that allows you to search all Gopher sites for menu items (files, directories, and other resources).

viewer

A program Mosaic launches as needed to display a file in a format it cannot handle internally. For instance, Mosaic launches an MPEG player program to display an MPEG video file in a separate window because it cannot interpret this format.

visit

To you access a World Wide Web document via a hypertext link. The anchor of a document that has been visited has a different appearance than the anchor of a link you haven't accessed.

W3O

An organization created by the Massachusetts Institute of Technology (MIT) and CERN to direct the development of the World Wide Web.

WAIS

See "Wide-Area Information Servers."

Wide-Area Information Servers (WAIS)

A very powerful search-and-retrieval system for information in databases (or libraries) across the Internet. WAIS databases are gradually being adopted for general information storage and retrieval by the Internet community.

WAN

See "Wide Area Network."

Wide Area Network (WAN)

A grouping of computers that are connected over communication lines, usually in a wide geographic area such as a state, country, or continent.

World Wide Web (WWW)

A hypertext-based system for finding and accessing Internet resources.

WWW

See "World Wide Web."

XBM

XBM refers to the X Bitmap graphics file format, which is the standard for bitmap image files in the X Window System. XBM files contain simple, two-tone images. XBM is one of only two formats in which inline images can appear in an HTML document. See also "GIF."

X Window System

A network-based windowing system, originally developed at the Massachusetts Institute of Technology (MIT); X is most frequently run in combination with the UNIX operating system.

INDEX

About the Authors

Dale Dougherty is manager of O'Reilly's Digital Media Group. He is publisher of the *Global Network Navigator*. He is also an editor and writer for O'Reilly & Associates. Among other books, Dale has written *sed & awk*, *UNIX Text Processing* (with Tim O'Reilly), *Using UUCP & Usenet* (with Grace Todino), and *Guide to the Pick System*.

Richard Koman is an editor for the *Global Network Navigator*. He is also technology editor for *Communication Arts*, a national graphic design magazine, and former editor of *Online Design*, a California monthly covering electronic design, graphics, and multimedia. He has covered design, publishing, and printing technology for a variety of publications.

Paula Ferguson is a writer for O'Reilly & Associates, as well as the editor of *The X Resource: A Practical Journal of the X Window System*. In addition to co-authoring this book, she has updated various volumes in the X series, including *Volume 6A, Motif Reference Manual*. Paula has also developed and taught courses on Motif for the Open Software Foundation and worked on various other interface-design and software development projects. Paula graduated from M.I.T. in 1990 with a B.S. in computer science and engineering. In July of 1994, she moved from Somerville, Massachusetts, to Boulder, Colorado, with her two cats. Now when she's not working in her home office, she's outside rock climbing, cycling, hiking, or skiing.

Colophon

Our look is the result of reader comments, our own experimentation, and feedback from distribution channels.

Distinctive covers complement our distinctive approach to technical topics, breathing personality and life into potentially dry subjects.

The image featured on the cover of *The Mosaic Handbook for the X Window System,* "The Pilot-House of the 'Great Republic'," may present an idealized view of the solitary sailor. A wheel this size would certainly take the full strength of two people to operate. In addition, there would doubtless be many people bustling about at any given time. Assuming that the ship pictured here is moving, this idyllic scene of contemplation is very unlikely to have happened.

A solitary journey through the Internet, however, is quite possible with Mosaic and the World Wide Web. Solitude is certainly not a requirement, however.

Edie Freedman designed this cover. The cover image is adapted from a 19th-century engraving from the Bettman Archives. The cover layout was produced with Quark XPress 3.3 using the ITC Garamond font.

The inside formats were designed by Edie Freedman and implemented in sqtroff by Lenny Muellner. The text and heading fonts are ITC Garamond Light and Garamond Book. The illustrations that appear in the book were created in Aldus Freehand by Chris Reilley, and the screenshots were processed in Adobe PhotoShop using Photomatic. This colophon was written by Clairemarie Fisher O'Leary.

INTERNET

Books from O'Reilly & Associates, Inc.

FALL/WINTER 1994-95

The Whole Internet User's Guide & Catalog

By Ed Krol
2nd Edition April 1994
574 pages, ISBN 1-56592-063-5

The best book about the Internet just got better! This is the second edition of our comprehensive—and bestselling—introduction to the Internet, the international network that includes virtually every major computer site in the world. In addition to email, file transfer, remote login, and network news, this book pays special attention to some new tools for helping you find information. Useful to beginners and veterans alike, this book will help you explore what's possible on the Net. Also includes a pull-out quick-reference card.

"An ongoing classic."
—*Rochester Business Journal*

"The book against which all subsequent Internet guides are measured, Krol's work has emerged as an indispensable reference to beginners and seasoned travelers alike as they venture out on the data highway."
—*Microtimes*

"*The Whole Internet User's Guide & Catalog* will probably become the Internet user's bible because it provides comprehensive, easy instructions for those who want to get the most from this valuable electronic tool."
—David J. Buerger, Editor, *Communications Week*

"Krol's work is comprehensive and lucid, an overview which presents network basics in clear and understandable language. I consider it essential."
—Paul Gilster, *Triad Business News*

!%@:: A Directory of Electronic Mail Addressing & Networks

By Donnalyn Frey & Rick Adams
4th Edition June 1994
662 pages, ISBN 1-56592-046-5

This is the only up-to-date directory that charts the networks that make up the Internet, provides contact names and addresses, and describes the services each network provides. It includes all of the major Internet-based networks, as well as various commercial networks such as CompuServe, Delphi, and America Online that are "gatewayed" to the Internet for transfer of electronic mail and other services. If you are someone who wants to connect to the Internet, or someone who already is connected but wants concise, up-to-date information on many of the world's networks, check out this book.

This is the fourth edition of this directory, now in a simplified format designed to allow more frequent updates.

"The book remains the bible of electronic messaging today. One could easily borrow the American Express slogan with the quip 'don't do messaging without it.' The book introduces you to electronic mail in all its many forms and flavors, tells you about the networks throughout the world...with an up-to-date summary of information on each, plus handy references such as all the world's subdomains. The husband-wife team authors are among the most knowledgeable people in the Internet world. This is one of those publications for which you just enter a lifetime subscription."
—Book Review, *ISOC News*

The Mosaic Handbooks

Mosaic is an important application that is becoming instrumental in the growth of the Internet. These books, one for Microsoft Windows, one for the X Window System, and one for the Macintosh, introduce you to Mosaic and its use in navigating and finding information on the World Wide Web. They show you how to use Mosaic to replace some of the traditional Internet functions like FTP, Gopher, Archie, Veronica, and WAIS. For more advanced users, the books describe how to add external viewers to Mosaic (allowing it to display many additional file types) and how to customize the Mosaic interface, such as screen elements, colors, and fonts. The Microsoft and Macintosh versions come with a copy of Mosaic on a floppy disk; the X Window version comes with a CD-ROM. All three books come with a subscription to The Global Network Navigator (GNN)™, the leading WWW-based information service on the Internet.

The Mosaic Handbook for Microsoft Windows

By Dale Dougherty & Richard Koman
1st Edition October 1994
234 pages (est.), ISBN 1-56592-094-5
(Foppy disk included)

The Mosaic Handbook for the X Window System

By Dale Dougherty, Richard Koman &
Paula Ferguson
1st Edition October 1994
220 pages (est.), ISBN 1-56592-095-3
(CD-ROM included)

The Mosaic Handbook for the Macintosh

By Dale Dougherty & Richard Koman
1st Edition October 1994
220 pages (est.), ISBN 1-56592-096-1
(Floppy disk included)

Internet In A Box

Produced by Spry, Inc.
Available late September 1994
UPC 799364 01100
(sold only in the US and Canada)

Internet In A Box™ is the first shrink-wrapped package to provide a total solution for PC users to get on the Internet. *Internet In A Box* provides instant connectivity, a multimedia Windows interface, a full suite of applications, and a complete online guide to the Internet. The box contains:

- Two ways to connect to the Internet: five-minute automated connection via SprintLink or manual connection to any PPP provider in the US and Canada.

- A subscription to the Global Network Navigator (GNN)™, an online interactive guide to the Internet.

- Software: The Air Series applications, including Mosaic, electronic mail, Usenet news reader, drag-and-drop file transfer, gopher, and telnet.

- Three books that clearly describe how to use these resources: a special edition of Ed Krol's bestselling *The Whole Internet User's Guide & Catalog*, a *Getting Started* guide, and an *Install* guide.

Connecting to the Internet

By Susan Estrada
1st Edition August 1993
188 pages, ISBN 1-56592-061-9

This book provides practical advice on how to get an Internet connection. It describes how to assess your needs to determine the kind of Internet service that is best for you and how to find a local access provider and evaluate the services they offer.

Knowing how to purchase the right kind of Internet access can help you save money and avoid a lot of frustration. This book is the fastest way for you to learn how to get on the Internet. Then you can begin exploring one of the world's most valuable resources.

"A much needed 'how to do it' for anyone interested in getting Internet connectivity and using it as part of their organization or enterprise. The sections are simple and straightforward.... If you want to know how to connect your organization, get this book."
—Book Review, *ISOC News*

Learning the UNIX Operating System

By Grace Todino, John Strang & Jerry Peek
3rd Edition August 1993
108 pages, ISBN 1-56592-060-0

If you are new to UNIX, this concise introduction will tell you just what you need to get started and no more. Why wade through a 600-page book when you can begin working productively in a matter of minutes? It's an ideal primer for Mac and PC users of the Internet who need to know a little bit about UNIX on the systems they visit.

This book is the most effective introduction to UNIX in print. The third edition has been updated and expanded to provide increased coverage of window systems and networking. It's a handy book for someone just starting with UNIX, as well as someone who encounters a UNIX system as a "visitor" via remote login over the Internet.

"If you have someone on your site who has never worked on a UNIX system and who needs a quick how-to, Nutshell® has the right booklet. *Learning the UNIX Operating System* can get a newcomer rolling in a single session. It covers logging in and out; files and directories; mail; pipes; filters; background-ing; and a large number of other topics. It's clear, cheap, and can render a newcomer productive in a few hours."
—;login

Smileys

By David W. Sanderson
1st Edition March 1993
93 pages, ISBN 1-56592-041-4

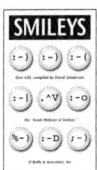

From the people who put an armadillo on the cover of a system administrator book comes this collection of the computer underground hiero-glyphs called "smileys." Originally inserted into email messages to denote "said with a cynical smile" :-), smileys now run rampant throughout the electronic mail culture.

"For a quick grin at an odd moment, this is a nice pocket book to carry around :-) If you keep this book near your terminal, you could express many heretofore hidden feelings in your email ;-) Then again, such things may be frowned upon at your company :-(No matter, this is a fun book to have around."
—Gregory M. Amov, *News & Review*

TCP/IP Network Administration

By Craig Hunt
1st Edition August 1992
502 pages, ISBN 0-937175-82-X

TCP/IP Network Administration is a complete guide to setting up and running a TCP/IP network for administrators of networks of systems or lone home systems that access the Internet. It starts with the fundamentals: what the protocols do and how they work, how to request a network address and a name (the forms needed are included in an appendix), and how to set up your network.

Beyond basic setup, the book discusses how to configure important network applications, including sendmail, the r* commands, and some simple setups for NIS and NFS. There are also chapters on troubleshooting and security. In addition, this book covers several important packages that are available from the Net (such as *gated*). Covers BSD and System V TCP/IP implementations.

"*TCP/IP Network Administration* provides a great service to network managers. Any network manager responsible for TCP/IP networking should keep a copy of this inexpensive reference nearby."
—*Network Computing*

Managing Internet Information Services

By Cricket Liu, Jerry Peek, Russ Jones, Bryan Buus & Adrian Nye
1st Edition Winter 1994/95 (est.)
400 pages (est.), ISBN 1-56592-062-7

This comprehensive guide describes how to set up information services to make them available over the Internet. Providing com-plete coverage of all popular services, it discusses why a company would want to offer Internet services and how to select which ones to provide. Most of the book describes how to set up email services and FTP, Gopher, and World Wide Web servers.

"*Managing Internet Information Services* has long been needed in the Internet community, as well as in many organi-zations with IP-based networks. Although many on the Internet are quite savvy when it comes to administering these types of tools, MIIS will allow a much larger community to join in and perhaps provide more diverse information. This book will be a welcome addition to my Internet shelf."
—Robert H'obbes' Zakon, MITRE Corporation

sendmail

By Bryan Costales, with Eric Allman & Neil Rickert
1st Edition November 1993
830 pages, ISBN 1-56592-056-2

Although sendmail is used on almost every UNIX system, it's one of the last great uncharted territories—and most difficult utilities to learn—in UNIX system administration. This book provides a complete sendmail tutorial, plus extensive reference material. It covers the BSD, UIUC IDA, and V8 versions of sendmail.

"The program and its rule description file, sendmail.cf, have long been regarded as the pit of coals that separated the mild Unix system administrators from the real fire walkers. Now, sendmail syntax, testing, hidden rules, and other mysteries are revealed. Costales, Allman, and Rickert are the indisputable authorities to do the text."
—Ben Smith, *Byte*

DNS and BIND

By Cricket Liu & Paul Albitz
1st Edition October 1992
418 pages, ISBN 1-56592-010-4

DNS and BIND contains all you need to know about the Internet's Domain Name System (DNS) and the Berkeley Internet Name Domain (BIND), its UNIX implementation. The Domain Name System is the Internet's "phone book"; it's a database that tracks important information (in particular, names and addresses) for every computer on the Internet. If you're a system administrator, this book will show you how to set up and maintain the DNS software on your network.

"At 380 pages it blows away easily any vendor supplied information, and because it has an extensive troubleshooting section (using nslookup) it should never be far from your desk—especially when things on your network start to go awry :-)"
—Ian Hoyle, BHP Research, Melbourne Laboratories

MH & xmh: E-mail for Users & Programmers

By Jerry Peek
2nd Edition September 1992
728 pages, ISBN 1-56592-027-9

Customizing your email environment can save time and make communicating more enjoyable. *MH & xmh: E-Mail for Users & Programmers* explains how to use, customize, and program with the MH electronic mail commands available on virtually any UNIX system. The handbook also covers *xmh*, an X Window System client that runs MH programs.

The second edition added a chapter on mhook, sections explaining under-appreciated small commands and features, and more examples showing how to use MH to handle common situations.

"The MH bible is irrefutably Jerry Peek's *MH & xmh: E-mail for Users & Programmers*. This book covers just about everything that is known about MH and *xmh* (the X Windows front end to MH), presented in a clear and easy-to-read format. I strongly recommend that anybody serious about MH get a copy."
—James Hamilton, *UnixWorld*

Practical UNIX Security

By Simson Garfinkel & Gene Spafford
1st Edition June 1991
512 pages, ISBN 0-937175-72-2

Practical UNIX Security tells system administrators how to make their UNIX system—either System V or BSD—as secure as it possibly can be without going to trusted system technology. The book describes UNIX concepts and how they enforce security, tells how to defend against and handle security breaches, and explains network security (including UUCP, NFS, Kerberos, and firewall machines) in detail. If you are a UNIX system administrator or user who deals with security, you need this book.

"Timely, accurate, written by recognized experts...covers every imaginable topic relating to Unix security. An excellent book and I recommend it as a valuable addition to any system administrator's or computer site manager's collection."
—Jon Wright, *Informatics*(Australia)

O'Reilly & Associates—
GLOBAL NETWORK NAVIGATOR

The Global Network Navigator (GNN)™ is a unique kind of information service that makes the Internet easy and enjoyable to use. We organize access to the vast information resources of the Internet so that you can find what you want. We also help you understand the Internet and the many ways you can explore it.

In GNN you'll find:

Navigating the Net with GNN

 The *Whole Internet Catalog* contains a descriptive listing of the most useful Net resources and services with live links to those resources.

 The *GNN Business Pages* are where you'll learn about companies who have established a presence on the Internet and use its worldwide reach to help educate consumers.

 The *Internet Help Desk* helps folks who are new to the Net orient themselves and gets them started on the road to Internet exploration.

News

 *NetNews* is a weekly publication that reports on the news of the Internet, with weekly feature articles that focus on Internet trends and special events. The Sports, Weather, and Comix Pages round out the news.

Special Interest Publications

 Whether you're planning a trip or are just interested in reading about the journeys of others, you'll find that the *Travelers' Center* contains a rich collection of feature articles and ongoing columns about travel. In the *Travelers' Center*, you can link to many helpful and informative travel-related Internet resources.

 The *Personal Finance Center* is the place to go for information about money management and investment on the Internet. Whether you're an old pro at playing the market or are thinking about investing for the first time, you'll read articles and discover Internet resources that will help you to think of the Internet as a personal finance information tool.

All in all, GNN helps you get more value for the time you spend on the Internet.

 The Best of the Web

The *O'Reilly Resource Center* was voted "**Best Commercial Site**" by users participating in "Best of the Web '94."

GNN received "Honorable Mention" for "**Best Overall Site**," "**Best Entertainment Service**," and "**Most Important Service Concept**."

The *GNN NetNews* received "Honorable Mention" for "**Best Document Design**."

Subscribe Today

GNN is available over the Internet as a subscription service. To get complete information about subscribing to GNN, send email to **info@gnn.com**. If you have access to a World Wide Web browser such as Mosaic or Lynx, you can use the following URL to register online: `http://gnn.com/`

If you use a browser that does not support online forms, you can retrieve an email version of the registration form automatically by sending email to **form@gnn.com**. Fill this form out and send it back to us by email, and we will confirm your registration.

AUDIOTAPES

O'Reilly now offers audiotapes based on interviews with people who are making a profound impact in the world of the Internet. Here we give you a quick overview of what's available. For details on our audiotape collection, send email to **audio@ora.com**.

"Ever listen to one of those five-minute-long news pieces being broadcast on National Public Radio's 'All Things Considered' and wish they were doing an in-depth story on new technology? Well, your wishes are answered." —Byte

Global Network Operations

Carl Malamud interviews Brian Carpenter, Bernhard Stockman, Mike O'Dell & Geoff Huston
Duration: 2 hours, ISBN 1-56592-993-4

What does it take to actually run a network? In these four interviews, Carl Malamud explores some of the technical and operational issues faced by Internet service providers around the world.

Brian Carpenter is the director for networking at CERN, the high-energy physics laboratory in Geneva, Switzerland. Physicists are some of the world's most active Internet users, and its global user base makes CERN one of the world's most network-intensive sites. Carpenter discusses how he deals with issues such as the OSI and DECnet Phase V protocols and his views on the future of the Internet.

Bernhard Stockman is one of the founders and the technical manager of the European Backbone (EBONE). EBONE has proven to be the first effective transit backbone for Europe and has been a leader in the deployment of CIDR, BGP-4, and other key technologies.

Mike O'Dell is vice president of research at UUNET Technologies. O'Dell has a long record of involvement in data communications, ranging from his service as a telco lab employee, an engineer on several key projects, and a member of the USENIX board to now helping define new services for one of the largest commercial IP service providers.

Geoff Huston is the director of the Australian Academic Research Network (AARNET). AARNET is known as one of the most progressive regional networks, rapidly adopting new services for its users. Huston talks about how networking in Australia has flourished despite astronomically high rates for long-distance lines.

The Future of the Internet Protocol

Carl Malamud interviews Steve Deering, Bob Braden, Christian Huitema, Bob Hinden, Peter Ford, Steve Casner, Bernhard Stockman & Noel Chiappa
Duration: 4 hours, ISBN 1-56592-996-9

The explosion of interest in the Internet is stressing what was originally designed as a research and education network. The sheer number of users is requiring new strategies for Internet address allocation; multimedia applications are requiring greater bandwidth and strategies such as "resource reservation" to provide synchronous end-to-end service.

In this series of eight interviews, Carl Malamud talks to some of the researchers who are working to define how the underlying technology of the Internet will need to evolve in order to meet the demands of the next five to ten years.

Give these tapes a try if you're intrigued by such topics as Internet "multicasting" of audio and video, or think your job might one day depend on understanding some of the following buzzwords:

- IPNG (Internet Protocol Next Generation)
- SIP (Simple Internet Protocol)
- TUBA (TCP and UDP with Big Addresses)
- CLNP (Connectionless Network Protocol)
- CIDR (Classless Inter-Domain Routing)

or if you are just interested in getting to know more about the people who are shaping the future.

Mobile IP Networking

Carl Malamud interviews Phil Karn & Jun Murai
Released Spring 1994
Duration: 1 hour, ISBN 1-56592-994-2

Phil Karn is the father of the KA9Q publicly available implementation of TCP/IP for DOS (which has also been used as the basis for the software in many commercial Internet routers). KA9Q was originally developed to allow "packet radio," that is, TCP/IP over ham radio bands. Phil's current research focus is on commercial applications of wireless data communications.

Jun Murai is one of the most distinguished researchers in the Internet community. Murai is a professor at Keio University and the founder of the Japanese WIDE Internet. Murai talks about his research projects, which range from satellite-based IP multicasting to a massive testbed for mobile computing at the Fujisawa campus of Keio University.

Networked Information and Online Libraries

Carl Malamud interviews Peter Deutsch & Cliff Lynch
Released September 1993
Duration: 1 hour, ISBN 1-56592-998-5

Peter Deutsch, president of Bunyip Information Services, was one of the co-developers of Archie. In this interview Peter talks about his philosophy for services and compares Archie to X.500. He also talks about what kind of standards we need for networked information retrieval.

Cliff Lynch is currently the director of library automation for the University of California. He discusses issues behind online publishing, such as SGML and the democratization of publishing on the Internet.

European Networking

Carl Malamud interviews Glenn Kowack & Rob Blokzijl
Released September 1993
Duration: 1 hour, ISBN 1-56592-999-3

Glenn Kowack is chief executive of EUnet, the network that's bringing the Internet to the people of Europe. Glenn talks about EUnet's populist business model and the politics of European networking.

Rob Blokzijl is the network manager for NIKHEF, the Dutch Institute of High Energy Physics. Rob talks about RIPE, the IP user's group for Europe, and the nuts and bolts of European network coordination.

Security and Networks

Carl Malamud interviews Jeff Schiller & John Romkey
Released September 1993
Duration: 1 hour, ISBN 1-56592-997-7

Jeff Schiller is the manager of MIT's campus network and is one of the Internet's leading security experts. Here, he talks about Privacy Enhanced Mail (PEM), the difficulty of policing the Internet, and whether horses or computers are more useful to criminals.

John Romkey has been a long-time TCP/IP developer and was recently named to the Internet Architecture Board. In this wide-ranging interview, John talks about the famous "ToasterNet" demo at InterOp, what kind of Internet security he'd like to see put in place, and what Internet applications of the future might look like.

John Perry Barlow
Notable Speeches of the Information Age

USENIX Conference Keynote Address
San Francisco, CA; January 17, 1994
Duration: 1.5 hours, ISBN 1-56592-992-6

John Perry Barlow—retired Wyoming cattle rancher, a lyricist for the Grateful Dead since 1971— holds a degree in comparative religion from Wesleyan University. He also happens to be a recognized authority on computer security, virtual reality, digitized intellectual property, and the social and legal conditions arising in the global network of computers.

In 1990 Barlow co-founded the Electronic Frontier Foundation with Mitch Kapor and currently serves as chair of its executive committee. He writes and lectures on subjects relating to digital technology and society and is a contributing editor to *Communications of the ACM, NeXTWorld, Microtimes, Mondo 2000, Wired,* and other publications.

In his keynote address to the Winter 1994 USENIX Conference, Barlow talks of recent developments in the national information infrastructure, telecommunications regulation, cryptography, globalization of the Internet, intellectual property, and the settlement of Cyberspace. The talk explores the premise that "architecture is politics": that the technology adopted for the coming "information superhighway" will help to determine what is carried on it, and that if the electronic frontier of the Internet is not to be replaced by electronic strip malls, we need to make sure that our technological choices favor bi-directional communication and open platforms.

Side A contains the keynote;
Side B contains a question and answer period.

O'Reilly on the Net—
ONLINE PROGRAM GUIDE

O'Reilly & Associates offers extensive information through our online resources. If you've got Internet access, we invite you to come and explore our little neck-of-the-woods.

Online Resource Center

Most comprehensive among our online offerings is the O'Reilly Resource Center. Here, you'll find detailed information and descriptions on all O'Reilly products: titles, prices, tables of contents, indexes, author bios, CD-ROM directory listings, reviews...you can even view images of the products themselves. We also supply helpful ordering information: how to contact us, how to order online, distributors and bookstores around the world, discounts, upgrades, etc. In addition, we provide informative literature in the field, featuring articles, interviews, bibliographies, and columns that help you stay informed and abreast.

To access ORA's Online Resource Center:

Point your Web browser (e.g., `mosaic` or `lynx`) to:

`http://gnn.com/ora/`

For the plaintext version, `telnet` or `gopher` to:

`gopher.ora.com`

Ora-news

An easy way to stay informed of the latest projects and products from O'Reilly & Associates is to subscribe to "ora-news," our electronic news service. Subscribers receive email as soon as the information breaks.

To subscribe to "ora-news":

Send email to:
listproc@online.ora.com

and put the following information on the first line of your message (not in "Subject"):
subscribe ora-news "your name" **of** "your company"

For example:
subscribe ora-news Jim Dandy of Mighty Fine Enterprises

FTP

The example files and programs in many of our books are available electronically via FTP.

To obtain example files and programs from O'Reilly texts:

`ftp` to:

`ftp.uu.net`
`cd published/oreilly`

or
`ftp.ora.com`

Email

Many other helpful customer services are provided via email. Here's a few of the most popular and useful.

Useful email addresses

nuts@ora.com
 For general questions and information.
bookquestions@ora.com
 For technical questions, or corrections, concerning book contents.
order@ora.com
 To order books online and for ordering questions.
catalog@ora.com
 To receive a free copy of our magazine/catalog, "ora.com" (please include a snailmail address).

Snailmail and phones

O'Reilly & Associates, Inc.
103A Morris Street, Sebastopol, CA 95472
Inquiries: **707-829-0515, 800-998-9938**
Credit card orders: **800-889-8969**
FAX: **707-829-0104**

O'Reilly & Associates—
LISTING OF TITLES

INTERNET

!%@:: A Directory of Electronic Mail
  Addressing & Networks
Connecting to the Internet: An O'Reilly Buyer's Guide
Internet In A Box
MH & xmh: E-mail for Users & Programmers
The Mosaic Handbook for Microsoft Windows
The Mosaic Handbook for the Macintosh
The Mosaic Handbook for the X Window System
Smileys
The Whole Internet User's Guide & Catalog

SYSTEM ADMINISTRATION

Computer Security Basics
DNS and BIND
Essential System Administration
Linux Network Administrator's Guide (Fall 94 est.)
Managing Internet Information Services (Fall 94 est.)
Managing NFS and NIS
Managing UUCP and Usenet
sendmail
Practical UNIX Security
PGP: Pretty Good Privacy (Winter 94/95 est.)
System Performance Tuning
TCP/IP Network Administration
termcap & terminfo
X Window System Administrator's Guide: Volume 8
X Window System ,R6, Companion CD (Fall 94 est.)

USING UNIX AND X

BASICS

Learning GNU Emacs
Learning the Korn Shell
Learning the UNIX Operating System
Learning the vi Editor
SCO UNIX in a Nutshell
The USENET Handbook (Winter 94/95 est.)
Using UUCP and Usenet
UNIX in a Nutshell: System V Edition
The X Window System in a Nutshell
X Window System User's Guide: Volume 3
X Window System User's Guide, Motif Ed.: Vol. 3M
X User Tools (10/94 est.)

ADVANCED

Exploring Expect (Winter 94/95 est.)
The Frame Handbook (10/94 est.)
Making TeX Work
Learning Perl
Programming perl
sed & awk
UNIX Power Tools (with CD-ROM)

PROGRAMMING UNIX, C, AND MULTI-PLATFORM

FORTRAN/SCIENTIFIC COMPUTING

High Performance Computing
Migrating to Fortran 90
UNIX for FORTRAN Programmers

C PROGRAMMING LIBRARIES

Practical C Programming
POSIX Programmer's Guide
POSIX.4: Programming for the Real World
  (Fall 94 est.)
Programming with curses
Understanding and Using COFF
Using C on the UNIX System

C PROGRAMMING TOOLS

Checking C Programs with lint
lex & yacc
Managing Projects with make
Power Programming with RPC
Software Portability with imake

MULTI-PLATFORM PROGRAMMING

Encyclopedia of Graphics File Formats
Distributing Applications Across DCE and
  Windows NT
Guide to Writing DCE Applications
Multi-Platform Code Management
Understanding DCE
Understanding Japanese Information Processing
ORACLE Performance Tuning

BERKELEY 4.4 SOFTWARE DISTRIBUTION

4.4BSD System Manager's Manual
4.4BSD User's Reference Manual
4.4BSD User's Supplementary Documents
4.4BSD Programmer's Reference Manual
4.4BSD Programmer's Supplementary Documents
4.4BSD-Lite CD Companion
4.4BSD-Lite CD Companion: International Version

X PROGRAMMING

Motif Programming Manual: Volume 6A
Motif Reference Manual: Volume 6B
Motif Tools
PEXlib Programming Manual
PEXlib Reference Manual
PHIGS Programming Manual (soft or hard cover)
PHIGS Reference Manual
Programmer's Supplement for R6 (Winter 94/95 est.)
Xlib Programming Manual: Volume 1
Xlib Reference Manual: Volume 2
X Protocol Reference Manual, R5: Volume 0
X Protocol Reference Manual, R6: Volume 0 (11/94 est.)
X Toolkit Intrinsics Programming Manual: Vol. 4
X Toolkit Intrinsics Programming Manual,
  Motif Edition: Volume 4M
X Toolkit Intrinsics Reference Manual: Volume 5
XView Programming Manual: Volume 7A
XView Reference Manual: Volume 7B

THE X RESOURCE

A QUARTERLY WORKING JOURNAL FOR X PROGRAMMERS

The X Resource: Issues 0 through 12
  (Issue 12 available 10/94)

BUSINESS/CAREER

Building a Successful Software Business
Love Your Job!

TRAVEL

Travelers' Tales Thailand
Travelers' Tales Mexico
Travelers' Tales India (Winter 94/95 est.)

AUDIOTAPES

INTERNET TALK RADIO'S "GEEK OF THE WEEK" INTERVIEWS

The Future of the Internet Protocol, 4 hours
Global Network Operations, 2 hours
Mobile IP Networking, 1 hour
Networked Information and
  Online Libraries, 1 hour
Security and Networks, 1 hour
European Networking, 1 hour

NOTABLE SPEECHES OF THE INFORMATION AGE

John Perry Barlow, 1.5 hours

O'Reilly & Associates—
INTERNATIONAL DISTRIBUTORS

Customers outside North America can now order O'Reilly & Associates books through the following distributors. They offer our international customers faster order processing, more bookstores, increased representation at tradeshows worldwide, and the high quality, responsive service our customers have come to expect.

EUROPE, MIDDLE EAST, AND AFRICA
(except Germany, Switzerland, and Austria)

INQUIRIES
International Thomson Publishing Europe
Berkshire House
168-173 High Holborn
London WC1V 7AA
United Kingdom
Telephone: 44-71-497-1422
Fax: 44-71-497-1426
Email: danni.dolbear@itpuk.co.uk

ORDERS
International Thomson Publishing Services, Ltd.
Cheriton House, North Way
Andover, Hampshire SP10 5BE
United Kingdom
Telephone: 44-264-342-832 (UK orders)
Telephone: 44-264-342-806 (outside UK)
Fax: 44-264-364418 (UK orders)
Fax: 44-264-342761 (outside UK)

GERMANY, SWITZERLAND, AND AUSTRIA

International Thomson Publishing GmbH
O'Reilly-International Thomson Verlag
Attn: Mr. G. Miske
Königswinterer Strasse 418
53227 Bonn
Germany
Telephone: 49-228-970240
Fax: 49-228-441342
Email: ora_de@ora.com

THE AMERICAS, JAPAN, AND OCEANIA

O'Reilly & Associates, Inc.
103A Morris Street
Sebastopol, CA 95472 U.S.A.
Telephone: 707-829-0515
Telephone: 800-998-9938 (U.S. & Canada)
Fax: 707-829-0104
Email: order@ora.com

ASIA
(except Japan)

INQUIRIES
International Thomson Publishing Asia
221 Henderson Road
#05 10 Henderson Building
Singapore 0315
Telephone: 65-272-6496
Fax: 65-272-6498

ORDERS
Telephone: 65-268-7867
Fax: 65-268-6727

AUSTRALIA

WoodsLane Pty. Ltd.
Unit 8, 101 Darley Street (P.O. Box 935)
Mona Vale NSW 2103
Australia
Telephone: 61-2-9795944
Fax: 61-2-9973348

NEW ZEALAND

WoodsLane New Zealand Ltd.
21 Cooks Street (P.O. Box 575)
Wanganui, New Zealand
Telephone: 64-6-3476543
Fax: 64-6-3454840
Email: woods@tmx.mhs.oz.au

O'Reilly & Associates, Inc.
End-User License Agreement